Fado

Fadó

Tales of lesser known Irish History

Rónán Gearóid Ó Domhnaill

Matador
9 Priory Business Park
Kibworth Beauchamp
Leicestershire LE8 0RX, UK
Tel: (+44) 116 279 2299
Fax: (+44) 116 279 2277
Email: books@troubador.co.uk
Web: www.troubador.co.uk/matador

ISBN 978 1783061 976

British Library Cataloguing in Publication Data.
A catalogue record for this book is available from the British Library.

Typeset in 11pt Aldine401 BT Roman by Troubador Publishing Ltd, Leicester, UK

Matador is an imprint of Troubador Publishing Ltd

For Lina, Órla and Manus.

*"You that would judge me, do not judge alone
this book or that, come to this hallowed place
where my friends' portraits hang and look thereon;
Ireland's history in their lineaments trace;
think where man's glory most begins and ends
and say my glory was I had such friends."*[1]

William Butler Yeats

contents

Introduction

The title of this book is *Fadó* from the Gaelic meaning "a long time ago" and will be familiar to many of a certain age who will recall how a story in Irish class often started off with the words *fadó fadó in Éirinn* (a long long time ago in Ireland). I started writing this book when I began work as a tour guide, a job that brought me to almost every corner of this island, which, although a small country, has so much to offer. There are already several current books out on Irish history and with this book I wanted to focus on the lesser known events which also convey the wealth of our Irish culture. Some events such as Fontenoy were once well known and this book is intended to rekindle interest and awareness in the Irish contribution to European events.

History itself is at times difficult to write about and it is nigh on impossible to remain neutral. Interpretations are constantly changing. A British history of Ireland is somewhat different to an Irish one. Indeed, Nietzsche remarked "There are no facts, only interpretations".[2]

As a tour guide it can be awkward to explain Irish history; a massacre here, a murder or injustice there; talking about Irish history it can seem that I am anti-English. Britain is a nation that indeed treated us most unjustly in the past but has also offered a home to millions of Irish and links today between the two countries as the visit of Queen Elisabeth II in May 2011 showed, are strong and friendly.

We also have the problem of Irish identity and defining what a true Irishman is. I have tried to give attention to Irishmen and women of different hues. Who were the Irish patriots of 1916? Those who fought in Belgium and France, "for the freedom of small nations", as soldiers of the British army or those who fought against the British army on the streets of Dublin Easter week? Was William Melville a great Irishman or a traitor? It is interesting to note that in the late 19th century, indeed until 1916, many Irish were seemingly happy living within the British Empire.

Should this book be solely about Irish Catholics or are Irish Protestants allowed to get a look in? It is often said that John F. Kennedy was the only American president of Irish descent, yet what about the American presidents of Ulster Scots descent? The Irish Unionist tradition is quite divisive. Until the 1990s those who fought for the British in the two world wars were regarded as traitors, in recent years the tide has turned in their favour, but the wearing of the poppy is still frowned upon and confined as with most monuments from the world wars on this island, to Protestant churches.

Another question I pondered when writing this book was should it be limited to people and events that happened exclusively in Ireland or should the Diaspora be included? I felt I could not write about Irish history without acknowledging the huge Irish Diaspora. Ireland has exported its people for centuries whether as missionaries or mercenaries. Many fared quite well, and some such as Lola Montez even brought down a king. America offered a home to millions of Irish though it would be disingenuous of me to say that they were always as welcome and as popular as they are today, which is why I felt the need to include the "San Patricios" and the "Molly Maguires". Given that a military career was the main way to advance oneself in life it hardly comes as a surprise that so many of these episodes relate to military history. The Austro-Irish episodes were inspired by my lengthy sojourn in Vienna.

Women played a pivotal role in Irish history, especially in early Ireland and have often been neglected, which is why I included a variety of them, including pirates such as Anne Bonney, the cunning Máire Rua, innocents like the Colleen Bawn and even the hangwoman Lady Betty. Their depiction as fearsome hags, as in the case of the Morrigan, may be the Christian influence trying to dissuade people from worshipping them.

I am grateful to my late father and the summer vacations during which we travelled to a different part of the country every year. It was not possible to drive past an old castle without stopping to investigate. If the castle or ruin was locked we would go into the nearest village and the keeper of the key was found. While there are many well known historical sites, there are also an abundance of sites which are less frequented and equally fascinating. As a result of my father's passion for history, it was a subject I found easy at school and I went on to study the subject at Univerity College Galway and the University of Dresden.

These episodes from Irish history have been arranged as far as possible in chronological order, and I have tried to limit each episode to around a thousand words. Each article is intended to provide all the necessary information within a minute or two. It is also possible to open this book and start reading from anywhere, which is ideal for people waiting for a bus. It is also easier to remember a chapter rather than a page number. While the book presupposes a basic understanding of Irish history I have included a small time line of Irish history. I have also given impulses for further research and given locations as exactly as I could. Ordnance Survey maps will further assist the curious here, as well as talking to locals who know the folklore. There are still Armada wrecks awaiting exploration, hidden treasures deposited by Highwaymen awaiting to be found and overgrown, long forgotten monuments with tales to tell.

Rónán Gearóid Ó Domhnaill, Dublin 2013

timeline of irish history

8000 BC	The arrival of the first People
5000BC	The building of Newgrange
600 BC	The arrival of the Celts
AD	
432	The arrival of St Patrick
795	The arrival of the Vikings
1014	The battle of Clontarf
1169	The arrival of the Normans
1593	The Nine Years War
1607	The Flight of the Earls
1609	The Plantation of Ulster
1649	Oliver Cromwell comes to Ireland
1690	The Battle of the Boyne
1691	Introduction of the Penal laws
1798	United Irishmen Rebellion
1800	Closure of the Dublin Parliament
1828	Catholic Emancipation
1845	The Great Famine
1916	The Easter Rising
1922	The foundation of the Irish Free State and Northern Ireland. Civil War.
1939-46	The Emergency. Ireland remains neutral
1949	Declaration of the Irish Republic
1973	EEC membership
1998	The Good Friday Agreement
2011	The Visit of Queen Elisabeth II

CROM CRUACH

Ireland was perhaps the only country in Europe where Christianity was introduced without bloodshed. The old pagan religions were absorbed into Christianity with the coming of Patrick and some of their festivals, such as *Samhain* (Halloween), live on to this day. It is no coincidence that Christians remember their dead at the same time our pagan ancestors did. Patrick, incidentally, was not the first Christian in Ireland and was preceded in 429 by Palladius. The arrival of the Christians in the fifth century brought about change. The druids despised Patrick and referred to their competitor as "Tálcheann", meaning "Adze head".

The main adversary Patrick had was Crom Cruach, the harvest God, a deity who demanded human sacrifices. He was said to have been introduced by King Tigernmus[3]. Given that nothing was committed to writing by either the Celts in Ireland or foreign visitors, as Caesar did with the Celts of Gaul, little is known about human sacrifices in this country. Reference to sacrifices is alluded to in various tales of mythology and the Fomorians seemingly demanded such sacrifices. There is an 8th century tale about Cú Chulainn rescuing a maiden from the Fomorians left out for them on a beach in what is believed to be the earliest European tale of a dragon slayer.[4]

A stone idol, the main one on the island, covered in gold in honour of Crom Cruach stood at the "Plain of Adoration" in County Cavan. Patrick put a stop to human sacrifices and destroyed statues erected in his honour. The name Crom Cruach comes from Cruach meaning mound or mountain, preserved in the Irish name for Croagh Patrick (Cruach Phádraic), while "crom" means crooked. He was so called because he carried the

1

sheaf of the harvest wheat on his back.[5]Cruach used as an old Irish adjective could however also mean "bloody". He was also known as Crom Dubh "Crooked-black" and Cenn Cruaich "Head mound". He has strong associations with Eagle Mountain, which became a place of pilgrimage for Christians, known to them as Croagh Patrick. Whether a natural phenomenon or a marvel of pagan engineering it is not known, but Croagh Patrick is home to the Rolling Sun of Boheh.[6] It can be witnessed there twice a year on 18th April and 24th August, important dates in the equinox calendar. At sunset the sun is seen to apparently roll down the northern slope of the mountain over a period of twenty minutes. It can be witnessed from the Boheh Stone or St Patrick's Chair along the pagan pilgrim route to the south east.[7]A *Dinsenchas* poem by an unknown author in the 12th century *Book of Leinster* gives a description of a gold figure surrounded by twelve stone figures which stood on the plain of Magh Slécht in County Cavan. *Dinseachas* poems explained how a certain place name came into being. The poem goes as follows:

"Here used to stand a lofty idol, that saw many a fight, whose name was the Cromm Cruaich; it caused every tribe to live without peace.

Alas for its secret power the valiant Gaedil used to worship it: not without tribute did they ask of it to satisfy them with their share in the hard world.

He was their God, the wizened Cromm, hidden by many mists: as for the folk that believed in him, the eternal Kingdom beyond every haven shall not be theirs.

For him ingloriously they slew their hapless firstborn with much wailing and peril, to pour their blood round Cromm Cruaich.

Milk and corn they asked of him speedily in return for a third part of all their progeny: great was the horror and outcry about him.

To him the bright Gaedil did obeisance: from his worship—many the crimes—the plain bears the name Mag Slecht.

Thither came Tigernmas, prince of distant Tara, one Samain eve, with all his host: the deed was a source of sorrow to them.

They stirred evil, they beat palms, they bruised bodies, wailing to the demon who held them thralls, they shed showers of tears, weeping prostrate.

Dead the men, void of sound strength the hosts of Banba, with land-wasting Tigernmas in the north, through the worship of Cromm Cruaich—hard their hap!

For well I know, save a fourth part of the eager Gaedil, not a man—lasting the snare—escaped alive, without death on his lips.

Round Cromm Cruaich there the hosts did obeisance: though it brought them under mortal shame, the name cleaves to the mighty plain.

Ranged in ranks stood idols of stone four times three; to beguile the hosts grievously the figure of the Cromm was formed of gold.

Since the kingship of Heremon, bounteous chief, worship was paid to stones till the coming of noble Patrick of Ard Macha.

He plied upon the Cromm a sledge, from top to toe; with no paltry prowess he ousted the strengthless goblin that stood here."[8]

Sacrificing the first born child was believed to yield a good harvest.[9] Worshipping Crom Cruach was apparently a dangerous affair and during the prostrations one *Samhain* night, King Tigernmus himself and three quarters of his followers destroyed themselves. Worship of the pagan deity continued until Patrick destroyed the idol with a sledgehammer. He was evoked for several centuries after his demise in the phrase "dar crom", the Gaelic equivalent of "by Jove".

Crom Cruach was of course not the only deity worshipped by our pagan ancestors. Just outside Killarney on the Cork Kerry border are the Papas of Anu (670m), two peaks representing breasts. Anu was believed to be the Morrigan or war goddess who was evoked to ensure fertility and prosperity. In order not to offend her, farmers in the area referred to her "Gentle Annie". Fires were lit in her honour in midsummer. In County Galway on the shores of Lough Corrib human sacrifices were made to the panther god Taryn, where the people of Glann annually sacrificed a virgin on the hill of Doon.[10] Queen Medbh, mythical queen of Connacht and Goddess of the land is said to be buried in a cairn at the top of Knocknarea in County Sligo.

In 1921 a stone dating from the Iron Age was discovered buried close to an Iron Age stone circle in County Cavan.[11] It was covered in La Tène designs. The name La Tène comes from a Swiss archaeological site of the same name and refers to the Iron Age culture all over Europe between 450BC and 100BC. It became known as the Killycluggin Stone and is now on display in the County Cavan Museum in Ballyjamesduff. The stone shows evidence of being hit with a sledgehammer, corroborating what Patrick, who has many associations with the area, is supposed to have done.

celtic women

The role of women in early Irish society is an interesting one and often overlooked. Given that the Celts wrote nothing down, our knowledge of them is limited to Roman writings and what has survived. Celtic women were different to other cultures of the time and could occupy high positions in society, which was not usual for women in other European societies. They were able to govern and were active in political and religious life. They were also physicians, judges and poets. They had sexual freedom and chose their own partners.[12]

In Early Irish Literature they are depicted as strong willed and independent figures. The image portrayed of women in Early Irish literature is often that of strong warriors. It may not have been far from the truth and Boudicca led a revolt against the Romans in Britannia around 60AD. Roman writers describe how Celtic women fought alongside their husbands. There are accounts of several amazons in the old Irish literature. You have the figure of Scáthach, for example, who was both amazon and clairvoyant and trained Cú Chulainn. Fionn MacCumhaill received his training in arms from two female druids in the Slieve Bloom Mountains on the present day Laois Offaly border.

The first person to set foot on the island was Cessair, daughter of Noah, who came forty days after the Great Flood and is said to be buried at Knockma near Tuam, County Galway.[13]Our ancient Celtic ancestors lived in close communion with the land and many of the Gods worshipped were female. Indeed, the island itself is named after the Goddess Ériu, goddess of the land, and her two sisters Banba and Fódla. She was the daughter of Ernmas of the Tuatha Dé Danann, or the people of Anu, who would later become

5

the *sí* or the faerie. Anu was a fertility Goddess associated with the south and The Paps of Anu in County Kerry are named after her. Ériu, or Éire to give her modern Irish name, was the wife of Mac Gréine, meaning "son of the sun". When the Celts arrived around 600BC she went to meet them and proclaimed that the island would be theirs for all time. The Vikings added the suffix "land" to the mix and the name eventually became Ireland. The Romans on the other hand were not interested in visiting and contented themselves with calling the country "Hibernia" or "cold place". In the Cork and Kerry region the Cailleach Bhearra, or the hag of Bearra, was revered. Her image of a hag may well be Christian influence designed to create animosity towards the old ways. According to legend, if the hero slept with her she would grant him favours. Another Goddess of the land, who features in the 8th century epic *The Táin,* was Queen Medbh. Though married to Aillill, it was Medbh who was the real queen, and he seemed to tolerate her many lovers. She is said to be buried at Knocknarea in County Sligo and her influence was so strong that Shakespeare referred to her as Queen Mab, Queen of the faeries. The faerie women are also shape shifters. The Morrigan or war witch often takes the form of a raven when she lands on the shoulder of the dying Cú Chulainn. Another female faerie, the *bean sí* or death messenger, instilled nocturnal fear in many old Irish families until belief in her subsided in the 20th century. Even some counties such as Armagh were named after goddesses. The Ulster County is named Ard Macha after Macha who, in order to save her husband's honour, raced against the king's horses while pregnant. She won and gave birth to twins, then died.

The reputation of the "Irish mammy" who would do anything for her sons was as strong then as it is now and best reflected by Mongfind, who poisoned the High King, drinking the same poison herself to lull him into a false sense of security. With the king, and herself dead, her son could take the high kingship. She would be revered long after her death by the pagan Irish, especially around the feast of *Samhain*, now called Halloween.[14] Nessa convinced the king of Ulster to give his kingship to her son Connor (Mac Neassa). The names of rivers in Europe usually have ancient origins. The names of towns may have changed but the names of rivers have stayed more or less the same. Many of them seem to be named after women. For example, the River Boyne is named after Boann, a lover of the Dagda, one of the chief Gods, who drowned in it. The river Corrib that flows through Galway, though named after Orrib, a pseudonym for the God of the sea Mannanán Mac Lir, was until the 20th century known as the Galway River.[15] Gailla was said to be a princess of the Fir Bolg and drowned in the river. The name Galway is an anglicised version of her name. The longest river in this country, the Shannon, is named after the Goddess Sionna,[16] who sought out the enchanted hazelnuts of wisdom.

Divorce was not unusual and part of Old Irish Law, which was enforced until the collapse of the Gaelic nobility at the turn of the 17th century.[17]A famous divorcee was the 16th century Gráinne Mhaol (Grace the Bald) so called because she cut her off her hair in order to go sailing with her father and later became known as the Pirate Queen. She married Richard Burke in 1566 and the couple remained together for a probationary period of one year.[18]At the end of the year she locked herself into Rockfleet Castle and called out a window to Burke, "*Richard Burke, I dismiss you.*"[19] which was sufficient to end the marriage.

While the men possess the brawn it is the women who possess the brains. Figures such as Cú Chulainn may be fearsome warriors, but they are not terribly clever and it is the women who make the difficult decisions. While, in the continental tradition, the man goes in search of love, this is not the case with Celtic women. This is especially true of the *sí* or the faerie folk. Fann, for example, goes to the mortal world because she desires Cú Chulainn. Niamh turns up in the Killarney area on a white horse and takes Oisín away with her. Mortal women too have their way of winning their man and Gráinne challenges Diarmaid's code of honour if he does not run away with her. She later challenges his manhood before they become lovers.

Medieval French authors, adapting Celtic tales of King Arthur and other Celtic heroes to a European audience, had to change the role of women to suit their audiences. The image of the powerful amazon who took whatever man she pleased had to go. Thus the helpless damsel in distress was born. The strong faerie woman was also reinvented as beautiful but evil.

The Cathach

The *Cathach* is Ireland's oldest surviving book, predating the Book of Kells by almost two centuries. It has a long and somewhat turbulent history and a battle was fought over its creation. The 6th century Psalter, the second oldest Latin Psalter in the world, is the Latin version of the Hebrew psalms is a copy of an older book and is associated with St Columba, or Columcille as he is known in Irish.

According to his biographer St Adomán, Columcille, whose name means "dove of the church" was born in 521 in Gartan County Donegal of royal blood, like most of the Irish saints. He died in Iona in 597, aged 75. He was related to the O'Donnell clan and is said to have had the gift of second sight. The city of Derry is named after him, the Irish name for the city being *Doire Cholm Cille*.

Colmcille was something of a bookworm and when he heard his former master Finian of Moville had just returned from Rome bringing with him a copy of St. Jerome's Gallican version of the psalms he set off to have a look. He was allowed to borrow the book and over a number of days secretly made a copy, without Finian's permission. When word got back to Finian he demanded the return of both the book and its copy. Colmcille refused to comply and the matter was put before the High King, Diarmuid Mac Cerbaill (†565) at Tara, the ancient residence of the High Kings in County Meath.[20] Mac Cerbaill was the last High King to follow the old pagan rituals of the *ban-feis* or marriage to the goddess of the land.[21] Today this matter would be referred to as a breach of copyright and this was probably the first case in history. He considered the matter and decreed *"to every cow its calf and to every book its copy"*. In other words the copy was to be returned to Finian.

Colmcille was unwilling to accept the judgment and returned north where the O'Donnells and the O'Neills assembled to take on the High King. Using the book as a shield they fought Diarmuid at Cúl Dreimhne in the shadow of Ben Bulben County Sligo in 561. The slaughter that followed sickened Colmcille and three thousand are believed to have been killed.[22] He went to his *anamchara* or soul friend St. Laisran for advice. His friend advised him to do penance for the deaths he had caused and to baptise as many as had fallen on the field that day. He was also to go into missionary exile and never return to Ireland. Colmcille left Ireland and founded a monastic settlement on the island of Iona where the more famous *Book of Kells* would later be written.

The infamous copied book was carried into battle by the O'Donnell clan thereafter and became known as the *Cathach* or battler. It was housed in a special shrine or *cumdach* which is now on display in The National Museum in Dublin.[23] The shrine dates from the late eleventh century and was made in Kells on the orders of Cathbharr Ó Domhnaill and Domhnall Mac Robartaigh, the Abbot of Kells. The Mac Robartaigh clan became the guardians of the *Cathach* and it was stored at the O'Donnell stronghold of Ballyshannon.

It was carried into battle by the Mac Robartaighs at the battle of Fearsod Mór in 1567, when the O'Donnells fought the O'Neills. Before a battle it was customary for a cleric to wear the Cathach in its *cumdach* around his neck and then walk three times around the troops of O'Donnell.[24]

After the disaster of Kinsale in 1601 the *Cathach* did a great deal of travelling, appearing and disappearing over the centuries. It was carried away from Donegal in 1690 by Daniel O'Donnell who took it with him to France. When he died in 1735 the *Cathach* was given to Irish Benedictine monks in Ypres in Belgium. It was given to them on condition that only an O'Donnell of standing could claim it. In 1813 it was passed on to the O'Donnells of Newport, where it was opened for the first time in centuries. No one knew what to expect. There were some who argued that anyone who opened it would be cursed.[25] Inside the damp Cathach, the earliest example of Irish writing, composed on vellum pages, was revealed. Fifty eight sheets were found, containing the text of Psalms 30:10 to 105:13 with each measuring 270mm by 190mm.

When the last herediaty keeper died in 1843 the *Cathach* was presented to The Royal Irish Academy for safe keeping for the people of Ireland. In 1920 it was sent to the Britsh Museum for restoration where the leaves were carefully separtated. It is still on display at the Royal Irish Academy on Dawson Street in Dublin.

saint brendan

Saint Brendan, also known as Brendan the Navigator was one of Ireland's so-called twelve apostles and patron saint of sailors. A biography of his seven year sea voyage was produced in the Middle Ages. Written in hiberno-Latin it proved to be something of a best seller and was translated into sixteen languages. The book described islands west of Ireland, which, given that the world was considered to be flat and Ireland lay on its edge, was a fantastic notion. In later centuries after the discovery of land to the west, scholars wondered if the saint had travelled as far as America. The theory that an Irish monk could have sailed the Atlantic was scoffed at until the English explorer Tim Severin proved in 1977 that it would have been possible.

Brendan was born in Fenit, County Kerry around 484 and baptised by Saint Erc. Traces of his name remain in the locality and a mountain used by the pagans was called Mount Brandon (953m) in his honour. He was sent into fosterage with Saint Ita, a typical Gaelic custom among the nobility, to which class most of the Irish saints belonged. Even in his youth he did a considerable amount of travelling and studied under Saint Jarlath in Tuam, County Galway and Saint Enda on Inishmore in Galway Bay. He was ordained a priest in 512.

He began establishing churches at places such as Clonfert in County Galway. The monastery he founded was replaced by a medieval cathedral which still stands and is famed for its magnificent carved doorway.[26] The monasteries were known as cities and were ruled by the abbot. The day began with the matin around 2:30am, followed by the laud around 5am. The first prayer of the day would then be said at 7am.[27] Like his contemporaries, Brendan was interested in spreading the word of God, but instead of going to the continent he took to the seas. Brendan sailed along the coast visiting hermits on their lonely islands, such as at Scellig Mhicil, off the Kerry coast. He also sailed to Wales and St. Malo in Brittany where his friend the saint, also a seafarer and after whom the city is named, lived. Brendan may even have sailed to North Africa where, according to the 14th century *Mappa Mundi* or map of the world, six small islands bear his name. A St Brendan's Isle was said to be somewhere to the west of Europe.[28]

The famous biography of Brendan *Navigatio Sancti Brendani Abbitis* appeared long after his death. The oldest surviving copy dates from the 10th century but was probably written two centuries before this. As a literary genre the *Navigatio* is based on the pagan Irish *immram*, which usually involved a journey over water into the unknown. A typical *immram* tale would be *Immram Brain*[29] The *immram* motive is present in Celtic literature such as *Tristan and Isolde* where Tristan sails aimlessly adrift being guided only by fate. In the Christian setting the monks are usually looking for the Promised Land of the Saints or the Earthly Paradise. The *Navigatio* also contains motives found in *Sinbad the Sailor*, such as landing on whale believing it to be an island.

According to the *Navigatio,* Brendan and his friends embarked on a seven year voyage in pursuit of the Promised Land and sailed until they reached the Isle of Saints. His adventure took him from Kerry up along the Irish coast to the Hebrides and Faeroes, then over Iceland where he spent the winter. From there they sailed towards Greenland. While much of the book seems to be fantasy and borrowing from traditions and cultures, it does contain some interesting aspects. These aspects could only be really fully appreciated by sailing the presumed route in a similar vessel, which is exactly what Tim Severin did. There is, for example, the description of "The Isle of Smiths", where the smithy was angry at the sight of the monks and hurled fire at them. Tim Severin believed the monks were witnessing a volcano erupting in the Iceland region, something that would not have been part of their knowledge.[30]The monks visited the "Island of Sheep". The word Faroe itself means Island of Sheep. There is also a Brandon Creek on the main island of the Faeroes that the local people believe was the embarkation point for Brendan and his crew.

Similarly, when the monks encountered "The Crystal Pillar" it could possibly have been the Greenland iceberg belt. The "Island of Saints" is a fog enshrouded island which could have been Newfoundland.

Irish monks did have settlements that far north. Indeed, Tim Severin pointed out that a village on the Faeroes used to bear Brendan's name. Around the year 625 Irish monks were living on the Faroe Islands and about a century later were known to have moved to Iceland. Though no archaeological remains have been found in Iceland, the 12th century *Book of Icelanders* claims that Irish monks, who were referred to as Papars, were already living on the island in the 9th century, and were among the first people to inhabit Iceland.[31]

Brendan would have sailed in a coracle made of animal hides and greased to make it waterproof. A similar boat called a *namhóg* (or *currach* further north in the Galway region) made of canvas stretched over a wooden frame and tar to make it waterproof is still used in the region. Based on period descriptions, Severin built a replica of the boat. The voyage was to take him all the way to Newfoundland, which he reached in June of 1977. He subsequently wrote a fascinating book of his adventure called *The Brendan Voyage*. The boat is still on display at Craggaunowen, County Clare.[32]

Brendan himself died at his monastery at Anngahdown, County Galway in 577. He did not want his body used as relic and it was conveyed secretly for burial to Clonfert Cathedral,[33] County Galway. At Fenit Harbour, Tralee, a substantial bronze sculpture has been erected recently in his honour.

saint cillian

I first heard about St Cillian when I was told to bring a group of Germans to Mullagh, County Cavan, where he was born.[34]Mullagh is an unassuming settlement but the heritage centre there makes the visit worthwhile.[35]Though not terribly well known in this country he is in Germany, where he met a somewhat grisly end. Cillian (sometimes spelt with a k) was a missionary during the golden age of wisdom and learning, which flourished until the arrival of the Normans, when Europe was cast into the turmoil of the Dark Ages. The continent had been ravaged by hoards of barbarians and needed re-evangelising, so "The Island of Saints and Scholars", as Ireland was known, sent missionaries such as St. Gall (550-646), after whom the Swiss city of St. Gallen was named. It is near here that one of the earliest Irish poems, *Panguar Bán*, a love poem between a monk and his cat, was written.[36]

Cillian was born in Mullagh in 640 and became a missionary in 686. He was sent to Franconia which today forms part of northern Bavaria. He was one of many Irish monks on the continent. Later monks included Johannes Scotus Eriugena (815-877) whose knowledge of Greek astounded the royal court of France. Greek, though taught in Ireland, was not widely taught on the continent at the time. Scotus is best known to Irish people as having adorned the old five pound note.[37]

Details of Cillian's activities are delivered to us in the Martyrology written between 842 and 856 by Hrababus Maurus, Abbot of Fulda, Archbishop of Mainz and theological writer. The Irish monks in Würzburg were quite active and The Würzburg glosses contain examples of Early Irish dating from around 750. Glosses were used as explanations of a text usually written in the margin or between the texts. Irish monks were also celebrated for their high level of agriculture.

Though Cillian had managed to convert Duke Gozbert of Würzburg, he failed to convert his wife Gailana and she became a dangerous enemy. Gailana had been married to Gozbert's brother and Gozbert took her for a wife when his brother died. Though the union would have been permitted under Roman law it was not under Church law of the time and Cillian saw it as a violation of scared scripture.[38] Discretion was not a strong point Cillian possessed and he made no secret of his dissatisfaction with the union. Word soon got back to Gailana and she waited until Gozbert was away from Würzburg before taking revenge. She ordered her soldiers to go to the square where the Irish evangelist was fishing for souls and to behead him. His companions Saint Colman, not to be confused with another Colman who met a grisly fate in Austria centuries later, and Saint Totnan met with the same fate. All three bodies were burnt in the royal stables but the heads were saved from the flames. A Cillian cult grew out of this incident and their skulls were inlaid with precious stones and preserved. In 752 Bonifactius declared the three remaining skulls relics and Cillian became patron saint not only of Würzburg but also Heilbronn. He was and continues to be evoked by those who suffer from eye diseases and rheumatism. A statue of Cillian portraying him as a bishop is in the main square and every St Cillian's day, on 9th July, the relics are paraded in a glass case through the streets of Würzburg.

.

SAINT VIRGIL OF SALZBURG

Ireland's contribution to the cultural renaissance that followed The Dark Ages has largely been forgotten outside of Central Europe. One of the lesser well known saints, but a major contributor to this renaissance was St Virgil, Virgil or Virgilius being the Latin form of Fergal. He was a man very much ahead of his time who would go on to become the Patron Saint of Salzburg, in Austria, where he is still revered to this day.He was born of noble birth around 700. Where exactly he was born is not known, though some sources suggest Trim, County Meath, and he was educated at the monastery of Iona.[39] After becoming a monk and a priest he became the abbot of a monastery at Aghaboe in County Laois in the late 730's.[40]He decided to travel to the Holy Land and this decision marked a turning point in his life. It was not unusual at the time for Irish monks to go abroad as Europe was in need of evangelisation and culture, as discussed in the previous chapter. It was largely due to these missionaries that Christianity not only flourished once more, but Central Europe experienced a cultural renaissance not seen since the Roman Empire. En route to Jerusalem in 741, Virgil came to the court of Pipin at Compaigne. Pipin was the father of the emperor Charlemagne and both men were champions of the faith. Pipin welcomed Virgil and his followers and employed them as consultants. In 744, Pipin sent Virgil and his companions to the court of his brother-in-law, Ottilo, Duke of Bavaria, whose dukedom was only partly Christian. While Southern Germany and Austria are today strongly Catholic areas, in the 8th century they were on the edge of the Christian world and in desperate need of missionaries. From there Virgil was sent to Salzburg, where he founded a monastery and became Abbot-Bishop of St. Peter's Monastery, while his fellow Irishman Sidonius became the third bishop of Passau. It was in Salzburg that Virgil was to remain for the next forty years spreading the word of God.[41] Virgil, however, was the only saint operating in the area. St. Boniface, a Saxon missionary who was primate of Germany controlled the diocese of Bavaria, to which Salzburg belonged, and the two saints soon became rivals.

Part of the problem was that Virgil was doing things "the Irish way". Boniface had structured the church so that it looked towards Rome. The early Irish church, however, saw itself more independent of Rome and was not hierarchical, the abbots being regarded as independent authorities.

The first dispute arose over baptisms. Priests at the time were poorly trained and ill educated. Their Latin was equally poor and when Boniface learnt that their Latin grammar was weak he declared baptisms in Virgil's diocese to be invalid. Virgil disagreed and the matter came before Pope Zachary, who supported Virgil, stating that ignorance of Latin did not invalidate baptisms.

Apart from being a holy man, Virgil was one of the most learned men of his age. As well as being a brilliant theologist and philosopher Virgil was a renowned mathematician and astronomist. His knowledge of geography earned him the nickname "Geometer". This was in a time when very little was known of the physical world. He believed that the world was round as opposed to flat. This was nothing new and the Ancient Greeks such as Pythagoras and Aristotle had argued this, centuries before. Virgil was however among the first Christians to believe and propagate this. Very few people had access to the ancient Greek manuscripts and as a result these theories were not widely known. Other theologians such as St. Augustine and Virgil's compatriot Dungal, astronomer to the Emperor Charlemagne, also believed in a spherical earth but refuted the notion of the antipodes.

The Irish, influenced by Saint Brendan the Navigator and the earlier pagan *eachtra* and *immram* stories, believed that people lived on the other side of the world.[42] This was of course several centuries before Columbus and mediaeval depictions of such people portrayed them as deformed creatures, with legs growing upwards out of their heads.

Boniface interpreted Virgil's teachings that these people were not of the "race of Adam" and therefore not in need of salvation. Boniface, perhaps stinging from the previous year's baptismal humiliation, seized his opportunity to report him to Pope Zachary in 748, who ordered him to set up a church council to investigate Virgil.[43]

It was a charge that would have to be proven and few knew more about the antipodes than Virgil. The pope was not expected to rule in his favour and excommunication loomed. Fortunately for Virgil the Pope died and the matter was apparently forgotten. It did not appear to stain his career as he was made bishop of Salzburg, though when exactly is not known. The area was not big enough for both saints and Boniface went to Frisia, in present day Holland, where he was martyred in 754. From Salzburg Virgil dispatched missionaries to what is now the Czech Republic and Hungry and, acquiring land, set about building churches.[44]

In 774 he laid the foundation stone of Salzburg's cathedral and dedicated it to Saint Rupert.

Virgil died in 784 and was canonized in 1233. In 1288 his remains were interred under the altar of Salzburg Cathedral, where they still remain. Though he made a contribution to science, all of his writings "disappeared" after his death and his scientific work was soon forgotten about. He is commemorated in Germany and Austria on 24th September and in the rest of the world on 27th November.[45]

Ísolde

The modern Dublin suburb of Chapelizod hardly gives any indication to any ancient link to one of Europe's most famous love tales *Tristan and Isolde*. Many, including the Dubliners themselves are unaware that the place name has nothing to do with lizards and the heroine of the Europe's most tragic love tales was a Dubliner. I have followed the tales for years and my interest in it was first awoken while doing a seminar on *Tristan and Isolde* at the University of Vienna many years ago. It was then that I first became familiar with the Celtic roots of the story, which tied into my research on Irish legends.

We have no proof that she ever existed. According to the popular legend Isolde was a Viking princess from Dublin and the daughter of King Aonghus, who is supposed to have lived before the Vikings established the settlement of Dublin in 988 where the Dublin City Municipal Building now stands.[46]Nobody knows for sure just how old the tale is, but the more ancient elements probably have Pictish roots. In 9th century Dublin there was a tower, somewhere around the present Temple Bar area, called Isolde's Tower,[47] which was later rebuilt by the Normans. The street leading up to where the tower once stood, now Exchange Street, is still called Isolde's street in Irish.[48]

The version of the tale I am most familiar is probably also the most complete and was written by Gottfried von Strassburg around 1215. It was this version that Richard Wagner used when he composed his opera *Tristan and Isolde*. It is essentially a mish mash of various Celtic legends. Earlier versions were composed by Thomas of Britain around 1160 and the 12th century Norman poet Béroul. A film version, albeit one very loosely based on the original tale, was made in 2006 with Sophia Myles playing Isolde.

The tale is something of a *ménage à trois* between the elderly King Mark of Cornwall, his nephew Tristan of Brittany and Isolde of Dublin. Isolde is depicted as having fairy like beauty and both she and her mother, also called Isolde, have healing powers. Mark wants to marry Isolde and sends his nephew to woo her on his behalf. There are parallels here with *Diarmaid and Gráinne*, but while there are elements of the tale which were known as far back as the 9th century the only complete surviving copy of the *Tóraíocht* dates from 1650 so it can never be proven that *Tristan and Isolde* was taken from the *Tóraíocht*.

Brangaine, Isoldes's lady in waiting is given a love potion which will make Isolde fall in love with the elderly king. Tristan and Isolde mistakingly drink the love potion en route to Mark and fall for each other. They try to hide their love but find it imposssible. Mark is furious and banishes his beloved nephew. The two lovers go on the run and are pursued by the jealous Mark and the tale enivitably ends in tragedy.

GORMLAITh

Gormlaith[49] was born in Naas, County Kildare around 955 and was considered something of a beauty. She is also regarded as something of a Helen of Troy figure who was blamed for starting the Battle of Clontarf in 1014. She was married three times, divorcing each husband, whenever she saw a better opportunity to further her son. Divorce was legal under the Gaelic Brehon laws.

Though the Vikings initially came to plunder and pillage, by the 10th century they had begun to settle down and established Ireland's oldest town of Waterford as well as other towns such as Dublin and Limerick. Intermarrying with the Gaelic inhabitants was not uncommon. While still a teenager, Gormlaith was married to Olaf Cuarán, several years her senior. Marriage at the time was for bearing children or forming political alliances. She bore him five children, including Sitric Silkenbeard, who would go on to become King of Dublin. Not long after their union, Olaf came High King of all Ireland. His position was challenged by Malachy of Meath who became High King in 980. Malachy was considerably younger than Olaf and the opportunistic Gormlaith was quick to recognise that he could advance her position much more than Olaf. She helped Malachy become King of Dublin and Olaf was exiled to Scotland. Thus Gormlaith married for the second time, becoming Malachy's wife while her son Sitric became King of Dublin in 994.

There was another more powerful force emerging from the west, and Brian Boru, the leader of the tribe known as the Dalcassians, who would later become the O'Briens and Kennedys from the banks of the Shannon at Kincora (later Kilalloe), challenged Malachy. Boru became High King in 1002 and it was the first time Ireland was united under a native leader. Gormlaith married Brian Boru and his daughter Sláine married Sitric.

Gormlaith continued her scheming and continued to advance the position of her sons. Maelmora went to visit Kincora and, though initially warmly received, he was insulted and he left with his followers. From then she started to conspire against Boru. Boru grew tired of her meddling and divorced her around 1012. She went back to Dublin where she worked on deposing Boru, and incited her brother Maelmora and Sitric against him. In response Boru and his ally, Gormlaith's former husband Malachy, laid siege to Dublin. Gormlaith is referred to as 'Kormlada' in the 13th century Icelandic saga *Njáls Saga,* set in the period between 960 and 1020.[50]Chapters 155 and 156 of the saga describe the Battle of Clontarf. According to the saga Gormlaith egged on her son Sitric to kill Boru and to seek allies. She ordered Sitric to gather the support of other Vikings and Sigurd of the Orkneys, as well as Amlaff and Broder from the Isle of Man.[51] They were not going to come for nothing and *Njáls Saga* says:

> *"So they parted on the understanding that Earl Sigurd gave his word to go; but King Sigtrygg promised him his mother and the kingdom."*[52]

According to the saga, Gormlaith was willing to pay any price in order to defeat her ex husbands. The Vikings promised to come to Dublin for Palm Sunday. Maelmora gathered his allies. Sitric remained in the city. Exact figures are not known but it is believed that up to 20,000 were on each side, which for a medieval battle was a huge amount. Boru laid siege to the town of Dublin and made camp in the area of Kilmainham and the Phoenix Park.[53]

According to the saga it was revealed to Brodir in a prophecy not to fight before Good Friday and that Boru would win, but fall in battle. *Njáls Saga* says:

> *"Brodir tried by sorcery how the fight would go, but the answer ran thus, that if the fight were on Good-Friday King Brian would*

*fall but win the day; but if they fought before, they would all
fall who were against him. Then Brodir said that they must not fight
before the Friday.*"[54]

Much has been made of the battle as a fight between Christianity and Paganism, the Irish and the Dane but it seemed to be something more of a personal power struggle.

The actual battle of Clontarf was not fought in the area we know today as Clontarf, which was part of the sea at the time, but more in the Ballybough area. The Liffey at the time was not walled as it is today and was much wider. The copy of a Viking mooring post, known as "The Stein" [55]beside Pearse Street Garda Station gives an impression of just how wide it would have been. The Vikings wore shirts of chain mail, which helped them in battle but hampered them in retreat and many drowned trying to reach their boats.

Gormlaith lost her youngest son Sigurd in the battle. Sigurd carried a banner, made by his mother in the shape of a raven and it had always brought him victory, but his luck had run out that day.

Though Brian won the day, the prophecy was fulfilled and Brodir, hiding in Tomar's woods, which stretched from Drumcondra down to the Liffey, killed the great Brian Boru. Traditionally the spot where this happened is believed to be where Mountjoy Square now stands. The Irish were careful to capture Brodir alive and give him an agonising death. *Njáls Saga* does not spare the details:

*"Wolf the Quarrelsome cut open his belly, and led him round and
round the trunk of a tree, and so wound all his entrails out of
him, and he did not die before they were all drawn out of him."*[56]

Malachy would reign once more as High King until he died in 1022. Gormlaith herself lived on after the battle of Clontarf, leading a rather withdrawn life, dying in a convent in 1042. Sitric outlived her and his legacy lives on in structures such as Christchurch Cathedral.

Dunmore Cave

Dunmore cave is a limestone show cave in County Kilkenny not far from Kilkenny city and is one of several show caves the country has to offer. The entrance, 12m wide and 6m high, is in itself spectacular. It is not the biggest cave in the country, but contains a quarter of a mile of passages and at its deepest point is 46 m. It also has some fine calcite formations. One of the stalactites, measuring nearly 6m tall, is known as the Market Cross. It opened as a show cave in 1967 and is home to a sizeable bat colony. The cave closed for archaeological work from 2000-03 and it is these excavations and the thousand year old massacre that occurred here which I intend to focus on.

The first mention of caves at Dunmore is in the Irish Triads, which covered a variety of topics such as nature, geography, law, custom and behaviour which were written in the 9th century. The cave was known then as Dearc Fearna or the "Cave of the Alders" and found itself in the kingdom of Ossory. The kingdom had been established by Cerball MacDunlainge (who died in 888) and while he lived the Vikings knew better than to attack his territory, having been slaughtered by his men when they attacked Ossory in 860.[57] The area was easy to access and close to the Viking town of Waterford. The marauding Vikings may have been raiding a monastery at the time. The annals however just mention a massacre and say nothing of any sacking.

The Annals of the Four Masters, an iconic history of Ireland written by Michael O'Clery of Donegal and others and completed in 1636, mention a massacre that took place there in the year 928. The event was also mentioned in *The Annals of Innisfallen*, a chronicle documenting events in Ireland between 433 and 1450 and written in Lough Leane in County Kerry. Accounts of massacres are commonplace in the annals. What is fascinating about this particular one is that the landscape where it is said to have taken place has remained virtually unchanged in a millennium. The annals state:

> "Godfrey, grandson of Imhar, with the foreigners of Ath Cliath, demolished and plundered Dearc Fearna, where one thousand persons were killed in this year as is stated in the quatrain: 'Nine hundred years without sorrow, twenty-eight, it has been proved, Since Christ came to our relief, to the plundering of Dearc-Fearna.'"[58]

Human remains have been uncovered in the cave since 1699. The earliest reports come from George Berkeley, who wrote a report in 1706 detailing what he came across when he visited the cave, but it was not published until 1871. He mentioned finding very few skulls as they had probably been removed by earlier souvenir hunters. James Graves and Peter Burtchaell had discovered large quantities of human remains, which they collected. In his reports, Foot meticulously documented his findings, and also called on references from the writings of researchers over the preceding 120 years.[59]

In 1944 the remains of 44 people were found within the cave. In the 1970's Viking coins dating from round 928 were found along with human remains in a dark recess far at the back of the cave, known as the market cross chamber. Rarely do archaeologists find artefacts that correspond so closely with the description of the annals. Yet more remains were uncovered in 1996. Radio carbon dating on the remains dated them to around 930AD, when the massacre was said to have happened. Many of the remains were women and children, who had presumably sought refuge in the cave, only to find themselves trapped and with no way out.[60] What is strange about the remains is that they did not show scars or stab marks, which you might expect in a massacre. The dark caves offered an ideal hiding place and the Vikings would not have risked going in when they could light a fire at the mouth and kill their prey with smoke inhalation. As many as a thousand are believed to have died and the cave became a tomb.

A hoard of Viking coins were discovered in 1999 and are now on display in the National Museum in Dublin.[61] The hoard created a mystery for archaeologists. The Viking coins, all dating between 860 and 930 were discovered in market cross chamber. All of the coins, save two were minted in Northern England, where other Viking settlements existed. The other coins were from as far afield as Armenia.[62]It still remains a mystery as to how and why they were deposited there.

saint colman

Until 1663 when he was replaced by Saint Leopold, the Patron Saint of Austria was an Irish man, Saint Colman. Very little is known about who exactly he was, though it is believed that he was a king's son from somewhere in the south of Ireland. It was the year 1012 when a stranger calling himself Colman or Coloman wandered into the village of Stockerau in Lower Austria, North of Vienna. He was on his way to the Holy land when his horse lost a shoe and he needed the service of the local smithy. In a time when people did not venture far from their native villages and everyone knew everyone, strangers stood out. This particular stranger spoke a strange tongue and wore strange clothes. The neighbouring Bohemians had often attacked the area and the villagers took Colman to be one of their spies sent to do a reconnaissance.

Perhaps bitter and angry with previous incursions, a mob gathered around the Irishman and he was thrown into jail, where they tortured him, but to no avail. He wouldn't talk their language and persisted in speaking his unknown language. They brought him before the local judge, but Colman's attempts to explain himself *as Gaeilge* and with gestures made no impression on the judge, who sentenced him to death by hanging.

He was dragged to barren elder tree and they hanged him between two murderers.

It was the usual practice of the time to leave the corpse hanging to act as a deterrent. In the case of Colman his body hung on the elder tree for eighteen months.[63]

Unlike the other corpses however, it did not decompose and appeared to be as fresh as the day he died. Nor had the ravens and crows plucked out his eyes. The barren elder tree had also started to blossom. The villagers wondered at this but more was to come.

In the village there was a man called Rumaldus and his son suffered from severe gout.[64] Rumaldus could do nothing about it until one night he was told in a dream to rub the afflicted area with a piece of flesh from a hanged man's body. It was a common belief at the time that a hanged man's body brought luck and cured certain ailments. Very often certain bodily parts were removed for this purpose. This is exactly what Rumaldus did and the corpse he chose was Colman's. While he was cutting off a piece of flesh, warm blood flowed out as if the body was still alive. He brought it home and the afflicted area had scarcely been rubbed three times when the boy stood up and was cured. Truly amazed by what had happened, Rumaldus went back to where Colman was hanging and is reported to have seen that there was no trace of any incision made on the corpse.

The locals took this as evidence that Colman was no spy, but a holy man. They realised then that they that they had been a bit hasty in hanging the stranger and had treated him with great injustice. The least they could now do was to give him a decent Christian burial and he was buried in a small church nearby. Not long after this his origins were established when one of Colman's servants travelling from Ireland, trying to trace the whereabouts of his unfortunate master, turned up in the village.

The village basilica was not to be Colman's final resting place. The following year the Danube broke its banks and flooded the entire area causing massive destruction. The only place the water shunned was Colman's grave, which remained a green dry island. The local prince was deeply impressed upon hearing this and decided the holy man's body should be reinterred in more suitable surroundings. It is said that when his grave was opened a smell arose that gave joy to all who smelt it and that the body still had shown no signs of decomposition. Thus the remains were transferred to Melk in Lower Austria in 1014. Leopold II of Austria made Melk into a Benedictine monastery in 1089 and Colman, though never officially canonized, became its patron saint.

Word spread of the saint's remains and people travelled from afar to see them. A Colman cult thrived and no less than four popes granted indulgences to those who evoked his name. It was highly desirable for a nobleman to have holy relics in his kingdom and tended to increase his standing greatly.

Perhaps with this in mind King Stefan of Hungary wanted the remains to be brought to Hungary. When his request was turned down he threatened to start a war. In order to avoid bloodshed the Austrian's reluctantly handed over the remains. The Hungarians were ecstatic that the miracle worker's remains had come to their country. Instead of a blessing, however, Stephan's kingdom was hit by plagues and famine, which the king believed to be an act of punishment and he had the remains returned to Melk in 1016. Colman became patron saint of Austria in 1244. He also became patron saint of those sentenced to death by hanging, travellers and cattle, protected against foot ailments and the plague. Popular images of him show a man wearing pilgrim's clothes of hat, cloak, and walking stick and are still quite numerous.He was not only revered in Austria, but also in Bavaria, Swabia and Hungary, where several churches bear his name. Farmers' daughters used to call upon him to send them a good husband. Though he was replaced as Austria's national saint by Saint Leopold in 1663 he still retains popularity. There is still an annual blessing of horses and cattle at Melk on his feast day on the 13th October. It is not only in Melk that traces of Colman are to be found. Beside the North side entrance of Vienna's famous St. Stephen's cathedral there is a stone, which once had traces of blood on it.[65] This is said to be the stone on which Colman was executed.Though it seems hard to believe that a single Irishman could have accidentally attracted so much attention he is still revered today a thousand years after his execution. In recent years he has become a symbol of the need for us to listen to one another. He looked different and spoke differently and such people still arouse suspicion and can very easily fall victim to intolerance.

Diarmait mac murchada

Diarmait Mac Murchada (1110-1171) or Dermot MacMurrough as he is known in English was the king of Leinster and the man responsible for establishing the link between Britain and Ireland. He has been much vilified as a result. How to view Mac Murchada depends on which contemporary source you consult. While Irish sources are less than flattering, Norman sources tend to be less critical. The Old French poem *Le Chansun de Dermot li Quens* or *The Song of Dermot and the Earl*, was possibly written by Morice Regan, who was the interpreter for Mac Murchada.

> *"In Ireland, at that time*
> *There was a king of suchlike valour:*
> *Very powerful and rich was he*
> *He loved the generous, he hated the mean."*[66]

His father was killed in battle in 1115 by the Dublin Vikings and buried with a dog to add insult to injury. Mac Murchada would not forget this. He was inaugurated as head of his clan at the age of fifteen. The inauguration stone, called the *Leac Mic Eochadha*, or Kehoe's Flagstone, was at Loggan Lower in North West Wexford.[67] His inauguration would have been similar to that of any Irish King or chieftain at the time. Unlike other European countries the eldest son did not automatically become king, but a candidate would be chosen by the ruling clan the *derb-fine*. The candidate would stand on the stone, while an *ollamh* would read aloud the laws of his people. He would then be given a long slender white rod, the symbol of his authority and he would turn three times to the left

31

and right, surveying his kingdom. His followers would then shout out his name. His kingship could be taken away from him by any of his clan, including his own son, who had enough support. Many of these inauguration stones were later smashed to pieces.[68] Mac Murchada had two wives, which was usual under Gaelic law, the second of whom gave birth to his famous daughter Aoife. He had two legitimate sons, Domnall Caemhánach (killed in 1175) and Énna Cennselach (blinded 1169). According to the Brehon laws nobody with any kind of blemish could become king and blinding Énna was one way of ensuring this. In some ways he was lucky as some heirs to the throne were castrated. The High King[69] Turlough O'Connor began seizing Mac Murchada territory and flexing his muscle against the young Diarmait. Things changed in 1131 when the high king was attacked from all sides when his enemies joined together and checked his expansion.

Mac Murchada was a patron of the arts and built monasteries at Baltinglass and a priory at All Hallows, where Trinity College now stands. He was also responsible for the compilation of *The Book of Leinster*, a collection of poems and a vital source of early Irish legends, now housed in Trinity College. It was around 1140 that Malcahy, the former primate of Ireland, went to Clairvaux and brought back with him the Cistercians, who wanted to reform the church in Ireland, which seemed to act independently of Rome. It was orders such as the Cistercians that would welcome the Normans.

By the 1150s Mac Murchada had become a powerful figure. There had always been a large amount of antipathy between Diarmait and Tiernan O'Rourke, King of Bréifne in northern Connacht. Matters came to a head when Diarmait abducted O'Rourke's wife Dervorgilla while he was on pilgrimage at Lough Derg.[70] It has been suggested that it was a voluntary abduction. By law Mac Murchada was bound to pay an honour fine to O'Rourke, which he failed to do and made many enemies as a result. He returned her to O'Rourke after a year, which increased the humiliation. She is known to have led a quite secluded life thereafter and became a patron of the church, financing Mellifont Abbey in County Louth and "The Church of the Nuns" at Clonmacnoise.

O'Rourke got his revenge when he marched with a coalition force on Leinster and Mac Murchada was banished from his kingdom. He found refuge in Wales and went to Bristol looking for the elusive King Henry II, who would either be found in England or in his French territories. The Normans were a very different people. They had subdued England and Wales after Hastings in 1066 and built a series of strong stone castles. They were powerful enough to help Mac Murchada regain his kingdom and when he eventually found Henry he was pleased that help would be offered. Soon eminent Norman families would assume power in Ireland, the most famous being Fitzgerald.[71] In Wales he found support from the Earl of Pembroke, otherwise known as "Strongbow". Strongbow had no interest in Mac Murchada's problems but was in the prospect of getting land and titles. Mac Murchada offered him the hand of his thirteen year old daughter, Aoife. That meant that he would become King of Leinster when Mac Murchada died. At least that was how it worked in the Norman world.

The arrival of the Normans was a milestone in Irish history and would establish a link, not always a happy one, between Britain and Ireland. They came to Ireland with the blessing of the pope who had issued a papal bull known as the Laudabiltier.[72]Nicholas Breakspeare, also known as Pope Adrian IV, was a friend of Henry and had granted Henry the island of Ireland in 1155, sending him an emerald ring as symbol of his office. Though the king toyed with the idea of conquering Ireland he soon forgot about it.

The Normans were far superior in terms of arms and equipment. They wore chain mail, which the Irish did not have. They had knights, while the Irish had mounted cavalry on ponies, which only had the advantage over boggy terrain. The longbow was not used by the Irish and was devastatingly effective. The first force arrived at Bannow Island just off the Wexford coast. The Viking town of Wexford was the first to fall. They did not put up much resistance and the population was spared. Waterford was different and fought fiercely against the invader. Waterford, Ireland's oldest town was taken by Raymond le Gros. He had arrived with a tiny force but managed to beat a much larger Irish force by driving captured cattle against them, creating panic in their ranks. Seventy local dignitaries were taken at Waterford. And though they could have fetched a ransom they were put to the sword. Strongbow arrived in August of 1170 and amidst the ruins and smouldering fires he claimed his bride who was young enough to be his granddaughter. The marriage, against all the odds, was a success, which was a good thing for Mac Murchada as, under Irish law, a woman could refuse to marry or continue the marriage, which was unimaginable in Norman culture. The event is commemorated in a painting by the 19th century artist Daniel Mclise now hanging in the National Gallery in Dublin.

Mac Murchada went to Dublin. The Annals of Innisfallen state:

"Mac Murchada and the same foreigners plundered Áth Cliath. All Mide, both church and lay property, was also plundered and burned by the oversea men."[73]

Henry II came to Ireland in 1171 as he feared Strongbow was becoming too powerful. Strongbow and Aoife settled in Dublin where traditionally a tomb of a Norman knight in Christchurch cathedral is said to be his grave.[74] Mac Murchada died in 1171 in Ferns, County Wexford at the abbey he founded and is said to be buried on the grounds. His obituary in the *Annals of the Four Masters* is less than charming and suggests he was diabolically possessed:

"Diarmait Mac Murchada, king of Leinster, who had spread terror throughout Ireland, after putting the English in possession of the country, committing excessive evils against the Irish people, and plundering and burning many churches among which were Kells,

Clonard and others, died this year of an intolerable and uncommon disease. He became putrid while living, by the miracles of God, through the intervention of Columcille, Finian and the other saints of Ireland for having violated and plundered their churches. He died at Ferns, without making a will, without penance, without the Eucharist and without Extreme Unction, as his evil deeds deserved."[75]

ᕼOlᎩ ᗯEllS

Holy Wells are to be found all over Ireland and form a common feature on Ordnance Survey maps. Many, known for their curative properties have been visited for centuries and still continue to attract pilgrims, while others have been long forgotten about and even destroyed. They are a fine example of how old pagan ways blended in with the new Christian faith. It has been suggested that some rituals performed at these sites only date back to medieval church rituals, but many wells in this country are to be found at former pagan gathering places. There are about three thousand holy wells around the country. References to wells and their curative properties go back centuries. Texts from the 12th century describe how Dian Cecht, the God of healing, used a healing well to heal the wounded after the Battle of Moyturra, a mythical battle fought in pre Celtic times in Sligo between the Fir Bolg and Tuatha Dé Danann.[76] He blessed a well called Slane, located to the west of Moyturra and east of Loch Arboch, where the Tuatha Dé Danann could bathe when wounded and which healed them. The well could heal any wound but decapitation. Dian Cecht's healing powers were invoked in Ireland as late as the 8th century.

Trees at holy wells may originally have stemmed from pagan tree worship. A white thorn is very often found beside a holy well. It is not uncommon to find rosary beads or even rags attached to the tree. As the rag decays so too does the sickness the pilgrim wishes to have lifted. Wells with fish such as trout or eels were believed to be especially potent. Votive offerings such as religious medals, statues or coins are still common.

Some wells are found in the mountains. Mám Éan in Connemara for example is located at the top of a mountain pass. It was built on the site of a Lughnasa, summer harvest thanksgiving festival site. In Clonmacnoise in front of the old hospital there is a bullaun stone, used to grind herbs. The water contained within the stone is said to contain a cure for warts and many visitors have supported this claim. Tobar Moling at Mullinakill County Kilkenny also treated skin ulcers.[77] St. Mullins in County Carlow was associated with St. Moling and was a major place of pilgrimage during the Black Death. Pilgrims walked through a stream against the current, a practice that continued until the 19th century, and ate the clay from the ground there.

In West Kerry near the village of Camp people from all over the country flocked to Tobar na nGealt in Gleann na nGealt or "Valley of the Insane". Nobody knows how the area got its name, but according to folklore it used to be called Gleann Volcáin, after Volcán who fled there in insanity after the Battle of Ventry. The water contains traces of lithium and eating the water cress which grows there was believed to help mental well being. Oddly, no saint is associated with this particular well.

The most famous well in County Clare is St Bridget's Well near the village of Liscannor. It contains a well house packed with votive offerings and memorial cards from all over the world. St Bridget's well at Bridewell in County Roscommon was known to support women wishing to become pregnant. In the days when doctors were both expensive and a rarity these wells gave solace to a desperate population. St Attracta's Well at Monasteraden near Ballaghdereen, County Roscommon was also used for this purpose. The well had stones known as serpents' eggs, which were fondled as part of the ritual.[78]

Not far from Letterkenny, close to the Rock of Doon, the inauguration site of the O'Donnells of Donegal there is a holy well, which is still venerated especially on New Year's Eve. A togher, a Bronze Age road through the bog, was uncovered which suggested the site was visited from very early times. When I visited the well on one of my tours I saw a rag tree full of objects including a baby shoe, perhaps symbolising the desire from one visitor to have a baby. Father Moore's Well in Rathbride near Newbridge County Kildare is still well visited. Father Moore (1779-1826) had the ability to cure people and before he died he blessed the well. There are three stones in the middle of the well which form part of the ceremony that pilgrims perform in order to have their request granted. The more famous St. Bridget's Well is located not very far away.

Until the 20th century it was usual for people to gather at the wells on pattern days. A pattern day was a particular day of the year commemorating the particular saint after whom the well was named. It may come as a surprise to Dubliners that the county has more than a hundred holy wells.[79]Most Dubliners are unaware that there is a holy well in the heart of the city on the grounds of Trinity College. It is called St. Patrick's Well and is underneath the Nassau Street entrance, said to have been formed by St Patrick himself. It is in this well that frogspawn was placed and from here Ireland got its frog population in the 17th century. A holy well on Dalkey Island was believed to hold a cure for scurvy. Saint Catherine's Well in Drisoge, Drumcondra, Dublin was known for curing toothaches, sore eyes and chin cough. In 1928 its location was described as being on the northern bank of the river Tolka under a kitchen floor, but it has since disappeared.[80] Sadly many were destroyed during the Celtic Tiger era.

ᏖᏂᎬ ᏰᏞᎪᏨᏦ ᎠᎬᎪᏖᏂ

The Black Death ravaged this country, as it did all of Europe in the 14th century yet, unlike the Great Famine centuries later it did not affect Gaelic Ireland, in fact it had the opposite affect.

It was by no means the first disease to strike this country. The Middle Ages was a time of plagues and pestilence, where life was harsh and short. The *Annals of Clonmacnoise* mentions a plague that struck the settlement. St. Ciarán himself, the founder of the settlement, died of yellow fever in 545. Indeed, the plague came and went right up to the 18th century and memories of it are preserved in the nursery rhyme "Ring a Ring a Rosy". It was the Black Death however that claimed the most lives. It has been estimated up to 60% of Europe's population succumbed to the disease. In the space of a century between 75 million and 200 million are believed to have perished. Figures for Ireland are hard to come by, as many of our Public Records were destroyed when the IRA burnt the Customs' House in 1921. It is, however, believed that up to 14,000 died from the Black Death in Dublin.

The plague came from China and entered Europe from The Great Silk Route and the ports. All the ports had grain houses which the rats sought out once the ship docked. The rats carried fleas which excreted the disease into whatever host they were feeding on. The plague was spread by the black rat, which these days has largely been replaced by the brown rat. The rats carried the plague carrying fleas known as *Xenopsylla cheopis*. The plague took on different forms. In the first form people suffered an infection of the lungs known as pneumonic plague, which led to breathing difficulties and death followed within two days. The second form caused boils to appear under the armpits, which oozed pus and bled when opened. The groin was also affected. The Italian writer Boccaccio described these lumps as being as big as apples.[81] Another typical feature was where the skin became covered in black spots.

Transmission of the plague was facilitated in towns by the unsanitary living conditions in which urban dwellers, both Normans and English lived. A typical town consisted of open sewers, contaminated water supplies, animals and rats roaming the streets. Diseases such typhoid from contaminated water and smallpox were already rampant. In the surrounding countryside famines as a result of crop failure were not uncommon. Malnourished children were particularly susceptible to the disease.

There are many first hand accounts, in this country which are mostly ecclesiastical. John Clyn, a Franciscan friar from Kilkenny, describes the terrible period in his *Annals of Ireland* and states that it came to Ireland in July 1348, having reached Bristol the previous month.[82] It entered the country via the ports on the East coast at New Ross, Waterford, Dublin and Drogheda. It was so contagious that whoever touched the afflicted person also got the disease. This meant that many would not have received the last rites. It struck Kilkenny between Christmas and March. With so much death around him Clyn must have believed the end of the world was nigh. His account ends in 1349 when he himself presumably succumbed to the disease and in the final entry is the following:

> "*So that notable deeds should not perish with time, and be lost from the memory of future generations, I, seeing these many ills, and that the whole world encompassed by evil, waiting among the dead for death to come, have committed to writing what I have truly heard and examined; and so that the writing does not perish with the writer, or the work fail with the workman, I leave parchment for continuing the work, in case anyone should still be alive in the future and any son of Adam can escape this pestilence and continue the work thus begun.*"[83]

People did not understand what was happening and they were told that the Black Death was a punishment from God for man's wickedness. People turned to prayer and thousands went on pilgrimage to holy wells, known for their curative waters. Clyn states that a favourite place of pilgrimage were curative waters at St Mullins in Carlow.

Prayer was certainly a better option than the primitive medicine that existed at the time and the doctors could only offer bloodletting and improving the surrounding air as a possible remedy. It is not sure where the victims were buried in this country and unlike other cities such as London no Black Death graves have been uncovered here, though it is believed that some may have been buried in an area in The Liberties known as "Blackpits".[84]

The horror and suffering of the time was reflected in statues of the period. Surviving stonework from this period shows stone carvings of people in agony. Tombstones from this period show a skeleton, so called cadaver tombstones.

There are different reasons why Gaelic Ireland was less affected than the Anglo Norman population. The latter lived in towns which, given the poor sanitary conditions, were optimal breeding grounds for the disease, while the Irish tended to live in bogs and on mountains, which seemed to form natural barriers against the disease. The Irish population was also a good deal more dispersed. The Black Death had a catastrophic affect on the English speaking population of the country and English influence outside the Pale waned and the Gaelic culture flourished.[85]

The worst of the plague subsided. Why and how is not known but the introduction of quarantine pest houses for those afflicted and ships containing the plague, would surely have helped. The ports on the east coast were now associated with the Black Death and as a result trade suffered. This was, however, good news for the ports on the west coast which had not been affected to the same extent and it is no coincidence that the ports of Dingle, Galway and Sligo experienced great prosperity in the proceeding century.

ᚱHE ᚷALLOᚷLASS

"The merciless Macdonwald,
Worthy to be a rebel, for to that
The multiplying villainies of nature
Do swarm upon him, from the Western isles
Of kerns and gallowglasses is supplied."

Macbeth
(Act One, scene 2)

The galloglass was a highly skilled fighting man and mercenary who operated in this country from the mid 13th century until the collapse of the Gaelic culture in the 17th century. They had a fearsome reputation and their razor sharp double handed axe was much feared amongst their enemies.

The galloglass originated in Scotland, which was also Gaelic speaking. These elite mercenaries were referred to as foreigners because they had intermarried with Norse settlers. The word galloglass itself comes from two words: *gall* meaning "foreign" and *óglach* meaning "soldier". A highlander without land had few options and most of them were natural warriors, learning martial skills from an early age. Without any farms, the life of the mercenary was the most attractive. The average galloglass was strong and tall and work as a mercenary became something of a family business.

Several clans, such as the MacDonnells from Kintyre, the MacCabes from Arran and McSweeneys from Knapdale were dispossessed in the 14th century Scottish wars of Independence and moved over to Ireland.[86] While the Irish chieftains had part time soldiers, they were basically farmers called up at time of war and might easily flee in panic if the situation became too stressful. The galloglass could be relied upon to hold the line or at worst make an orderly retreat.

The Galloglass claimed not to fear death. In the field of battle they were more inclined to give quarter if the enemy surrendered without much resistance but massacred all before them if strongly opposed. Otherwise they were regarded as cruel and lacking in compassion. They usually served for the period of a quarter of a year and were paid in cows and land accordingly.

Though mainly serving the Gaelic lords, the galloglass also served the Anglo Normans and Lord Deputy and were billeted within the Pale. The 16th century also saw the introduction of the Redshanks from the Western Isles.[87] They were given the nickname because under their kilts they went barelegged no matter what the weather. They mostly came from the clans of Macleod, Maclean, MacDonald and Cambell. They were paid in land and beef and hired for longer periods than the regular galloglass. The English were concerned by the vast number of highly trained mercenaries in the country and often gave captured galloglass no quarter. Over 700 of them were executed in 1571 following the first Desmond Rebellion.

The group of galloglass was led by a constable, a man who was obeyed without question. Usually the constable was a man who had proved himself in battle and always fought at the front. The lord whom they served usually had them billeted among his tenants. They had the right to as much food and drink as they wanted and they usually ate pork, beef and butter and were known to have voracious appetites. Not only did they eat the unfortunate family out of house and home but they also took anything that took their fancy. Galloglass violence against civilians was tolerated and the man of the house could not really object. It is unlikely that they were seen as welcome guests and must have been an unbearable burden on families who could barely feed themselves. They were generally feared and obeyed by all and the only ones they would accept orders from was their employer or constable. Disobeying them would be a capital offence.

Their weapons included a long double handed axe with a six foot handle and double handed sword, the so-called *cliabh mór* or claymore. Unfortunately few examples in good condition of these fine weapons exist in his country. The galloglass wore heavy coats of mail in battle and padded jackets off the battlefield. Each galloglass had a servant boy who carried his coat of mail when not in battle and cooked for him.[88]

There are several depictions of galloglass on contemporary tombs such as Felim O'Connor's tomb in Roscommon Abbey. Albrecht Dürer made the most famous illustration of the galloglass, after he encountered them while in the Spanish Netherlands around 1521.[89]

The introduction of gunpowder and the plantations signalled the end of an era for the galloglass. The Flight of the Earls, when the Gaelic nobles left Ireland, meant they no longer had any employers and though their days were numbered in this country some of them continued to ply their trade abroad and are known to have served in the Thirty Years War in the service of Holland and France. They made a brief comeback in Ireland when galloglass such as Alasdair MacColla fought for Eoin Rua O'Neill at the battle of Benburb in 1646. MacColla was however also involved in massacring innocent civilians, both here and in Scotland.[90] Their name lives on in some place names. Milford in County Donegal is known as *Baile na nGallóglach,* meaning town land or settlement of the galloglass.

ᏖᏂᎬ ᏰᎪᏖᏖᏞᎬ Ꮎᖴ ᏦᏁᎾᏟᏦᎠᎾᎬ

Knockdoe, in the parish of Lackagh, four miles north east of Claregalway, just outside Galway city was the scene of one of the bloodiest battles in Irish history. It is believed that up to 5,000 people lost their lives during the course of the battle, which only lasted a few hours.[91]

The battle was the result of a clash of interests between two Norman families, the Burkes of Clanrickard in South Galway and the Fitzgerald's of Kildare, both of whom had by the 16th century become more Irish than the Irish themselves.[92] The War of the Roses had kept King Henry VII out of Irish affairs, and this enabled the king's representative Gearóid Mór Fitzgerald, eighth Earl of Kildare, to consolidate his power. His influence however was weakest in the West.

Ulick Finn Burke of Clanrickard, who had been elected as chieftain in 1485, had emerged as the most powerful chieftain in the West and was unwilling to accept Gearóid Mór's authority. Subsequently, he formed an alliance with O'Brien of Thomond and the Munster clans. In an effort to win over Burke, Gearóid Mór offered him his daughter Eustacia in marriage. While Burke took her as his wife, he mistreated her and this, according to *The Book of Howth,* was the cause of the conflict. There were however other factors that caused Gearóid Mór to march against his son-in-law.

Burke had attacked and destroyed the castles of O'Kelly, Lord of Hymany, at Monivea, Garbally and Castleblakeney. Furthermore, Burke was living in open adultery with the wife of O'Kelly. O'Kelly went to Gearóid Mór to complain of these outrages and so an army was gathered. The Burkes of Mayo and most of the northern clans also declared their support for Gearóid Mór.

Gearóid Mór was also supported by approximately eighty English soldiers from The Pale, which was at odds with a law the English had passed in 1498, declaring that English soldiers were not to be used in private wars between Irish chieftains. It was a law he was supposed to uphold but he also realised he needed all the support he could get if he were to check Burke's challenge to his ambitions of becoming the dominating figure in Ireland.

In the summer of 1504 Ulick Burke entered Galway,[93] which was in breach of the town's charter. His presence in Galway disrupted trade and the freedom the Galwegians had been granted by the English kings. Thus the fuse for battle had been lit and Gearóid Mór marched his army west.

News of his march reached Burke, who marched out to where the hostile army had taken up position. The two armies faced each other a mile to the North of where the parish church of Lackagh now stands. In all about 10,000 people took part in the battle, with 6,000 supporting Gearóid Mór and 4,000 supporting Ulick Burke.

The galloglass formed the backbone of both armies and the MacSweeneys were the main galloglass clan. They fought on opposing sides at Knockdoe, with one branch serving the O' Donnells of Donegal and another Burke of Clanrickard. They were famous for their use of the razor sharp axe which accounted for the large number of casualties. Indeed, Knockdoe itself comes from, Cnoc Tua meaning Hill of the Axes.

Gearóid Mór deployed his troops in such a way that their right flank was protected by a stone wall and his left by archers. Ulick formed his army into a solid block with his two flanks protected by the galloglass. Accounts of the battle, most notably *The Annals of the Four Masters* and *The Book of Howth* are somewhat sketchy as to what went wrong, but at some stage the tide of battle turned against Burke. Ballybrone on the banks of the River Clare was the scene of the greatest slaughter. Of the nine battalions of galloglass that had taken part, only one left the field.

It is said of Knockdoe that it was the first time gunpowder was used in Ireland and one of Ulick Burke's men was beaten to death by a new weapon called a gun, when he strayed into the wrong camp.[94] Burke's troops fled the field and despite attempts to regroup for another battle his troops went their separate ways. Gearóid Mór held the field and the next day he ransacked Claregalway Castle, taking two of Ulick's sons and a daughter prisoner. From there he marched unopposed into Galway where he rewarded his men with thirty large barrels of wine.

As a result of his victory, the pinnacle of his career, according to the Fitzgerald chroniclers, Gearóid Mór was able to extend English influence into the west, while Ulick Burke's power was destroyed and he himself faded into obscurity. The Burkes of Mayo prospered at his expense and three branches of the O'Kellys west of the river Suck were established at Moylough, Gallagh and Mullaghmore, where they would retain power until the end of Gaelic Ireland. Today a number of cairns still adorn the summit of the 130 metre hill where the dead are said to be buried.

a dark year for galway

Following the disaster of the Spanish Armada the remnants of the fleet sailed down along the Irish coast and had the misfortune to encounter the worst storms in ten years. To add to their misfortune their maps, especially with regard to Connacht, were deeply inaccurate, with only half the province actually appearing on their maps. Of the estimated 5,000 members of the fleet who perished in Ireland just over a fifth lost their lives in Connacht and twelve ships found their watery grave along the Connacht coast.

The Spanish saw the native Irish as savages. Indeed, Captain Cuellar's[95] account, describing his treatment upon reaching land, does little to dispel this image. The English feared the Spanish would invade Ireland and the order went out that no quarter was to be given to any Spaniards landing in Connacht and the man who would oversee this in Connacht was Governor Richard Bingham.

Bingham had been appointed governor of the province in 1584. He was a soldier and seaman who had served both with and against the Spaniards and been involved in English naval manoeuvres against the Spanish at Smerick in 1580. Connacht was relatively peaceful and any sign of rebellion was brutally crushed. It was not long before Bingham became known as "the flail of Connacht".

In September 1588 two ships were sighted off the Aran Islands, but were unable to land in the poor weather. It is not known what became of them. An unnamed Spanish vessel sailed into Galway bay and anchored around Bearna. A party went inland bringing wine with them which they hoped to barter for food and water. It is probable that they knew the coastline well as they had managed to avoid running aground. Galway was the centre of wine trade in

Ireland with the continent. The city was also loyal to the crown and the landing party was met by a mixed group of Galwegians and English troops who ordered the Spanish to lay down their arms. Edward Whyte, a clerk of Bingham's Connacht Council, who spoke Spanish, recorded that the townspeople took them and the mayor of Galway was willing to spare their lives if they would yield up their goods and ship. However, the captain, seeing how his men were being treated, sailed away. Whether or not the ship made it back to Spain is not known.

The *Falco Blanco Mediano*, a 300 tonne ship carrying 103 men on board 16 guns was wrecked on a reef near Freaghillaun in Ballynakill Bay between Clifden and Renvyle. The survivors were looked after by the Connely clan.[96] Bingham had issued a proclamation that all Spaniards were to be surrendered to the English under pain of death and through his network of spies news of the Spaniards' arrival would have soon reached him.

The survivors were transferred to the O'Flahertys of Ballynahinch who brought them to their clan leader Sir Murrough O'Flaherty at Aughnanure. Murrough had been recently knighted by the Queen Elisabeth and was anxious not to antagonise the English in Galway. The survivors were handed over to the garrison at Galway without much delay.[97]

There were several Spanish noblemen amongst the prisoners, the most famous being Don Luis de Cordoba, his nephew Don Gonzalo and the captain Pedro de Arechaga.

Another sept of the O'Flahertys under Tadhg na Buile[98] was involved with another wreck. He had his castle at Ards near Carna, at the head of a natural harbour. Only a small part of a wall now remains as a reminder of this time. The clan knew the sea well. It was at *Duirling na Spáinneach* near Ards in Mweenish Bay that the *Cocepcion Delcano* went ashore. One night in rough weather the crew saw fires on the shore. Thinking the fires were to guide them in they followed them, little realising that Taghg na Buile deliberately intended to drive the ship aground and plunder what remained. It carried two hundred and twenty five men on board and its captain Juan Delcano went down with the ship. Again the survivors were beaten and robbed. The guns from these wrecks were soon recovered by Sir George Carew. Those who survived were brought to Galway, among them Don Diego Sarimento.

In Galway the jails were soon overflowing. Spaniards from wrecks in Mayo had also been sent to The City of the Tribes. They numbered between 300 and 350. Sir William Fitzwilliam, the Lord Deputy of Ireland, had given the order to execute all Spaniards regardless of rank and even to use torture. He came from Athlone to Galway to personally oversee the executions. It is highly probable that his motive was also to get his share of the spoils and he ordered the O'Flahertys to hand over anything of value they had stolen from the Spanish.

Robert Fowley, Captain Nathaniel Smythe and John Byrte along with several assistants were chosen to act as the main executioners. Three hundred Spaniards were taken to a hill at St Augustine's Monastery, now called Forthill, where the grisly deed was to be performed. The Augustinians gave the condemned men the last rites and then to the horror of the Galwegians they were beheaded.[99]

Forty noblemen were set aside for ransom with Don Diego Sarimento and Captain Archega included in their ranks. When news of this reached Fitzwilliam he was furious and ordered them to be executed immediately. The order was carried out. Included in the executions were six Dutch boys, who had been on the ships. It is said that two Spaniards were saved and hidden in the city. This is probably a reference to De Cordoba and his nephew, whose lives were spared. De Cordoba made no secret that he was a wealthy man and there is little doubt that is what kept them alive. They were both repatriated after a ransom was paid. Unsurprisingly, his sojourn in Ireland left him bitter towards the Irish.

The women of Galway made burial shrouds[100] for the corpses and the Pope, learning of what had happened, wrote a letter to Galway, forgiving them. The question remains however, could the

Galwegians have done more for the Spaniards? While it is true that most people in Connemara would have had scarcely enough food for themselves, let alone for a few hundred Spaniards, their actions seem to promote self-interest over showing kindness to strangers.

Today there is little trace in Galway city of these terrible events and most Spaniards and Galwegians are oblivious to what happened so long ago. Forthill is still in existence and is the city's oldest cemetery. Thirty seven Spaniards are said to be buried in a corner of the cemetery and a plaque serves as a reminder to this grisly episode in the city's history.

ᏚᏂᎬ Lynch window

There is an intriguing monument in Galway city known as the Lynch memorial window, which reminds the visitor of a crime that occurred several centuries ago. It may not have happened but the truth should not get in the way of a good story.

Galway was ruled by fourteen merchant families of Norman stock, whom Cromwellian troops would later call the "Tribes of Galway", a moniker that has remained. Their coats of arms are omnipresent in the narrow streets of the medieval city and the name Lynch is forever connected with stern unwavering justice.

Galway considered itself something of a city state modelled on the Italian examples. Though surrounded by the Gaelic culture the city of Galway was English speaking and loyal to the crown. Through trade with Spain it became a rather wealthy city and became well known in Spain. It is said that some Spaniards would ask in what part of Galway Ireland was located.

Lynch was mayor of Galway, as indeed were many of his family. His Spanish business partner wanted his son Gomez to see a bit of the world and like many other Spaniards wanted to learn English, so it was decided to send the young Spanish gentleman to Galway, where he would avail of the hospitality of the Lynch family. Gomez was introduced to the mayor's son, Walther Lynch, a popular youth of similar age, and the two soon became friends. As often is the case a woman came between friends. Walther had his sights set on a girl called Agnes. When he saw Gomez coming out of her house he suspected the worst and was consumed by jealousy. He pursued the Spaniard, who ran towards the Claddagh (from the Gaelic *cladach* meaning rocky sea shore) and catching up with him stabbed him to death and threw his body into the sea. The tide soon washed up the body and Walther's hat was found at the scene. Walther himself had absconded to the woods and became the prime suspect. He knew the game was up and surrendered himself to justice.

The mayor was faced with a dilemma. He had promised his Spanish business partner that his son would be safe in Galway. As mayor he was also the local magistrate with power over life and death and he was forced to condemn his only child to death. At the time felons had to be brought through the town to be brought to jail. It was feared his friends would try to free him. Walther was a popular figure and no hangman wanted anything to do with his execution. Lynch had to see justice done and from the window of his house hanged his only son. It is said that Pope Alex VI sent a gift of rosary beads to the grieving father as consolation, though there is no official record of this.

Mayor Lynch is said to have died in 1519 and was buried in the nearby church of St Nicholas where there is a Lynch memorial window commemorating this illustrious family. When the Cromwellian soldiers ransacked the city in the 17th century local lore has it that they desecrated the Lynch graves at the back of the Franciscan Abbey, robbed the corpses and fed the remains to the local dogs.

In 1854 a Lynch monument was erected on the site of the old house which had been demolished ten years previously. A skull and cross bones serving as a *memento mori* dates from 1621 and is not connected to the Lynch family in any way. Though comprised of a melange of historical remnants from all over the medieval city, generations of tour guides, including myself, informed the visitor that Lynch had hanged his son from that very window. The fact that the infamous window is sixteenth century and the incident is said to have happened a century previously should not get in the way of a good story. The plaque carefully states that the execution took place on that spot rather from the actual window. It reminds me of when a tour guide was showing a group around the nearby church of Saint Nicholas, where Columbus is reputed to have prayed in 1477 when he visited the city. The church was probably the closest church to the medieval harbour at the end of Quay Street, but a tourist wanted to know in which pew the great Columbus had prayed. It happened that a professor of archaeology was in the church at the time and the guide asked him. The professor gave him a look and then pointed at a random bench. From that moment on groups were shown the exact pew where Columbus had prayed.

So is this where the term to "lynch" someone comes from? Unfortunately Galwegians are not the only ones to lay claim to this term and the Americans claim that the term comes from Colonel Charles Lynch (1736-96) of Virginia. It may also come from Captain William Lynch who was indemnified in 1782 for illegally punishing people.[101]

The house was still standing when James Haridman wrote his famous *Hardiman's History of Galway*, and he identifies the street as Lombard Street, known locally as "Dead Man's Lane".[102] The tale is also on display in the lobby of Lynch's Castle on Shop Street, an enduring symbol of Galway's splendid past. The seventeenth century would see major disruption to business as two major wars were fought and Galway, by being loyal to the crown, backed the wrong horse in both. It was impossible to do business in a climate of death and destruction and so the merchant families left the city, taking with them their wealth and marking the decline of the city. Some of the Lynchs settled in Bordeaux where they set up vineyards.

The story has inspired visitors to Galway. When James Joyce came to the city in 1912 he visited the monument which was right beside the childhood home of his partner Nora Barnacle at Bowling Green.[103] He would later use the name Lynch as a character in *Ulysses,* who leaves Stephen in the lurch. Historically speaking the tale may not be one hundred percent accurate, but it is a charming tale from a city that oozes charm.

FiacH mcHugh o Byrne

"Curse and swear, Lord Kildare,
Fiach will do what Fiach will dare
Now Fitzwilliam have a care,
Fallen is your star low
Up with halbert, out with sword,
on we go for, by the Lord
Fiach McHugh has given the word."
"Follow me up to Carlow"

Fiach McHugh O'Byrne (1534–1597) remains one of the forgotten chieftains of the Nine Year War (1592-1601) a war that destroyed the Gaelic clans and opened the way for the colonisation of the entire island. Like the Native Americans he fought to protect his land and his way of life. Indeed, the Elizabethan conquest of Ireland was a blueprint for the colonisation of the Wild West. First it was necessary to defeat the natives militarily, then to force them from their lands and colonise it with settlers and then "civilize" the natives. Wicklow in the 16th century, though close to Dublin, the seat of English power in Ireland, still remained untouched, largely because of its rugged and wild terrain.

The O'Byrnes controlled the territory around the Wicklow Mountains. The name Fiach itself is the Gaelic word for "raven". The clan made frequent raids on the Pale,[104] the area controlled by the English, and in order to curb this, the English started to build garrisons around Fiach's territory.

The Battle of Glenmalure[105] in 1580, fought during the Desmond Rebellion which swept through the southern half of the

55

country, was Fiach's biggest victory against the English. Lord Grey led his army of 2,000 westward through the Pale planning to attack Glenmalure through the Glen of Imaal. The English army was easy to spot from several mountain tops and therefore easy to ambush. According to *The Annals of the Four Masters* an accidental beat of the drum forewarned Fiach that the English were coming. Grey had expected to catch Fiach in the open and easily defeat him. He had not planned on guerilla attacks launched over inhospitable terrain by forces who knew the land. According to the Annals the English lost 900 men and the remnants of his force retreated to the safety of Rathdrum.[106]

A period of peace followed, with Fiach supplying hostages to the English as a sign of his cooperation, but no complete trust between Fiach and Dublin was ever fully established.In 1587 it was reported that Fiach had sent messages to Philip of Spain. This was the time of the Armada when the English were paranoid about an invading fleet. Help from Spain did arrive and a Spanish contingent of 700 landed at Smerwick in County Kerry and took position at a fort called Dún an Óir. Grey was sent Kerry to quash the Desmond Rebellion. He besieged Dún an Óir at Smerwick and called upon the soldiers to surrender. They were left with no other option and surrendered. Once they were disarmed they were massacred.[107] The massacre caused widespread revulsion and the displeasure of Queen Elisabeth herself.

Fiach married Rose O'Toole in 1573. She was regarded a great beauty of her time and was considerably younger than him.[108] A contemporary poet said of her that she was:

"A blazing meteor, wine of grape, flower of women… She glows with the fire of youth. She is the life and death of heroes."[109]

Fiach's sister Margaret Maol was married to Rory Og O'More, the Laois chieftain. Rose proved to be a skilled advisor and Fiach came to rely upon her advice. It was said that Fiach and Rose O'Toole helped plan Red Hugh O'Donnell's first escape from Dublin castle in 1591.[110] O'Donnell had been kidnapped by the English when he was sixteen to ensure his clan's loyalty to the crown. Unfortunately for O'Donnell, due to atrocious weather conditions the English reached him before Fiach did. In 1592 O'Byrne involved himself in a second escape attempt from Dublin Castle. In a dramatic prison break O'Donnell and two friends broke out of the castle by crawling through a sewer and made their way in the snow and ice to Glemalure. The event is now commemorated with a night hike challenge entitled "The Art O'Neill challenge" every January, where the participants, starting at Dublin Castle around midnight, follow the route the escapees more than likely took. The fugitives were guided to Glenmalure. One of the group, Art O'Neill perished and a cross at Granabeg under Table Mountain, which can still be seen, was erected at the spot long after the event.[111] O'Donnell recovered from his wounds and was sent back to Donegal where he commenced what became known as the Nine Years War. It was a war that initially started off in the Irish favour but the tide turned and it would mark the end of Ireland's Gaelic speaking nobility. The lack of unification among the Irish chieftains, with some siding with the Northern chieftains and others with the English, weakened the Irish cause and essentially the Irish themselves were the architects of their doom.

Lord Grey was succeeded as deputy by Sir John Perrot in 1584, and he in turn by Sir William Fitzwilliam in 1588. The authorities in Dublin feared Fiach would invade Dublin and as a result troops that could have been sent to fight O'Neill and O'Donnell were tied up in Dublin and Wicklow. There was a brief peace in 1595 but the Dublin authorities knew they had to kill Fiach in order to turn their complete attention to the northern chieftains

He was still a force to be reckoned with and The O'Byrnes launched an attack at Athy. His wife was captured in 1595 and convicted of treason by a Dublin jury and sentenced to be burned at the stake.[112] Her life was spared because she had been convinced to convey information to Fiach that his son Turlough was betraying him. Consequently O'Byrne delivered over Turlough who, refusing to engage in any more schemes to betray his father, was executed.

Fiach was in open revolt by 1594 and attacked Ardree Castle on the Barrow near Athy. In order to spread the rebellion he sent his nephew Owney MacRory O'More into Laois to destroy the Queen's County plantation. One Elizabethan commentator suggested that half the royal army in Ireland should be stationed around Fiach's territory, placed in garrisons at Ballinacor, Arklow, Wicklow and in Shillelagh. The English now began counter attacking and were in far greater numbers. Fiach still managed to lead a raid to the village of Crumlin outside of Dublin and set it ablaze. He was now being ruthlessly head hunted by Captian Lee. A traitor told the English where to find the elderly chieftain who tracked him down to a cave in Glenmalure and cut off his head.

O'Byrne's corpse was cut up and his head placed on a pike staff on the wall over Dublin Castle drawbridge, before being sent to London. His wife Rose was sentenced to burn at the stake but some sources state she lived until 1629.[113] His deeds were commemorated in a 19th century ballad by Patrick Joseph McCall "Follow me up to Carlow", also known as "The Marching Song of Feagh MacHugh". Following his death, the county of Wicklow, Ireland's youngest county, was created in 1608.

Myler Magrath

In a country where religion was deemed so important, changing one's religion, especially for reasons of pure opportunism, was frowned upon. Nobody could adapt more to the times than Myler Magrath and his lack of scruples make him, even today, a much reviled figure among both Protestants and Catholics.

He was born in Fermanagh in 1522 as Maolmhuire, which means "Servant of Mary" though contemporaries referred to him as *Maol gan Muire* (Servant without Mary) in reference to his abandonment of the Catholic faith. In English, he is generally known as Myler. He entered the Franciscans at the age of eighteen and lived through the troubled age of the Reformation. Henry VIII had established his own church in order to remarry and the new religion, along with English ways in general, were being established in Ireland. Though the English were being met with resistance McGrath watched to see which way the wind was blowing and chose his side accordingly.

He was sent to Rome to lobby for the brother of Shane O'Neill, who wanted to become Bishop of Down and Connor. Magrath decided he himself was just as good for the job and convinced the Vatican of this. Thus he was appointed Bishop of Down and Connor in 1565, something that did not endear him to the O'Neills.[114]

In May 1567 met with the Lord Deputy of Ireland, Sir Henry Sidney, at Drogheda, where he agreed to conform to the new church. Just because he changed religion did not however mean that he would give up his Catholic offices and he remained Bishop of Down and Connor until 1580 when the Vatican finally acted and declared him a heretic.

In 1570 he was appointed Bishop of Clogher by Queen Elisabeth and a few months later became Archbishop of Cashel. He functioned as a spy who reported to Dublin priests and bishops who were still practising Catholics as well as any rebel activity in the area. The English trusted his opinions and he became invaluable to them.

In 1571 he imprisoned some Franciscan priests at Cashel. James FitzMaurice FitzGerald threatened to burn to ashes everyone and everything connected with Magrath if they were not released. Magrath hastily complied.

He married Áine Ní Mhearra, who was a devout Catholic as were all of his nine children. It is said that one Friday she refused to eat meat. When Magrath asked why she would not eat meat with him she replied; *"Because I do not wish to commit sin with you."* *"Surely,"* he replied, *"you committed a far greater sin in coming to bed with me, a friar!"*[115]

Until the end of the Desmond Rebellions in 1583, Magrath remained in his province, while assisting the English government on the one hand and intriguing with the Catholic rebels on the other. In October 1582, he travelled to England bearing letters of strong recommendation, which cited his ability to provide valuable information on the rebels. Despite his allegiance to the authorities, Magrath never arrested the new Catholic Archbishop of Cashel, Kearney, who lived peacefully under his nose. However, Magrath continued to court favour with the authorities, and in 1584 he did arrest the Catholic Bishop of Emly, Murrough MacBrian, who died two years later in custody in Dublin Castle.[116] In 1591 Magrath again visited England. While there he spoke with the Prince of Breifne, Brian O'Rourke, whom he tried to convert to Protestantism. O'Rourke had been knighted by the English, who had later questioned his loyalty when he helped survivors of the Spanish Armada, including Francisco de Cuellar. He was not impressed by Magrath and cursed the bishop as he stood on the gallows waiting to be hanged, drawn and quartered at Tyburn.

It is no coincidence that Cashel is built like a fortress and the archbishop had reason to fear kidnapping. He lived in a keep adjoined to the cathedral. His excuse for having a private army was to protect himself after the murder of Bishop Walsh of Ossory in his palace in Kilkenny. [117]Like Pope Julius II, the Warrior Pope, Magrath was more himself when abroad on his horse dressed for battle than at home in his palace fulfilling his ecclesiastical duties. He was attacked on several occasions. In one incident an attacker had left him seriously injured on the road to Dublin. Visitations to his diocese in 1604 and 1607 showed ruinous churches, ill-educated clergy guilty of neglect of duty, and above all as many as seventy parishes held in benefit to members of his family, including one to his widowed daughter and one to his daughter-in-law. One contemporary wrote, "People in his diocese scarcely knew there was a God. His cathedral was no better than a hog-sty."[118] He kept for himself most of the revenues of his diocese and passed on to his clergy only a pittance. Archbishop Jones' sketch of the diocese of Cashel revealed the extent of Magrath's mishandling of church finances. Preachers were almost unheard of, churches were in ruins, and the education of children was neglected. In all the years that Magrath held his appointments he had made scarcely any effort to tend to the spiritual or physical fabric of the Protestant religion in his dioceses.[119]

The reader may wonder why the English were prepared to tolerate a bishop who behaved immorally, cared little for his religious duties and even had his children baptized as Catholics. The answer lies in the importance the administration attached to Magrath's services as an informer. The wind of change blew once more when Elisabeth died in 1603 and was succeeded by James. The English had now all but completely conquered the island by force of arms and had little use for the renegade bishop. Thus Magrath fell from grace and for a time was deeply troubled that he would be put on trial, but his incredible luck held out. Many in Ireland hoped he would reconcile himself with the Catholic Church. He died in

1623 at the age of 100 after having served 52 years as a bishop. It has been suggested that the character of Magrath in James Joyce's *Finnegans Wake* owes something to the reputation of Miler Magrath. His tomb is at Cashel and easy to find, though where he is buried is another matter. Aware that his grave might be desecrated the epitaph reads:

Venerat In Dunum Primo Sanctissimus Olim

Patricius Nostri Gloria Magna Soli

Huic Ego Succedens, Ultinam Tam Sanctus Ut

Ille

Sec Duni Primo Tempore Praesul Eram.

Anglia Lustra Decem Sed Post Tua Scepta

Colebam,

Principibus Placui Marte Tonante Tuis

His Ubi Sum Positus Non Sum, Sum Non Ubi Non

Sum.

Sum Nec In Ambobus Sum Nec Utroqcue Loci.

Patrick, the glory of our isle and gown,

First a bishop in the see of down

I wish that I, succeeded him in place

As bishop, had an equal grace,

I served thee, England, fifty years in jars

And pleased thy princes in the midst of wars.

Here where I'm placed I'm not; and thus the case is

I'm not in both, yet am in both the places.[120]

william Lamport

William Lamport (1615-1659) was a student, pirate, soldier, adventurer, spy and lover. Though not so well known in his native Ireland he is a celebrated figure in Mexico where he is recognised as an early contributor to Mexican Independence and known as Guillén Lombardo or Don Guillén Lombardo de Guzmán. He may even have been the inspiration for Zorro.

Lamport was born in Wexford Town around 1615 to a wealthy Old English merchant family. The Old English families had come to Ireland with the Norman Conquest in the 12th century and despite the Reformation had retained their Catholic faith. He was given the best education of the time by the Jesuits in both London and Dublin. By the time he was twenty-one he could speak fourteen languages. He was arrested for sedition in London in 1627 after he was caught distributing pro Catholic pamphlets. He escaped and made his way to France, but was captured en route by pirates and pressed into their service, taking part in the defeat of the English Navy at the siege of La Rochelle. He stayed with them for around two years until he got a chance to escape in Bordeaux and make his way to the Irish community in exile at La Coruña in Galicia. Taking on the name Guillén Lombardo he studied at the Colegio de Niños, the Irish school in Santiago.[121] In 1633 he entered military service when he joined an Irish regiment of the Spanish army and fought against the Swedes at the Spanish Netherlands. Europe was the time in the grip of the notorious Thirty Years War (1618-48). He distinguished himself at the Battle of Nördlingen in 1634 and led the Irish soldiers at the siege of Fuenterrabía (1638), a battle fought between the French and the victorious Spanish.

He went to Madrid where he worked in espionage. In 1639 he became involved in an invasion plan of Ireland. The Spanish however had unpleasant memories of previous ventures to Ireland and were reluctant to commit men and resources and the plan remained a pipedream. Lombardo began a relationship with a noble woman called Doña Ana de Cano y Leyva and when she became pregnant the scandal was such that he fell from grace and was sent as a spy to Mexico, then known as New Spain, in 1640.

Though part of high society, Lombardo sympathised more with the common people. He believed the actions of the Conquistadors were contrary to the ideals of Christian justice.[122] He opposed slavery and championed social equality in a society where class and ethnic divisions were pronounced. They were radical notions for the time in which he lived.

He drew up potential plans for Mexican Independence. The territory would have a monarch, democratically elected by the people. He believed that if Mexico retained its silver instead of sending it to Spain it would become a great power. His plans were philosophical and there is no evidence that he actually intended to drive the Spanish out. Nevertheless, it was the first Document of Independence in the New World and revolutionary. New ideas were dangerous and less appreciated by the notorious Spanish Inquisition. He was arrested in 1642 and charged with heresy. It was claimed that his visions of New Spain were induced by the drug peyote. He defied the Inquisition and by doing so had made a powerful enemy against whom he had little chance of winning.

He spent the next eight years in prison and managed to break out in 1650 in a daring escape attempt that added to his reputation. While on the run he posted pamphlets throughout Mexico City criticising the Inquistion. He was soon recaptured and the Inquistion was determined to break him and he spent the next nine years in solitary confinement. He tried to maintain a close relationship with God by writing psalms with homemade ink and a chicken feather as a quill and his bed sheets as a parchment. By the time the authorities had found out what he was up to, he had written 900 psalms in Latin.

The years of confinement, were taking their toll and he gradually went insane. The end came in 1659 when he was sentenced to the *Auto de Fé* or burning at the stake the standard way the Inquisition dealt with critics. Defiant to the end, he managed to strangle himself before the Inquisition could perform the macabre spectacle.

The figure of Zorro emerged in the 19th century when in 1872 Vincente Riva Palacio wrote "Memoirs of an Impostor"[123] where the figure of Don Guillén Lombardo leads a double life as a poet and dandy by day and a swashbuckling swordsman with an eye for the ladies by night. Interest was rekindled at the beginning of the 20th century when Mexican nationalism was strong and Lamport was recognised as a pioneer for Mexican Independence. His statue was included among the other Mexican patriots when *La Columna de Independencia* was unveiled in 1910. Johnston McCulley wrote his famous novel Zorro in 1919 and many believed that the character was based on Lamport to the extent that he was labelled "The Irish Zorro". An English biography was written by Gerard Ronan in 2004.

mÁiRe RuA

The ruin of Leamaneh Castle in county Clare is imposing and one of the most well known castles in the country. The locals there are always ready to tell visitors of the woman who lived there, one Máire Rua or 'Auburn haired Mary' as her name translates. She was born in 1615 in either Bunratty or Clonderlaw.[124] She was a shrewd woman who adapted herself to the conditions in the land, mangaing to hold onto her lands while others lost them.Aged around seventeen, she married Daniel Neylon of Dysert O'Dea in north Clare and they had three sons, William, Daniel and Michael. When her husband died in 1639 Máire assumed control of the estate.

It was not befitting to be a widow at such a young age and she married a second time to Conor O'Brien of Leamaneh in 1639, bringing £1,000 with her into the union. The couple had eight children. The Rebellion of 1641 spread from Ulster all over the country and the couple were identified by Gregory Hickman as having raided his cattle.

Leamaneh Castle was a 15th century tower house not far from Kilfenora.[125] Such tower houses, found all over the country, were built primarily for defence and as a place of residence they were dark and damp. The introduction of gunpoweder in the 16th century had made their purpose obsolete. By the 17th century most people were deserting such castles in favour of mansions. In the case of Leamaneh they built the mansion onto the towerhouse in 1648. The name "Leamaneh" comes from the Irish "Léim an Eich" meaning "Horse leap". According to legend she kept a wild stallion and her suitors were expected to ride the beast. One such suitor, Torach Ó Loughlainn managed to stay on and when Máire saw the stallion and mount return she closed the gates of Leamaneh. The stallion died while jumping the gates and hence the name "Léim an Eich".

Conor O'Brien was killed while leading a party against Cromwellian troops at Inchicronan in 1651. Those who fought against Cromwell were forced to forefeit their lands as punishment. She would have realised this and not long after her huband's death, dressed in her finery she went to Limerick offering to marry any one of Cromwell's officers. Thus she married for a third time to Cornet (junior officer) John Cooper. They had a son together, making it her thirteenth child.

Their estate was reduced in size around 1654 when Catholics from Ulster were transplanted to Clare. In 1662 she was accused of the 1642 murder of Thomas Bacon. Her powerful friends however interceded on her behalf and she was given a royal pardon.

Legends of her are numerous and willingly recited by the people of Clare. Many of them characterise her as a lustful and cruel woman. One such legend claims she "accidentally" pushed Cooper off the castle wall.[126] Like many figures from Irish history facts can be clouded by tall tales and fiction.

ᏪᏂᎬ ᏪᎬᎪᏮ ᎾᎱ ᎾᏞᎥᏉᎬᏒ ᏚᏞᎤᏁᏦᎬᏖᏖ

"Deo Gratias"
(Bishop Plunkett's response to his death sentence)

The town of Drogheda in County Louth contains an unusual relict, the head of Oliver Plunkett, once the Catholic Primate of All Ireland. He was born in 1629 in Loughcrew, County Meath, into a troubled country. The Gaelic nobility had fled to the continent leaving the country leaderless and both the Gaelic culture and Catholic religion were in the process of being erased.

His family were wealthy and he was educated in Dublin and continued his education in Rome in 1647, where he studied at The Irish College, becoming ordained in 1654. While he was abroad his native country was in dire straits. Responding to reports of massacres of Protestant settlers, both real and exaggerated, Cromwell came to Ireland to seek revenge. A large shift in the population happened when the native Irish were driven west of the Shannon, where the land was poorer, in a policy simplified as "to hell or to Connacht". Priests and civilians were kidnapped and sold as slaves to Barbados, where some of their descendents, "the redlegs", still live.[127]

Plunkett returned to Ireland in 1670 with the restoration of the king. He immediately set about reorganising the battered Catholic Church and built several schools. He established a Jesuit College in Drogheda in 1670. It was attended by 150 pupils, 40 of whom were Protestant, making it the first integrated school in Ireland.[128]

Catholics were distrusted in Britain. The term "Popery" was more than just a fear of Catholics but also the belief that Catholics intended to plot against the king and overthrow the Church of

England. The Guy Fawkes Gunpowder plot of 1605 had given credibility to such theories.

Plunkett refused to comply with the Test Act of 1673. It was impossible to be a practising Catholic and adhere to this act. According to the act only those who professed the faith of the established church, Protestantism, were eligible for public office. Plunkett's college at Drogheda was levelled and he was forced into hiding.[129] He was required to leave the country but refused.

Public anxieties in Britain were raised in the late 1670s by the issue of the royal succession. Charles II fathered no legitimate offspring. This meant that the crown would pass to his brother, the Duke of York, who had converted to Catholicism. The so-called 'exclusion crisis' was provoked by allegations made by Titus Oates,[130] a former Jesuit novice, of a "popish plot" to assassinate Charles II and place his brother on the throne. According to Oates it would be carried out by the Jesuits. The King himself was not impressed with Oates. The fantastical plot was given credibility by the mysterious death of Sir Edmund Bury Godfrey, the magistrate who first investigated Oates' claims. Plunkett was arrested in Dublin and imprisoned in Dublin Castle. He was tried at Dundalk for conspiring to bring French soldiers as part of the "Popish Plot". The charges could not be proven as the prosecution witnesses themselves were wanted men and failed to turn up in court. It soon became obvious that no jury in Ireland would convict the head of the Catholic Church in Ireland and Plunkett was sent to London for trial. Oates himself soon fell from grace and was arrested on charges of sedition. When James II came to the throne in 1685 he ordered him whipped through the streets of London five days a year for the rest of his life.[131]

The jury did not take long to return with a guilty verdict. Plunkett was found guilty of treason and promoting the Catholic faith. He responded with *"Deo Gratias"*. Those found guilty of treason could only expect one outcome-to be hanged, drawn and quartered. The process included half hanging until the victim lost consciousness. The sentence was carried out on 1st July 1681 at Tyburn. Plunkett was one of fifteen innocent men to be executed on flimsy accusations.

His remains were exhumed in 1683 and brought to a Benedictine monastery at Lamspringe, near Hildesheim in Germany and also Downside Abbey in England, while his head was brought to Rome. From there it was taken to Drogheda in 1725 and eventually went on display in 1921 in a small glass case in Saint Peter's Church.[132] Also on display in the same church is the door from the condemned cell of Newgate Prison, London where he was imprisoned. Oliver Plunkett was the last Catholic martyr in Britain. Beatified in 1920, he became Saint Oliver Plunkett in 1975.

the Limerick Germans

"One beautiful fair's day as I went through Baile Uí Shíoda
Who should I meet on the way only a Palatine's daughter
She asked me my name and where I was from. Said she:
'If you abandon The Mass you will get my hand in marriage
And have a pretty girl by your side if you want a Palatine'."

The above words are an English translation from a charming folksong song *Iníon an Phalaitinigh*[133] and recall an all but forgotten time when Germans lived in Ireland.

Eighteenth century Europe was a turbulent place and Western Germany, particularly the area along the French border now known as Rhineland-Pfalz, was ravaged by war. The Lutheran Palatines inhabiting the area suffered greatly from French attacks and Queen Anne, a champion of Protestantism, offered them refuge in Britain. In 1709 Eight thousand moved to Rotterdam, where English ships were to convey them to a safe haven. It turned out that there were two thousand Catholics in the group and they were turned away. Three thousand of the group sailed to The New World while the remaining three thousand Palatines were brought first of all to England, which was ill equipped to deal with them and then on to Dublin, where in the autumn of 1709, 871 families, numbering 3,073 arrived. It was hoped they would augment the Protestant population of rural Ireland.

Their time in Dublin was not happy one. They were overcharged for food, were sold watered down milk and given counterfeit money in change. This was so rife that the Lord Mayor of Dublin issued a proclamation promising to deal severely with the culprits.

From Dublin the Palatines were dispatched to sympathetic landlords in Gorey on the Abel Ram estate and also Carlow. By far the biggest colony however would turn out to be in Rathkeale County Limerick on the Southwell estate. Sir John Southwell, a Catholic landlord warmly embraced the concept of the colony and by 1714 over 130 families were living on Southwell's lands.[134]

Each Palatine received eight acres of land at a nominal rent of five shillings per acre and at leases of three lives. Each family was also allowed forty shillings a year for seven years to buy stock and utensils. This was quite generous, considering that the Irish tenants at the time were paying rents of thirty five shillings per acre. Such generosity did not prevail and in the 1740s many landlords increased the rent considerably, so much so that many Palatines left the country in favour of America. It was around this time that the colony in Gorey and Carlow all but vanished.

In addition to the land, every Palatine household received a musket to protect themselves from the Irish. The Palatine men joined a local Yeomanry calling themselves "True Blues" or "German Fusiliers". It turned out to be unnecessary as the native Irish left them in peace.

To earn a living they farmed the land and were known to grow hemp and flax as well as raise cattle. Their agricultural practices differed to that of the locals. While the Irish were wont to plant potatoes using the spade, the Palatines used horses and ploughs. They ploughed the land in spring, planted the potatoes in the furrows and covered them over again with the plough. Again at harvest they used the plough to dig out the potatoes. They were also renowned for their cider production.

They had a distinctive Germanic lifestyle until the 19th century. While their Christian names such as Adam, Ebenezer, Ernest, Frederick, Jacob, Jasper, Julius, Ethel, Rebecca and Julius, were distinctly German they tended to adopt more Irish names in the 19th century.

One of their customs was to be buried with their bibles, which accounts for the fact that while they spoke German, they had no bibles in the German language. They maintained their dialect until 1880 when the last speaker, Long Anne Teskey from Rathkeale, who was also a fluent Irish speaker, passed away at the age of 115. The name Teskey is still common in the Rathkeale area.

While it was expected that the Palatines join the Anglican Church, many turned to Methodism. They built a Methodist church at Ballingrane near Rathkeale in 1766 which was dedicated to the memory of Philip Embury and his cousin Barbara Heck. Both were from the area and when they left for America they became leading figures in the Methodist church. John Wesley, the founder of Methodism, made several missionary trips to Ireland and always made a point of visiting the Palatine communities of County Limerick.[135] The small cemetery in the churchyard still bears the graves of the Palatine community. The church had no bell so a cow horn, which still survives, was used to summon the faithful to service.

Largely due to their varied diet they were not greatly afflicted by the Great Famine of 1845. The dire state of the country, however, encouraged many to emigrate to America which further reduced the colony.

While in the eighteenth century they tended to marry only within the Palatine community, thereafter their reduced numbers forced them to marry outside the colony and as time went by they became more integrated with the Irish and their settlements diminished. Little remains of their settlement today, although in Killaheen there is still an old Palatine well. It consists of a trench cut into the ground deeper than the water table. The sides and the top are lined with stone and 18 stone steps lead down to the clear, cold water.

The colony failed to spread the Protestant faith to any large extent in the area and they failed to make linguistic impact. Consequently no Palatine words survive in the locality today. Their ancestors, however, are eager to keep their memory alive. Many Irish surnames such as Cole, Crowe, Young, Cooke, St. John, Bowen,

Laurence, Lowe, Miller, Everett, Ross, and Switzer have Palatine origins. The latter family became famous in the retail business.

The Irish Palatine association was formed in 1989. At an old disused railway building just off the N21 Limerick to Tralee road in Rathkeale, they have a Palatine heritage centre.[136]

ANNE BONNEY

The Caribbean in the 18th century was the golden age of piracy. One of the most feared pirates was a Corkonian called Anne Bonney[137]. She was born around 1698 in Kinsale as the illegitimate daughter of the lawyer William Cormac and Mary Brennan, one of his maids.[138] The ensuing scandal was not good for his business and he left to start a new life in the Americas and settled in South Carolina where he had a successful plantation.

It was to this kind of lifestyle Anne was raised in Charleston. She became bored with the dull life and craved adventure and started to hang around with the wrong crowd. At the age of 16 she married a lowly seamen and minor pirate from Bristol called James Bonney. Bonney was only after her inheritance, something of which her father was aware and he disinherited her before their wedding. In retaliation she is said to have burnt his crops. The newlywed couple went to New Providence in The Bahamas which was then a haven for pirates. For Anne the new lifestyle offered adventure that she could never had hoped for on her father's plantation. Her husband was also an informer and Anne distanced herself from him, preferring the company of other pirates. It was around this time that she met Captain Jack Rackham, otherwise known as Calico Jack because of his extravagant clothes. He was said to have been the first pirate to use the skull and crossbones as a flag. He is even more familiar in popular culture as the model for the pirate in the movie *Pirates of the Caribbean*.

At the time he was in the Bahamas because an amnesty had been announced for pirates. They were affecting trade and it seemed like the best way to stop piracy. The two soon began an affair and when Bonney found out he dragged Anne before the governor. Calico Jack offered to buy her divorce but James Bonney refused. It was illegal to buy a divorce, but at the time it was not unusual. The governor gave her the option of returning to her husband or getting a public flogging for adultery. She chose neither option and escaped with Calico Jack, sailing away dressed as a man on a ship he had just stolen.

She was the only woman on board but the crew respected her, not because she was the captain's mistress but more due to her fighting skills; she was a good shot and could use a sword quiet well. Her temper also made them keep their distance. Another woman, Mary Read, also disguised as a man, came on board. She had always worn male clothes, partially because her mother got an allowance from an aunt who thought she was a boy and disliked girls and partially because she believed men had it easier in life than women and could travel around easier.[139] The two were unaware of each other's sex until Bonney tried to seduce her. Together the two of them would go down in history as fearsome female pirates. It is rumoured that the pair had a lesbian relationship but nothing of this has been proven. Anne gave birth to a still born baby and recuperated in Cuba before returning to piracy.

Rackham had stolen a royal navy ship and was being pursued relentlessly by pirate hunter Jonathan Barnet. In 1720 a Royal navy man-o-war, *The Albion*, came across Jack's ship. A short battle ensued and the main mast was blown away, making escape virtually impossible. The crew were celebrating and had been drinking rum so they were in little condition to fight. The Royal Navy boarded the vessel and were confronted by Read and Bonney, who fought like hellcats and shot and swung their cutlasses at the boarding party, refusing to submit and urging the crew hiding below to join the fight.[140] They were eventually overpowered and brought to Jamaica where they were tried and sentenced to be hanged, the usual sentence for piracy. Calico Jack was hanged at Gallows Point in Port Royal and hung from a giblet in a cage as a warning to others. Before he died Bonney famously told him:

"Had you fought like a man, you need not have been hanged like a dog." [141]

The men had been tried separately and when it came to the trial of Read and Bonney they announced they were both pregnant and pregnant women could not be hanged. Their execution was postponed to see if they really were pregnant and, if so, until after they had given birth. Conditions in prison were atrocious and Mary died of prison fever while awaiting the birth of her child. There is no record of Anne's execution. Among the less fanciful accounts, The *Oxford Dictionary of National Biography* suggests that her father came to her rescue and, bribing the right officials, got her out of jail and she returned to his home at Charleston, South Carolina. Her story was told in Charles Johnson's (pseudonym for Daniel Defoe), *A General History of the Pyrates,* printed in London in 1724.[142]

She led a quiet inconspicuous life thereafter. It was there that she gave birth to her second child and married Joseph Burleigh and the couple had ten children. Though less exciting it was a safer and longer life. She died in 1782 and is said to be buried in South Carolina, though the exact location is unknown.[143]

seán na sagart - the priest-catcher

I first heard about the infamous Seán na Sagart from my good friend Diarmuid Clifford and, as luck had it, I was sent to Ballintubber Abbey the very next week as part of a tour where the helpful staff told the story. Eighteenth century Ireland was a turbulent place for Catholics and the Penal laws were strictly enforced. The laws had been introduced after the battle of the Boyne and were designed to establish economic, social and political supremacy of Protestantism by keeping Catholics in a state of incapacity. The laws hoped to eradicate Catholicism in Ireland within two generations and thus bishops and regular clergy were banished and no new priests were permitted to enter the country. The Penal Act of 1709 demanded priests take the *Oath of Abjuration*[144] and recognise the Protestant Queen Anne as Queen of England and Ireland. Any cleric who refused was deported. Out of an estimated two thousand priests in Ireland at that time, only thirty three priests swore the oath. Despite the harshness of these laws the majority of the population remained Catholic and the mass was still celebrated, albeit at secret locations such as Mass rocks. It was not unusual for the priest to wear a veil while saying mass. Thus any mass goer could honestly say they did not know who had said the mass. While mass was being said someone kept watch for the soldiers and an escape route was always at hand. People were equally vigilant for the infamous and widely despised priest-catchers.

The most famous priest-catcher in the west was Seán na Sagart. He was born John Mullowney in 1690 at Derrew, near Ballyheane in the parish of Ballintubber, County Mayo. Mullowney was by all accounts something of a scoundrel. His two passions were horse stealing and drinking. His former passion landed him in trouble with the law around 1715 and he came before a judge in Castlebar, almost certain to face the hangman's noose. The authorities however saw potential in him and realised a person of such low character was ideal for the purposes of priest-hunting. Thus, he was spared on condition that he became a priest-catcher, and it was not long before he became known as Seán na Sagart or John of the Priests.

Priest-hunters, or pursuivants as they were also known, operated in a similar way to bounty hunters. A Bishop was worth £100, a priest £20 and a monk or Jesuit £10. Some like Seán na Sagart had been coerced into doing so, others, former soldiers and spies, had volunteered, while others like the infamous Spaniard John Garzia in Dublin had been brought in from abroad. Though lucrative, it was a risky business. They were considered the lowest form of society and it was not unusal for a mob to chase them through the steets and beat them to death. The distribution of priest-hunters throughout the country was uneven and in some areas religious worship was overlooked, though Seán, operating in Mayo, could never be accused of being relaxed in his duties. Although he was held in poor regard, some opened their doors to him and he was a regular visitor to Newbrook House in Robeen, near Ballinrobe in South County Mayo, then the residence of John Bingham. He was reputed to be the most active priest-hunter in the west and his ill gotten gains were used to finance his heavy drinking and expensive tastes.

Though small in stature, Seán was quite strong and always armed with a knive and pistols. He was usually accompanied by mounted troops when he rode out on his business.In 1715 Seán gave testimony at Castlebar before the Grand Jury on the whereabouts of the Vicar General of Tuam Diocese, Francis Bourke and James Lynch, Titular Archbishop of Tuam. The document bore a cross for his signature, suggesting he was illiterate.

If he could not catch a priest he killed him. It is not unknown how many priests he killed, but it is recorded that he shot a Fr.

Andrew Higgins as he tried to escape after celebtraing mass near a cave at Pulnatheacken. Seán gave evidence that he saw priests being ordained in Laukill Wood, Aughagower. According to tradition Seán arrested and killed priests and brought the heads to the Sheriff in Castlebar. It is also said that the heads were thrown into a little lake in the parish of Ballintubber, Burriscarra and that it is called "Loch na gCeann" (Lake of the Heads).

By 1726 priest-hunting in places such as Dublin was a dying trade, but not so in the west where Seán was still plying his trade with a passion. He even used his own family to catch priests and once, when he wanted to catch a priest in Ballintubber, he convinced his sister, a widow and a devout Catholic by the name of Nancy Loughnan, that he was gravely ill and needed to confess before he died.

A priest, Father Kilger was duly sent for and arrived in disguise. As the priest knelt by the bed to pray he leant closer to hear his last confession. Seán suddenly jumped up and stabbed him. There was widespread revulsion and Seán knew the priest's nephew Friar Bourke would probably be at the funeral in Ballintubber.

The friar was indeed at the funeral, accompanied by two armed raparees John McCann and Fergus McCormick, who acted as his bodyguards. As the procession reached Ballintubber a troop of redcoats was seen moving in and out sprang Seán na Sagart from behind a bush. As he grabbed hold of the disguised friar he cried "tá mo chíos íochta agam", (my rent is paid) in reference to the bounty he would receive. The friar managed to break away from him and ran towards the Partry Mountains with Seán in pursuit. The pursuit is said to have gone on for the greater part of the day. Exhausted, the friar and the priest-hunter fought each other. John had followed the pair and in the struggle the friar stabbed Seán na Sagart, with McCann who was a relative of the murdered Father Higgins finishing the job.

Seán na Sagart was buried at Ballintubber Abbey, County Mayo. The locals took umbrage at this and they dug up him up and threw his corpse into nearby Lough Carra, but the local priest ordered the mortal remains to be reinterred, albeit in unconsecrated ground with the body facing north, where the sun never rises. An ash tree, which never bore fruit and became known as Seán na Sagart's Tree, marked its grave until it split the grave one hundred and fifty years later.

James Annesley

Robert Louis Stevenson's famous work *Kidnapped* was inspired by true events and the main character was based on the figure of James Annesley (1715-1760) from County Wexford. The novel *Kidnapped* was not the first fictionalised account of Annesley, but undoubtedly the most well known. The story itself is stranger than fiction. Indeed historians doubted much of the story as being true until recently. In 2010, A. Roger Ekirch wrote *Birthright:The True Story That Inspired Kidnapped* which proved a lot of the story was true.[145]

The word "kidnapped" itself was coined in the 18th century and referred to the all too common practice of stealing homeless children for sale abroad as slaves. Children were easy targets, easy to steal and once on board easy to control. Shockingly, in the eyes of the law, it was considered a minor misdemeanour.

The Annesleys were part of the Protestant Ascendancy, a wealthy minority that ruled the country. Originally from England, the Annesley family obtained a massive amount of land in Ireland during the Elizabethan conquest of the 16th century, when Captain Robert Annesley, from Buckinghamshire, was granted 2,600 acres in County Limerick after the natives had been resettled elsewhere.[146]

James Annesley was born in 1715 at Dunmain House, Dunmain, County Wexford, where his father Arthur Annesley, 5th Baron Altham (1689-1727) had extensive lands including much of New Ross. When James was two, his father threw his mother, Mary Sheffield out of the house, falsely accusing her of having an affair. Father and son moved to Dublin where the baron fell into debt. It is believed his father's mistress Sally Gregory disliked James and at age eight his father threw him onto the streets to fend for himself.

A butcher, John Purcell took pity on the boy and offered him a place to live in the summer of 1727. When his father died in autumn of that year James attended the funeral at Christchurch, although he had not been invited. He stood there in his tattered clothes and proclaimed that the deceased was his father and ran out the door. He may have done this for sentimental reasons or to let people know that there was an heir. He stood to inherit his father's wealth, something of which his uncle Richard was also aware.

Not long after the funeral strange men began hanging around Purcell's yard, but the butcher saw them off with his cudgel. The following April however, James, who was by then twelve years old was seized in Ormond Market, behind the present day Ormond Quay and brought to George's Quay where a ship was waiting to take him to America. Uncle Richard had made a deal with the ship's captain to sell James as an indentured servant once they reached America.

Indentured servants entered the New World willingly or as in the case of young James, less willingly. Paupers sought a better life in the New World and sometimes in return for their passage offered their services free of charge for a set number of years, usually between three to seven years. The majority were teenagers. When their period of indenture had been served they were free and they usually settled in the New World. It was a practice written about at the time, most notably by Daniel Defoe who mentions it in his work *Moll Flanders* and much later by John Steinbeck in *Cup of Gold* (1929). White slaves in the new world were nothing new and Cromwell had started sending Irish people as slaves to Barbados in the 1650s. Their descendents are still there and are known as "red legs".[147]

James found himself in Newcastle, Delaware, where he would spend twelve years as a slave. It is not known for how much he was sold, but the going rate was somewhere in the region of sixteen pounds. He was sold to Duncan Drummond a small-time merchant-farmer who was living in north western Delaware.[148] He escaped after five years but was recaptured and severely whipped.

When he eventually obtained his freedom he had no intention of creating a new life in the area and his only desire was to return home to claim his inheritance. He made his way to Jamaica where he enlisted in the royal navy as an able seaman and served abroad the *H.M.S. Falmouth*. On board he was recognised by an old friend from Dublin who vouched for his identity, which would have otherwise been dismissed as far-fetched.

By the time he returned to Dublin, something that no one, least of all, his uncle, had expected, he was the talk of the city. His uncle set about plotting his nephew's death and when James went to the races at the Curragh of Kildare a coach nearly ran him over. Accidents happened but when the coach turned and tried a second time it looked a little suspicious. James brought his case to court and at the time, taking nearly two weeks, it was the longest trial that had ever been heard in either Britain or Ireland with twenty-eight barristers participating. The case gripped the popular imagination and Uncle Richard was now regarded as a scoundrel who had wronged his nephew most terribly. Uncle Richard had never offered a consistent explanation for his nephew's sudden disappearance in 1728. He had told some people the boy died of smallpox, others that he died in the West Indies. The trial attracted considerable attention both in Britain and Ireland and fifteen different accounts of the trial were published.

James won his case, which was a cause of much celebration among Dubliners. As a result Parliament in Dublin tried to pass legislation to stop the kidnapping of homeless children, but the bill was overruled at the request of officials in London and kidnapping continued to be practiced until the 1820s.

Though James had won his case in Dublin he had to go to London to fight for his English estates before he could claim his inheritance. Unfortunately for him, Uncle Richard had not given up and knew the right people who would best know how to stall the proceedings, which would make them rich and bankrupt James.

James Annesley suffered an asthma attack half way through his legal battle and died at the age of 44. He was buried in Kent without ever getting the inheritance for which he had fought and suffered for so long. His uncle still held on to the estates but was now looked on as a schemer and scoundrel who became a social outcast and died within the year. Neither left an heir and the title 'Earl of Anglesey' became extinct.

His story continued to inspire and the first fictionalised account of his life appeared in 1743 when Eliza Haywood wrote *Memoirs of an Unfortunate Young Nobleman*, followed by Tobias Smollett's *Peregrine Pickle* in 1751, Sir Walter Scott's *Guy Mannering* in 1815 and Charles Reade's *The Wandering Heir* in 1872. Robert Louis Stevenson wrote his famous novel in 1886 and is today one of the twenty six most translated authors.

Fontenoy

"When on Ramillie's bloody field,
The baffled French were forced to yield,
The victor Saxon backward reeled
Before the charge of Clare's Dragoons.
The Flags we conquered in that fray,
Look lone in Ypres' choir, they say,
We'll win them company to-day,
Or bravely die like Clare's Dragoons."
(Clare's Dragoons)

Following the Treaty of Limerick in 1691 up to twenty thousand Irish soldiers followed Sarsfield into exile. A profession in soldiering was the best way to advance oneself at the time. The Irish Brigade, though committed to the fight against England, was a pawn in a larger political game and Louis like any ruler welcomed additional cannon fodder. Several Irishmen made a name for themselves in their adopted country. Richard Hennessy for example established the world famous cognac. Though the Irish Brigade was involved in several battles its most memorable victory was at Fontenoy, perhaps because they beat the English that day and the battle itself is regarded by many as an Irish victory over England.

The battle was fought on 11 May 1745 in what is now present day Belgium to the south east of the city of Tournai, as part of the War of Austrian Succession (1740–48) fought mostly between the British and the French.

At 2:00am on 11th May, the Allied regiments took up their stations. The British under the Duke of Cumberland, later nicknamed "the Bloody Duke" for his actions against the Scottish highlanders after Culoden, were supported by the Hanoverians, Austrians and Dutch.[149]

The French forces were led by Maurice de Saxe. A large battery of Allied guns began to bombard the French positions at long range. The allied bombardment had little effect however, as most of the French were in the woods or behind the swell of ground leading to their position, or fortified in Fontenoy. Nevertheless the English were gaining the upper hand and the battle was being lost, so the French began to retreat. In a last attempt to stop defeat Sax ordered in the Irish Brigade, consisting of the regiments of Clare, Dillon, Lally, Berwick Roth, and Buckley and Fitzjames' horse. They charged the English flank with fixed bayonets without firing, shouting out their battle cry of "*Cuimhnígí ar Luimneach agus ar fheall na Sasanach!*" (Remember Limerick and Saxon deceit!). The Irish brigade had the advantage of being fresh to the fight, while the English had been fighting all day. Two colours of the Cold Stream Guards were captured.[150] Such colours were battle honours and their loss was something of a disgrace. Fifteen cannon were also captured. The Irish Brigade managed to turn the tide of battle in favour of the French. The Brigade in their redcoats were at one stage attacked by French cavalry who mistook them for the English until they shouted out "*vive le roi*".

Though it was a victory it was a costly victory. One quarter of the officers, including Colonel Dillon, were killed, and one third of the men. It is estimated that the French lost 7,000, while the Allies lost around 12,000. It is not known how many Irish were among the ranks of those fighting on the English side. It was the highest casualty rate in Western Europe since the Battle of Malplaquet in 1709.

The Irish even won the respect of the enemy and George II is reputed to have cursed the (penal) laws which deprived him of such subjects.[151] News of the victory gave fresh hope to many in Ireland and all those who supported the Jacobite cause. It also prolonged the *Ancien Régime* by thirty years. The soldiers of the Irish Brigade had sworn loyalty to the King of France, not to the French people, which would lead to disbandment in 1792. Though an Irish Legion was formed in 1803 by Napoleon it could never match the glorious number of the Irish brigade at Fontenoy.

The artist Horace Vernet (1789-1863) painted a famous picture of the battle entitled *Bataille De Fontenoy,* and interest in the Irish Brigade was rekindled by the poetess Emily Lawless (1845-1913) in her poem *Fontenoy).*[152] Little remains of the battlefield today and the site itself has been dissected by a motorway. A Celtic cross was erected to commemorate the Irish who fell.[153]

Highwaymen

*"Tis of a highwayman a story I will tell
His name was Willie Brennan and in Ireland he did dwell.
Twas on the Kilwort mountains he commenced his wild career.
Where many a gallant gentleman before him shook with fear."*
"Brennan on the Moor"

The political and social upheaval of 17th and 18th century Ireland led to thousands of former soldiers taking up a life of banditry. The new order, the Protestant Ascendancy, which came into being after the Williamite wars of 1690, introduced discriminatory legislation, the penal laws designed to control the native Catholic population. It effectively made Irish Catholics second class citizens in their own country. Though feared by the Protestant Ascendency and hunted by the authorities highwaymen were loved by the common people, who had nothing worth robbing anyway. Known initially as Tories, raparees and highwaymen they were given grandiose titles of 'count' or 'captain'.

According to folklore they robbed from the rich and gave to the poor. Sometimes they watched as the rent was collected, robbed the collector and returned it to the tenants. In addition to robbing mail coaches they also robbed landlords and wealthy farmers.

From the mid 17th century those living in the woods harassed the British and became known as Tories, from the Irish *tórai* meaning raider. They were also known as rapparees, from the Irish *robaire*, meaning robber, though it is more commonly suggested that it referred to a type of short pike they carried.

There were a few notable rapparees. For example, Michael "Galloping" Hogan from Doon in East Limerick, close to the Slieve

Phelim hills, who became a raparee after the Cromwellian conquest. He is best remembered for guiding Patrick Sarsfield and his men to destroy the Williamite guns at Ballyneety in 1690. Following the Treaty of Limerick he went to serve France where he became a general. He was again forced into exile after a killing a brother officer in a duel, and he continued his military career in Portugal, where his descendants still live.[154]

Eamonn a' Chnoic, sometimes referred to as "Ned of the Hill", from Atshanboe County Tippeary was born around 1670 and had fought at the Boyne and Aughrim. When he shot a tax collector, who was harassing a widow, he was forced to hide out in the woods. There was a price on his head and greed for the money meant he could trust few people. In 1724 a reward of 200 pounds was on his head. He took refuge with a relative of his called O'Dwyer in Hollyford. While he slept O'Dwyer murdered him with a hatchet and took his head to Clonmel to claim the reward, only to discover that Eamonn a' Chnoic had been pardoned and he got nothing. Local lore says that he had been chivalrous towards a lady of the Butlers and she had influenced the pardon. His name lived on in a famous Irish poem "Eamonn a Chnoic" and the love song "Bean Dubh an Gleanna", believed to have been written by his wife Mary Leahy.

James Freney's family had been in County Kilkenny since the 13th century. They lost all their lands and property during the Cromwellian campaign. When the penal laws came into force life became even more difficult and he took to the roads having been proclaimed an outlaw in 1748. He surrendered in 1749 and was pardoned when he informed on his gang, who were sent to the gallows. He wrote a very successful autobiography *The Life and Adventures of Mr James Freney* in 1754 and featured as a character in William Makepeace Thackeray's 19th century work *The Luck of Barry Lyndon*, which in turn would be turned into a movie by Stanley Kubrick. By 1776 he had settled at the port of New Ross where he worked as a customs official, a post he held till his death in 1788. He was buried in Inistioge graveyard, county Kilkenny.[155]

Several songs written about raparees are still popular. Willie Brennan was made famous in the song *Brennan on the Moor* and operated between Clonmel and Killarney. A tale is told of how he was arrested by redcoats from the garrison in Fermoy. On the way to the barracks Brennan asked if they could stop at a shebeen. Unbeknown to the soldiers he was well known at the illicit pub. He asked the barmaid if she could give him some fire for his pipe, and she went away and returned with a loaded blunderbuss. He robbed the soldiers and escaped.[156] Despite his fame it is disputed how exactly he died. According to the song he was hanged in Clonmel, though other accounts state that he was shot by a Kerry lawyer Jeremiah O'Connor, whom he was trying to rob.[157]

Though its origins are somewhat unclear it is widely believed that "Whiskey in the Jar" alludes to Richard Power of Kilbolane near Charleville, whose sweetheart poured water into his pistols and summoned the soldiers. He was hanged in Clonmel in 1685.[158]

In the east the favourite haunts of highwaymen were the Dublin, Drogheda, Dundalk and Belfast roads and they waited for their quarry at taverns such as the Cat in The Cage tavern in Drumcondra, which is still in business.[159]

Count Redmond O'Hanlon was born around 1620 In Poyntzpass, County Armagh and was heir to the castle at Tandragee. He had served under Owen O Neill at the Battle of Benburb in 1646 and took to the hills of Slieve Gullion when his lands and property were confiscated. Almost everyone who was anyone in the area paid him protection money and at one stage he was bringing in more money than government tax collectors. In 1674 Dublin Castle sent a militia in pursuit of him, but they spent more time terrorising the peasants than pursuing their quarry. His main target was his former land, now in the possession of Henry St. John, who started evicting tenants. When St. John was shot in an affray with O'Hanlon's men in 1679 the hunt for him intensified. He was betrayed by one of his closest confidants, his foster brother Art O'Hanlon, who murdered him and received two hundred pounds from the Lord Deputy, the Duke of Ormond. Upon seeing his head on a spike outside Downpatrick jail, his mother composed a now famous *caoineadh* or lament.

In the Comeraghs in County Waterford William Crotty held sway and from a rocky outcrop that still bears his name he had an excellent view of the countryside and Waterford city. He was at large for several years and one way he managed to confuse his pursuers was to have his horse shod backwards. His hideout was in a cave which could only be accessed by a rope. It was there that he was safe and his wife kept watch while he slept. His downfall came when he stayed at a 'friend's' house in 1742, where he was got drunk and the soldiers were summoned. He was taken to Waterford city where he was hanged, drawn and quartered. He had hidden his loot under a certain rock in the Commeraghs, which has never been found. The authorities turned their attention to his wife and as they closed in on her, she jumped off the cliff.

In the west, Captain Gallagher from Swinford, County Mayo was active. On one ocassion he visited a landlord in Killasser and had him tear up and eat eviction notices he had prepared. He was betrayed as he spent Christmas at a "friend's" house at Attymass in the Ox Mountains.[160] Taken by the redcoats to Castlebar, as he mounted the scaffhold he revealed that his treasure was hidden under a rock in his home in Barnalyra, but it was never found.[161]

Some highwaymen were fortunate enough to survive their own execution. William Delaney was hanged in Naas but the hangman cut him down too soon and he was revived by friends. He was later caught in Kilkenny and this time the hangman did the job properly.[162]

By the 19th century changes such as urbanisation, the railways, enclosed fields and the introduction of traceabale banknotes instead of gold coins meant that the time of the highwayman had passed, though the deeds of these colourful characters live on in folkore and song.

ART O'LEARY

"Mo ghrá go daingean tú!
Lá dá bhfaca thú
ag ceann tí an mhargaidh,
thug mo shúil aire dhuit,
thug mo chroí taitnearnh duit,
d'éalaíos óm charaid leat
i bhfad ó bhaile leat."
Trans: My steadfast love!
When I saw you one day
by the market-house gable
my eye gave a look
my heart shone out
I fled with you far
from friends and home. [163]
Caoineadh Airt Uí Laoghaire

Art O'Leary (1747-1773) was an officer in the Austrian army who was murdered by redcoats in County Cork. Were it not for the love poem and lament his widow composed he would have been completely forgotten. *The Lament for Art O'Leary,* or *Caoineadh Airt Uí Laoghaire* to give it its original title, was one of the greatest Gaelic poems composed in the 18th century. It was written down from the oral tradition and describes Eibhlín's love for Art. Part of it was sung at the wake and part at his burial.

Eibhlín[164]Dubh Ní Chonaill (1743-1800) was born in Derrynane, County Kerry as one of twenty two children. She was an aunt to Daniel O'Connell, also known as "The Liberator" whose statue stands on O'Connell Street in Dublin. The family made their fortune from smuggling. Families such as the O'Connells formed part of what Daniel Corkery referred to as "The Hidden Ireland".[165]They wrote and spoke English fluently and outwardly appeared completely "civilised", even leaving out the Gaelic 'O' from their name in correspondence,[166] but Irish was the language they spoke amongst themselves. Eibhlín was married at the age of fifteen to a man of wealth called O'Connor,[167] but he died six months later, leaving the young widow quite well off.

About seven years later, while on a visit to her sister, she met Art who was a captain in the Hungarian Hussars in the market Square of Macroom. A plaque in the market square recalls this event. Against the wishes of her family, who considered him a hothead who could cause them trouble, she eloped and married Art O'Leary[168] in 1767. She left her family for him and they settled in Arthleigh, County Cork. Together they had three children. Art was not known for his modesty and walked around Macroom with his fine sword. All gentlemen carried them and the quality of the sword signalled their status. Art was, afterall, an officer and a gentleman and was unwilling to accept his status of second class citizen. Ireland of the time, however, was no place for a hothead unwilling to accept unjust laws and Catholics were obliged to conform or go abroad. The Penal Laws had been introduced by the Dublin Parliament to maintain an unequal *status quo* between Protestant and Catholic and stipulated that Catholics could not bear arms, receive an education, practice their religion or join the army. Art, like most of the Catholic gentry, received his education abroad.

A contemporary economist of the time Edmund Burke said of the Penal Laws that they were:

"A machine of wise and elaborate contrivance, as well fitted for the oppression, impoverishment and degradation of a people, and the debasement in them of human nature itself, as ever preceded from the perverted ingenuity of man."[169]

It was only a matter of time before Art would clash with the authorities. Matters came to a head at a local horse race. Art raced his fine brown horse, which he had brought over from Austria, and beat that of the local Magistrate, Abraham Morris. It is most likely that Art gloated over his victory and Morris did not taking losing in his stride. In order to humiliate Art he offered to buy the winning horse for the meagre sum of five pounds. One of the penal laws stipulated that if a Protestant wanted to buy a horse from a Catholic it had to be sold and for no more than this sum. The laws at this time were, however, being relaxed. Art refused and challenged Morris to a duel, which he declined. By refusing to sell the horse Art had broken the law. He could now be legally shot on sight and he went on the run.

He boasted in a tavern that he would kill Morris and was on his way to do so when he encountered a party of redcoats at Carraig an Ime.[170]Thinking he was out of range he taunted them. A soldier by the name of Green, who was later awarded for gallantry, proved otherwise and ended his life. His horse rode riderless home and Eibhlín knew immediately something had happened. She mounted the horse who took her to the scene. The lament describes how both an old woman and she drank Art's blood, which was apparently usual at the time. It was an ancient practice which Elizabethan commentators confused with cannibalism, but was done as a mark of respect to the deceased.

The wake was held and the corpse keened. The word keen comes from the Gaelic *caoin* meaning to cry. It was usual at such wakes to compose a lament extolling the deeds of the deceased. The mourning ritual was different to what foreign observers knew. In the 16th century Stanihurst wrote:

"They follow the dead corpse to the grave with howling and barbarous outcries."[171]

The killing created an outcry in the district. To avoid any litigation the horse was surrendered to Morris. Morris volunteered to stand trial for his actions, which was farcical as he knew he would be acquitted and, given that his judges were like minded individuals it came as no surprise that he was indeed acquitted. It was, however, by no means the end of the matter and Cornelius, Art's brother went to the home of Morris to serve his own justice. He fired a shot through the window, wounding Morris. A warrant went out for his arrest but by then Cornelius had long since left the country and forged a distinguished career for himself in America.[172] Morris died two years later, possibly of his wounds.

Art O'Leary was buried at Kilcrea, first of all outside the abbey, as Catholics were not interred in churchyards, and the inscription on his grave, composed by Eibhlín reads:

"Lo Arthur Leary, Generous, Handsome, Brave, Slain in his bloom, Lies in this humble grave. Died May 4th.1773.Aged 26 years."[173]

In recent years a small monument commemorating the spot where he was killed was erected.

the travel writings of roger lamb

While personal accounts of military service from ordinary soldiers are common place today in the 19th century it was unheard of. Given that most soldiers were illiterate, accounts were usually only written by officers. The most detailed account of Britain's war in America, however, was written by Dubliner, Sergeant Roger Lamb. He has largely been forgotten and he first came to my attention on a visit to the Army Museum in London. His account reads like a travel log and even for those not interested in military history his vivid descriptions of the Native American culture, their war dances and custom of taking scalps, as well as detailed description of wildlife of the North American continent provide fascinating reading.

He drew his first breath in Dublin as the youngest of eleven children in 1756, where exactly, he does not reveal,[174] but it would appear to have been near the North Wall, making him a Northsider. The first chapter of the book provides an interesting account of contemporary Dublin life. He recalls, for example, in 1766 walking along the South Wall, seeing criminals hanging on giblets near the light house. These were the Mugglins, four men convicted of piracy and murder and who hung there as a warning to others. After a month people started to complain of the smell and the sight of the decaying corpses and they were duly removed. He appears to be have been fascinated by swimming and recommended it as useful for surviving shipwrecks. He swam regularly in the Liffey at a spot where the Customs' House now stands. He describes Lower Abbey Street and Marlborough as places where "Club law" prevailed and he appears critical of the duelling culture prevalent in Dublin at the time.

He joined the British Army in 1773 aged seventeen and over six days was marched down to join the 9th Regiment of Foot, based in Waterford. Discipline was harsh and Lamb recalls bursting into tears when he first saw a man being flogged. Being literate, he had an advantage over his comrades and was given better jobs, which was essential as his sergeant very often stole the mens' pay to pay off his debts in the alehouse. He was one of 50,000 British soldiers to be sent to the Americas to quell The American War of Independence. During his eight years there he served on two major campaigns was captured twice and twice escaped from captivity to rejoin the British Army.

He first served under General Burgoyne in Canada, who invaded the Colonies from the north, intending to divide New England from the southern colonies. But as he moved southwards the Americans managed to block his supply routes and his army came to a standstill, eventually compelling him to surrender at the battle of Saratoga in 1777. It was the end of Burgoyne's career and he returned to England and became a playwright. His army, the "Convention Army", so called after the treaty or convention that was to be signed promising that the soldiers would never again take up arms against the Americans, was taken into captivity. Lamb does not record his time in captivity as being particularly harsh, though he does mention they were not given any blankets and his captors set the straw alight as soon as they saw a prisoner falling asleep. He and about a thousand others managed to flee and he made his way to New York where he was assigned to the Royal Welch Fusiliers[175]. This was one of the oldest regiments of the British Army, which fought in nearly every campaign of the war and now they were poised to move south to subdue the southern colonies. Lord Cornwallis, who would later become Viceroy to Ireland, commanded the Crown forces in the south. Lamb fought at Camden in South Carolina in 1780, a battle the British won. He carried the regimental colours and although he had little medical experience became the provisional regimental surgeon. He was so exhausted at this battle that another sergeant had to replace him. The sergeant who replaced him was killed by a nine pound cannon ball and Lamb considered that fate was on his side. While he was in the southern colonies he had opportunity to observe the way of life there. He gives a vivid description of slavery, pointing out the hypocrisy of the Americans who, while loving their freedom, practiced slavery, with the plantation owner regarding a slave like a farmer would regard livestock. At the battle of Guilford Court-House in North Carolina in1781 Lamb is credited with saving the life of Cornwallis.[176] While it was a battle the British won, Cornwallis suffered a crushing defeat that same year at Yorktown. The surrender at Yorktown marked the end of the war and Cornwallis was to become known as the man who 'lost America'.[177]With the cessation of hostilities, Lamb was sent back to Portsmouth in 1783, demobbed shortly afterwards and returned to Dublin where he was appointed schoolmaster of the Methodist Free School in Whitefriar Street, a position he held for thirty years. In his free time he took up writing, observing that people were more interested in tales of war than of peace. He wrote *A Journal of Occurrences* during the Late American War in 1809 and later *Memoir of My Own Life* in 1811, both of which were widely read. His books were to influence others and Robert Graves would later write two thinly fictionalised accounts of Lamb's experiences entitled *Sergeant Lamb of the Ninth* in 1940[178] and a sequel entitled *Proceed, Sergeant Lamb* in 1941, which dealt with the passions and frustrations of a distant war which mirrored many of Graves' own feelings for World War Two. In 1809 Lamb was awarded a pension of one shilling a day from the Chelsea Hospital, based at The Royal Hospital Kilmainham, in recognition of his military and literary services. He died in 1830.

Duelling

The notion of two people fighting each other is as old as time itself. In ancient Irish mythology Cú Chulainn fought his best friend Ferdia over a three day period. Over the centuries it took on different shapes, whether it was two champions fighting each other to decide the outcome of a battle or fighting and letting God be the judge. By the seventeenth century the custom of duelling had evolved and in Britain and Ireland duels were fought according to a code drawn up in Clonmel. The word duel itself comes from the Latin *duellum* meaning 'war between two' and usually entailed swords or pistols. The object of the duel was not necessarily to kill the opponent; many of them only went to first blood. It was seen much more as an exhibition of honour and bravery. It formed an important part of a young gentleman's education. Unfortunately friends who had had a falling out often ended up on the duelling field, the results of which often led to lifelong regret.

A set of rules was set out at Clonmel assizes (court), when delegates from the west of Ireland met at Clonmel in 1777 and came up with the *Code Duello,* or the twenty six commandments, a duelling code which became standard in Ireland and in Britain.[179] It would later become standard in the USA. As well as seconds, a surgeon was usually present. Though a flesh wound would be sought the opponent very often died of the wound that was inflicted.

John Rigby of Suffolk Street in Dublin was known throughout the country as one of the leading gun manufacturers in the country. Examples of his duelling pistols are on display in the National Museum at Collins Barracks in Dublin. The Read family on Parliament Street were known as the best providers of duelling swords.

There were several famous duels fought in this country. Richard Martin (1754-1834) MP for County Galway and co-founder of the RSPCA had the moniker "Hair-trigger Dick" and fought over a hundred duels.[180] In 1785 he had a falling out with his cousin, James Jordan, who then challenged him. Martin apologised, and arrived at the "appointed place" without his pistols. This would have been frowned upon according to the code. Jordan refused to accept Martin's apology and in the ensuing duel Jordan was killed. It left a lasting impression on Martin as the two had been very close and he was often heard to comment "unconsciously" at the dinner table, *"I could not have missed him."*[181]

Leonard McNally, a United Irishman, who betrayed the movement, fought a duel in the Phoenix Park with the Shears Brothers acting as his seconds, both of whom were later executed. McNally narrowly escaped with his life when the ball struck the buckle on his braces.[182]

Duels were commonplace in the military. In 1803 an argument over dogs led naval Captain McNamara to fight a duel with Colonel Montgomery. Both men were good shots and in the ensuing duel both were wounded, though Montgomery died of his wounds. McNamara, once recovered, was tried for murder but received the support of Admiral Nelson and was acquitted.

One of the most famous duels was between Daniel O'Connell and John N. D'Esterre on 1st February 1815 on Bishop's Court Demesne, County Kildare.[183] In a speech O'Connell gave in January 1815 as part of his Catholic Emancipation movement, he referred to the Dublin City Corporation as "beggarly". John D'Esterre, a Protestant, took umbrage and interpreted the remark as a personal insult. He called on O'Connell to retract his statement. O'Connell refused and satisfaction was demanded. As the two men fired their first shot, O'Connell's shot struck D'Esterre in the hip. At first it seemed as though D'Esterre had been slightly wounded but after he was carried to his house and examined by doctors it was discovered that the shot had entered his abdomen. He died two days later. The press of the time presented the duel as having religious motives though this was not the case. Though popular support for O'Connell increased, he was filled with remorse, wearing a black glove on the hand that killed D'Esterre whenever he entered a church thereafter. He also gave financial support to his widow and daughter and was known to tip his hat whenever he walked by the house.

Duels became forbidden by law, but the law was decided by lawyers and the gentry, the very people who engaged in the practice. By the 1840s the duelling culture had faded away from civilian life though it continued for some time in the military. There were a number of reasons for this. Organisations such as "The Friendly Brothers of St Patrick" and The Catholic Church were always against it. The establishment of the RIC meant that the law could be enforced and the development of more accurate pistols meant that duels would go further than merely first blood and the likelihood of killing the opponent was now much higher. Killing someone, even in a duel agreeable to both parties, was no longer considered a minor misdemeanour and severely punished.

ᚷhe whiᚷeʙoys

The Whiteboys was a secret society that flourished in the 18th century. They used violence to support rights for tenant farmers. The name comes from the Irish *Buachaillí Bána* and the white smocks they wore. One wonders if such smocks were not an inspiration for the Klu Klux Klan garb, though the latter was suposed to represent the ghosts of Shiloh. They were also known as *Levellers* and resisted the enclosure of commons or undeveloped lands by destroying newly erected walls.[184]

They were by no means the only secret society in Ireland at the time. The Peep O' Day Boys, so called for their early morning forays against Catholics were predessecors to the Loyal Orange Order.

The Whiteboys fought against rack rents or the extortionately high rents tenants had to pay, and the infamous tithe. At the time the local Catholic population was obliged to pay a tithe or church tax to the Church of Ireland, which, though it was the official religion of the island, was not the religion of the majority as most of the Irish remained Catholic. This tax led to much resentment and Protestant clergymen bore the brunt of this resentement.

Though their activities usually included attacks on property, cattle maiming, tarring and feathering, they were not adverse to using stronger phyical violence and carried out the occassional murder. The White Boy Act of 1762 was designed to curb their rise and Lord Drogheda was given the task of suppressing the association. It had little effect and the Whiteboys were seldom brought to justice for fear of retribution. The rural unrest continued into the 19th century. Travelling through the North Cork countryside, I came across a roadside monument, of which there are many in the area, commemerating the Battle of Keimaneigh, fought in 1822. The battle was immortalised in a song by local woman Máire Buí Ní Laoghaire *Cath Chéim an Fhia*.[185] A group of Whiteboys from Ballingeary went on a raid to the houses of loyalists in the Bantry area searching for arms, as only Protestants were allowed carry arms at the time. When the alarm was raised the Earl of Bantry and his yeomanry pursued the raiding party and caught up with them at Keimaneigh. The Whiteboys had taken to the heights and threw rocks down at the yeomanry, who were forced to flee. Six People, mostly Whiteboys, were killed in the affray. A yeomanry soldier was killed in the battle. He was decapitatted and the head was placed on a stick and waved at the opposition. Repurcusions ensued and forty suspected Whiteboys were arrested and nine were hanged. While the executions were taking place the local priest Fr MacSweeny addressed the crowd *as Gaeilge* condemning the Whiteboys.[186]Daniel O'Connell also did not support the Whiteboys, referring to them as "miscreants" and urging the authorities to wipe them out.

In 1823 the Tithe Composition Act meant that the clergy could demand money instead of food. In the Kilkenny parish of Graiguenamanagh in November 1830 a herd of cattle were seized as payment for the tithe. When the seized cattle were put up for sale the following month nobody was willing to buy them. The "no buyer" concept fitted well with Daniel O'Connell's campaign to achieve freedom through non-violence and the concept spread.

Anti-tithe meetings were held throughout Leinster. The authorities watched and waited to set an example. In May of 1831 the RIC opened fire on a crowd at a fair in Castlepollard, killing seventeen people.[187] In June, the Yeomnary shot dead fourteen people at a tithe sale in Bunclody, County Wexford. Shortly before Christmas 1831, the Whiteboys struck back, ambushing a police force near Knocktopher, Co. Kilkenny, resulting in a further fifteen deaths. The meetings grew larger. Over 200,000 were reported to have attended one in Co. Cork, while 120,000 were clocked at one in Co. Longford. The government began to clamp down, imposing heavy fines and police sentences on those whom they deemed to be leading the campaign.

The Whiteboys did to some extent manage to cap extortionate rent increases through threats and intimidation, as nobody would take over the property of the evicted family. They were feared by the gentry, who saw them as instigators for peasant revolt.

Though O'Connell achieved 'Catholic Emancipation' in 1829 with The Catholic Relief Act, it changed little for the peasantry, who continued to live in mud huts, were malnourished and could still barely afford to pay the rent. They ate only potatoes and disaster struck when the potato crop suddenly failed. Whiteboyism came to an end with the famine, an event that wiped out a million people. A further million left the country for America, where they were not always met with open arms. This led in turn to a new secret society-the Molly Maguires.

James Louis Rice

There were several attempts to rescue the French royal family from the guillotine in Paris. One of them involved an Irishman connected to the town of Dingle. I first heard about this while reading *The Last Colonel of the Irish Brigade*, a biography of Count O'Connell written in 1892.[188]James Louis Rice, son of Thomas Rice of Ballymacadoyle, came from a prominent Dingle family who had built a strong business in the wine trade in both France and Ireland. Like many Irish Catholic gentlemen of the time he received his education abroad and was sent to the Irish College in Louvain, Belgium, where it was intended that he become a priest.[189] He decided instead on a career as a soldier and went to serve the Austrian Habsburgs, seeing action against the Turks. He rose through the ranks and became a friend of the Emperor Joseph II.[190] The emperor's fourteen year old sister Marie Antoinette had married the fifteen year old French emperor Louis XIV in 1770. The two countries were traditional enemies and Rice was entrusted to bring messages between the siblings. In gratitude, the title of Count of the Holy Roman Empire was conferred on Rice in 1776.

The French Revolution in 1789 sent shockwaves throughout Europe. The monarchy had been overturned and European monarchs feared the same would happen in their own countries. Joseph II was naturally concerned about his sister. The royal family had been arrested and imprisoned in The Temple in Paris, but few believed they would be put to death. Rice and others came up with a plan to free Marie Antoinette. The plan was to take her in a closed carriage to Nantes, where a ship owned by the Rice family would be waiting to take her to Dingle, where she would recuperate. The upper floor of the Rice household in Dingle had been specially prepared for her. Today, it is one of the few Georgian houses in Ireland with a French influence. From Dingle she would go to Dublin, London, and Brussels and back home to Vienna. Everything, including bribing the jailers, had been arranged. At the last moment, however, she had a change of heart. She refused to leave either her husband or children. The plan, though well organised, could not accomadate them all and without her support it would not work. The emperor was somewhat indecisive in deciding which family members should escape with which escape attempt. Marie Antoinette wanted to keep the family together and they did eventually escape as a family on 21st June 1791, but were captured within a day at Varennes. According to popular lore, Louis, though travelling incognito, was recognised from his image on one of the coins.

Marie Antoinette was sent to the guillotine in October of 1793, her husband having been executed in January of that year. Her daughter survived but her son Louis XVII died at the age of ten after four years of solitary confinement in a dungeon.

Paris was a dangerous place and the reign of terror claimed several Irish lives. One of the most high profile Irishmen to be sent to the guillotine was General Arthur Dillon, commander of the Dillon Regiment. He was later rehabilitated and his name is inscribed on the north pillar of the *Arc de Triomphe*.[191] General James Ferdinand O'Moran of Elphin was guillotined in 1794.[192] The charges were flimsy and very often the result of a grudge. Thomas Delany was seventeen when he was accused of denouncing the revolution and brought to the guillotine. Father Pierre O'Brennan was executed on 23rd July 1794, for having spoken against the authorities and concealing some old title-deeds.

The Rice family home built in 1750 is still standing, as indeed are some old Rice graves in the old graveyard. It stands at Canon's Corner, the junction of Upper Main Street and Green Street. In 2010 the Dingle Historical Society erected a plaque to commemorate the event.[193]

Citizen Moore

While Ireland officially became a republic in 1948, it was not the first republic this island had seen. Another republic, the republic of Connacht existed as far back as the 18th century, albeit briefly.

The year was 1798, a time of rebellion inspired by events in America and France. An uprising had already taken place in Wexford which, after a few initial successes, had been brutally suppressed. Several months later the flame of insurrection was rekindled in Mayo when the somewhat youthful but experienced General Joseph Amable Humbert landed at Killala on 23rd August 1798. The province had hitherto been spared the ravages of war and it was a time that would later become known as "The Year of the French".[194]

For the French it was very much a win-win situation. They had committed just over a thousand troops to the venture and though regular troops, they were far from the elite of *grande armée*. A similar landing had been carried out in Fishguard two years previously. The expedition, though small in size, would have been of a big enough concern for the royal navy and tie up their ships, giving the French a freer hand in more important theatres of war.

George Moore was a Catholic landowner, one of the few in the country who, due to the harsh penal laws was compelled to seek his fortune abroad. He made his fortune in Alicante in Spain and returned to his native land when he realised the punitive penal laws had been relaxed.[195] He built a splendid Georgian mansion, Moore Hall at Lough Carra, Muckloon in County Mayo. This was against the advice of locals, who considered the site unlucky. Local folklore had it that when Brian Orbsen, King of Connacht was killed in 400AD his druid Drithliu sought refuge on Muckloon hill where Moore Hall now stood, and the same druid was hunted down and slain at that very site.[196]

His son John was born in 1767 and received the best education money could buy, studying at Liège and Paris before moving to Ireland, where he hoped to continue his study of law. The Moores were concerned that the sudden arrival of the French could bring about destruction of property and John Moore, the heir to Moore Hall, sought out Humbert to get assurances.[197]

Humbert was impressed by the educated Moore, who could also speak French. He realised Moore would make an excellent administrator and convinced him to join the venture. Thus John Moore assumed the somewhat grandiose title of "President of the Provisional Government of the Republic of Connacht". It was a move that perhaps should have been better considered and he would have declined the position had he known that the venture was doomed to fail. In the eyes of his Protestant neighbours he had just become a traitor to the crown.

The French left Killala and moved towards the Midlands. The expedition, though augmented by the local population, who were thrilled to get quality clothing in the form of uniforms, received no reinforcements and it was bound to fizzle out. The end came at Ballinamuck, County Longford on 8th September. The French, realising they were massively outnumbered, laid down their arms and surrendered. It was the last battle involving a continental European army fought on Irish soil. No surrender was accepted from the Irish. As regular soldiers the French were taken prisoner, marched through the streets of Dublin and repatriated. A different fate awaited the Irish and no quarter was given.

Moore's tenure as President ended on 4th September when he was arrested at the Republic's capital in Castlebar by Colonel Crawford and his cavalry in an event know as the "Relief of Castlebar", a moniker designed to soothe the pain of the humiliating "Races of Castlebar" when the English had fled before the advancing French.

Although later generations would look upon Moore as a patriot, the Dublin authorities were looking for vengeance. By collaborating with the king's foreign and domestic enemies he had committed treason and there was only one penalty for treason.

John Moore was arrested and thrown into gaol. His father was determined to save his son and persuaded the gentry to his side. Unlike other leaders his trial was delayed as it was feared that rebels still at large in Mayo would try to free him. His solitary confinement in prison, where he was denied exercise, took its toll on the young gentleman, not accustomed to such harsh conditions. His family tried to plea the *habeas corpus* act, an act which examined the lawfulness of a prisoner's detention.

Thus Moore escaped the court-martials which took place all over Connacht and usually resulted in hanging. The months passed and he lingered on in gaol, awaiting trial. The period of incarceration was crippling for the Moores, who spent over two thousand pounds on health and legal fees. As a result of the stress George Moore went blind from a stroke. The wealth of the Moores quite possibly saved John Moore from immediate execution. A trial could be embarrassing for all concerned and in December it was decided to send him into exile, a decision that angered those loyal to the crown. He was sent to Waterford, from where a ship would take him to the Americas. But it was not to be. Ireland's first president of Ireland died on 6 December 1799 aged 36 in the Royal Oak tavern in Broad Street Waterford.[198] There was no mention of foul play. Moore Hall itself was burnt down by the IRA in 1923 and today only the burnt out shell still remains.

His grave was long forgotten until it was discovered by chance in Ballygunner Cemetery, Waterford in 1960.[199] The following year his remains were exhumed and conveyed under Army Guard to Castlebar, where, at a ceremony with full military honours, John Moore was reinterred at the Mall in the centre of the town. The inscription on his grave reads:

"Ireland's first president and a descendant of St Thomas More, who gave his life for his country in the rising of 1798. By the will of the people exhumed and reinterred here with all honours of church and state."[200]

Lady Betty

The most notorious executioner in Irish history was a woman called Elisabeth Dolan, or McDermott, better known as Lady Betty. Very little is known of her background, and though she did exist, much of what is written about her appears to be folklore and hearsay. The only real account we are left with was written by Sir William Wilde who spent his childhood in Roscommon and wrote of her in *Irish Popular Superstitions*, published in 1852.

Originally a Kerry woman, she was born around 1750. She was married to a poor tenant farmer and when he died she was left destitute with three children. She would probably have been evicted and decided to move up north to Connacht to seek a new life, settling in Roscommon. Two of her three children died of starvation along the way and she devoted herself to her remaining son. She had learnt to read and write, which was unusual given her circumstances, and passed this skill on to her son. Life had dealt her several cruel blows and perhaps as a result of this she was known to be a bad tempered and mean spirited woman. Her son moved away to seek his fortune in America[201] and she was left broken hearted. Though he promised to come back to her some day, she knew she would never see him again. The years went by and she made a little money from offering lodgings to strangers. One night a well dressed stranger came to her door and he asked her for shelter. He offered her money and she noticed he had a purse full of gold coins. Greed overcame her and realising the stranger's wealth could change her circmstances she stabbed him to death as he slept.

Going through his papers she was suddenly horrorified when she realised that the man she had just murdered was her own son. Why he had not revealed himself is not known. She was taken to

Roscommon Jail. There was only one sentence for murder at the time and that was hanging. She cared little for her fate. Her son had been her life and not only had he died but she had played a part in the tragedy. Whether this event really happened is open to speculation and similair stories have been recorded throughout Europe, and it may be an urban legend to explain how she ended up in prison. Another version of the tale claims she murdered more than one lodger.

Public hangings were commonplace at the time and even minor crimes were punished this way. The day came for her to be executed and she went along with twenty five others to meet her maker.[202] The others were mostly Whiteboys. Whiteboys and Ribbonmen were secret societies common in 18th century Ireland. In some areas they had strong local support. The condemned awaited their fate but the hangman never came. Apparently no local hangman wanted to be associated with executing the popular Whiteboys and the sheriff was faced with a dilemma. Betty apparently stepped forward and proclaimed *"Set me free and I'll hang them all"*. The sheriff pondered a while and realised the only other person who could do this unpopular task was himself and he agreed to her request. She did the gruesome task without a shred of emotion and hanged all twenty five. The authorities were impressed and decided to keep her on as hangwoman and she operated throughout Connacht. Her duties also included public floggings and she soon became known as "Lady Betty".[203] As she was still a prisoner under sentence of death she received no wage, though she never wanted for food again. Hangings at the time were slow and agonising. Those with money would tip the hangman for a speedy demise, but Lady Betty was not interested in this. The gallows went through a small doorway on the third floor which looked out onto the market square, as hangings tended to draw crowds. It had a simple iron beam and pulley above and a small platform containing a trapdoor beneath, which shot away when Lady Betty pulled the lever, sending the condemned to their deaths. It was believed to be the longest drop in all of Ireland. It was only in the latter half of the 19th century that hangings became more scientific, delivering a swift death.

Lady Betty was pardoned for her own crime in 1802 but continued on with her grisly trade and still lived in the prison. She did not have much choice as executioners were despised, shunned and feared. According to Sir William Wilde, she drew a sketch of each of her victims as their legs danced in the air.[204] Charcoal drawings of her victims were also found on the walls of her quarters in the prison. The drawings were discovered after her death in 1807 and she was buried inside the prison walls. Her name was still used decades after her death by parents to scare their children.[205]

The prison itself closed its doors in 1840, when it became an asylum. Today only the facade remains and forms part of the Stone Court Shopping Centre.[206]

the colleen bawn

It was a story no playwright could resist, a young peasant girl falls in love with a gentleman only to realise too late that it is not true love and then tragedy strikes. The scene for the "romance" was County Limerick, not far from the Shannon.

John Scanlan, aged around twenty five, had served in the Napoleonic Wars as lieutenant and when he was discharged he took one of his subordinates, Stephen Sullivan as his servant. Ellen Hanley was the daughter of a small farmer at Ballycahane, near Bruree in County Limerick and was born in 1803.[207] She was something of a local beauty and her friendly, easy-going manner made her popular throughout the area. Her mother died when she was six years old and she was brought up by her uncle, John Connery, a rope maker. It is not clear under which circumstances John Scanlan made her acquaintance but he was doubtless captivated by her beauty. Before any kind of relationship could take place she insisted that he make an 'honourable' woman of her. He agreed to marry her, but on condition that it would be their little secret. She eloped with him in July of 1819, taking with her a hundred pounds and twelve gold guineas.[208] They were married by an excommunicated priest, which he believed would make the marriage invalid but suffice for him to have his wicked way with her. He was shocked, however, to learn that the marriage would be regarded as valid and he was stuck with her. They honeymooned briefly in Dublin where her money was soon spent, before returning to the area.

Though a great beauty, they both came from very different backgrounds and she would never be accepted by his family. It was something of a summer romance, if indeed it ever was a romance. His family was anxious that he find someone more suitable and arranged for him to be coupled with a woman of beauty from his own standing. Ellen Hanley was, however, still his legal wife and stood very much in the way of any such advancement.

Scanlan asked his servant Stephen Sullivan to take her out into the Shannon and murder her. Sullivan brought her out but could not bring himself to murder the young girl. Scanlon was insistent and Sullivan knew that that he had to obey his master and so he brought her out again. He shot her with a musket, clubbed her and stripped her. He then attached her to a stone and rope and dumped the body overboard. The following day Ellen Walsh, Scanlan's maid asked her master where his wife was and he told her she was with his sister in Kilkee. She noticed Scanlan was wearing Ellen Hanley's carved ring. Her suspicions were further aroused when she saw Sullivan's sister wearing a mantle that belonged to Ellen.

In autumn of 1819, six weeks after her mysterious disappearance, the naked body of a young girl was washed up on the shore near Moneypoint and news of the colleen bawn, from the Irish *cailín bán* meaning "fair girl", spread like wildfire throughout the area. Though severely battered, with teeth removed, she was still identifiable and Ellen Walsh recognised her mistress. Scanlan was located without difficulty, but his servant, who had sold Ellen's fine clothes, had disappeared.

The trial began in March of 1820, was presided over by Judge Richard Jebb and lasted only a day. It attracted considerable attention in the locality and there were those who believed Scanlan should not be on trial as she was "only" a peasant girl and he was her "better". An acquittal was expected. Scanlan was defended by one of the greatest legal minds of the time, one Daniel O'Connell. Though he protested his innocence the evidence of his maid Ellen Walsh, her broken-hearted uncle John Connery and John Driscol, who had found the body won over the jury. He was found guilty and sentenced to death by hanging to be carried out two days later. Death by hanging was considered a disgraceful way for a gentleman to die. His family tried to get a reprieve but a messenger would not be able to make a return journey to Dublin in only two days.[209]

He was taken from the Jail on 16th March to Gallows Green a mile from the prison in a horse and cart. At a bridge on the way the horses stopped, and though the escorting soldiers whipped and prodded them with their bayonets they would not budge and Scanlan had to walk the rest of the way. Some would have regarded this as a divine sign that the condemned man was innocent, though some believed his mother had bribed the cart driver to do exactly this. Even as the noose was placed around his neck Scanlan refused to admit any guilt.

How exactly the murder had taken place was revealed a few months later when Sullivan, or Clinton as he now called himself was located in Kerry. He had married a local woman and things were going fine until he committed fraud and found himself in prison. Prison is a place of great boredom and it is not clear whether he was recognised in jail or, as often is the case, spoke a little too freely and trusted too many people. He was brought back to Limerick where he had to answer for himself. He made a full confession, perhaps hoping that by putting the blame on his master he could save himself from the gallows, but his hopes in that matter were in vain.

Ellen Hanley was buried in Burrane cemetery,[210] between Kildysart and Kilrush. Several years later a Mrs. Reeves, from nearby Bessborough House, erected a Celtic cross at the head of the grave. When the story became popular her grave was marked on maps and the monument was chipped away by souvenir hunters.

A novel about the events, *The Collegians* was written by Gerald Griffin in 1829. This is turn was turned into a highly successful play *The Collen Bawn* by Dion Boucicault, which premiered in New York in 1860. Two years later the tale inspired Sir Julius Benedict to compose the opera *The Lily of Killarney*, which became a popular piece in Victorian England.

Today the tale is less well known nationally. The locals of Killimer, however, have endeavoured that her name not be forgotten and those who take the car ferry over to Tarbert in Kerry are reminded by a fine monument to a tragic episode.

117

RAFTERY

"Is Mise Raifteirí an file,
Lán dúchais is grádh,
Le súile gan solas,
Le ciúnas gan crá."[211]
"I'm Raftery the poet,
Full of hope and love,
With eyes without sight,
My mind without torment."

The lines of the above poem are well known to many Irish people who would have encountered them either in primary school or on the back of the five punt note. Most people do not realise that the famous poem was not penned by Antoine Ó Raifteirí (An-ton-a O Raftery) or Anthony Raftery as he is known in English. Indeed it was not even written in Ireland, but in America. The lines were penned by Seán Ó Ceallaigh towards the end of the 19th century in New York in homage to the great poet.

Raftery was the voice of the common people of Ireland, who were, in the 19th century, still largely Gaelic speaking. He was born around 1784 at Killaiden near Kiltimagh, County Mayo to the son of a weaver. Around 1788 his siblings contracted smallpox, which left him blind and all but he died. One of the last things he saw was his dead siblings being laid out. Though blind, he learnt to play the fiddle. Several musicians of the time such as Turlough O'Carolan[212] were blind and it provided them with a source of income. He also learnt poetry from an early age and was supported by his father's employer Frank Taafe. Much of our history and culture would have been transmitted through the medium of poetry and song and

118

though it may seem incredible to a modern audience he never learnt to read or write. Poetry and song was at the time mostly oral and he would have learnt and composed a vast amount of poems and songs to use in his repertoire.

Poets lived from patronage and Taafe supported the young poet. Things changed when Raftery was riding one of Taafe's best horses and, whilst jumping a drain, the horse's neck broke. Taafe was furious and banished the young poet from the estate. Years later Raftery would write *Cill Aodáin*, where he praised his former benefactor but it failed to make the desired impression on Taafe as he was of the opinion that he was not praised enough in the poem. Raftery took to wandering the province, mostly Galway and Mayo. He lived through somewhat turbulent times. It was a time of powerful and unjust landlords, the penal laws were still enforced, Whiteboys and Ribbon Men were active and the people rose in rebellion in 1798.

He felt injustice and reflected the mood of the people in his songs. In 1820 Anthony Daly, a carpenter from Kilrickle, was arrested for Whiteboy membership and was sentenced to hang. As he sat on his own coffin on the cart bringing him to the place of execution the crowd pleaded with him *as Gaeilge* to jump and they would hide him. Even the soldiers using the secret language said they would not shoot to kill him, but he refused as he did not want reprisals on the local population. Raftery witnessed this and immortalised the events in his poem *Antoine Ó Dálaigh*.

One of his most famous poems was *Eanach Dhúin*.[213] Annaghdown is a small village in County Galway on the shores of Lough Corrib. A group of men and women were making their way down the Corrib to a fair in a rotten and leaky boat that was overloaded. Around the Dangan area a sheep put his foot through the bottom, so one of the passengers blocked the hole with his coat.But when he went to stomp it in the bottom fell out the boat entirely. It was unlikely that many of them could swim and nineteen people drowned. Twelve others were saved by another boat.

Raftery's lament, which would have been sung, proved popular in the locality.

He immortalised the highwayman Liam Joyce in the poem *Casán Liam Deois* (The path of the highwayman Liam Joyce). He frequented the area around Carnmore airport just outside Galway city. Joyce was caught while trying to rob a farmer of his valuable hay and brought to Oranmore. It is not known whether he was hanged or transported to Australia.

Raftery strongly opposed the introduction of the national schools in 1830. The schools were designed to spread English influence into Gaelic areas and erode the native culture. Indeed children wore a stick around their neck and had a notch cut into it if they spoke Irish. A beating either by the school master or parents would ensue. Nothing was taught about Ireland and a poem, written on the board was recited daily:

"I thank the goodness and the grace
that on my birth have smiled
and made me in these Christian days
A happy English child."[214]

Raftery died in the house of Diarmuid O'Clunnian of Kileeneen on Christmas Eve of 1835. He was buried in Craughwell in a cemetery known locally as *Reilig na bhfile*. In 1900 a headstone was erected in his memory by W.B. Yeats, Lady Gregory and Edward Martyn, founder members of the Abbey Theatre in Dublin and key players in the Gaelic revival movement. His poems would have been forgotten about had it not been for scholars such as Douglas Hyde, Ireland's first president, who collected and published them. Raftery's passing marked the end of the centuries old tradition of the wandering bards.

the Resurrectionists

A somewhat macabre but highly lucrative business flourished in the first half of the nineteenth century and while the term body snatchers is commonly used today, those who stole cadavers to sell for medicinal research were more commonly known as "sack-em up men" or resurrectionists.

Medical students had been studying corpses since the 16th century. The bodies supplied were those of executed criminals. By the 19th century however, the number of people studying medicine had risen and demand far exceeded the supply, thus corpse robbing developed into a profitable business. Up to ten pounds was paid for a cadaver, a sum equivalent to a yearly wage for some. The body of a child was paid for by the inch, while a set of teeth would earn a pound. Given Dublin's proximity to the sea, Irish cadavers were also exported to England and Scotland in barrels and crates. Once dug up the corpse would be stripped, as to remove anything but the body was regarded as theft. Corpse robbing itself, though not entirely legal was not considered a serious offence. The corpse had to be fresh without any sign of decomposition. The corpse would then either be placed in a sack or placed on a cart and brought away. A famous Dublin memoir *Malachi Horan Remembers* recounts that the horses wore leather shoes to muffle any noise. Sometimes the corpse would be dressed in an old coat and, supported by two people, walked out, giving the appearance of a drunk being brought home by friends.[215]

The basic method the resurrectionsts employed was using a wooden spade, to create less noise, to dig at the head of the grave, placing the earth on a sheet to disguise their activities. The body would then be pulled from the grave and the earth carefully replaced. Another more refined method; whereby a tunnel would be dug a few metres away and a small boy would crawl into the tunnel and slip a noose around the neck of the corpse and slowly drag the body out, was also used. Thus it appeared that the ground had never been disturbed. Sometimes resurrectionists attended funerals, carefully noting where the body lay and sometimes gravediggers themselves were reurrectionists by night. It was usual at the time for relatives to remain behind after the funeral and watch over the grave of their loved ones to deter the resurrectionists.

Some resurrectionsts unintentionally provided a service to humanity. When Margorie McCall from Lurgan got the fever and died in 1705 she was buried in haste to stop the disease from spreading. Resurectionists dug her up a few hours later. Intending to steal her wedding ring, one of the group cut off her finger and to his horror the body stirred. She woke up and walked the short distance home, still dressed in her shroud, where her family were grieving their loss until they heard her familiar knock. It is said that her husband dropped dead from the shock. She lived for several years thereafter.[216]

The main source of bodies was Bully's Acre on the grounds of Kilmainham hospital. During the time of the Penal laws it was the only cemetery open to Catholics and as burial there was free it was used until the cholera epidemic of 1832 by Catholics from all walks of life. It was a somewhat lonely location and its low walls provided easy access. Though considered the lowest form of life, those who had dealings with resurrectionists were often highly regarded in society and the medical profession certainly did not frown upon the practice. Peter Harkan, a pathologist at a medical institute known as Crampton's School was caught body snatching with his students by a night watchman at Bully's Acre. He fled with the others but the watchman grabbed him by the legs while his students pulled him by the arms and though the students won the tug-o-war, he died of his injuries shortly afterwards in 1814.

One of the most famous bodies stolen was that of the champion fighter Dan Donnelly, who died in 1820 and was buried at Bullys' Acre. When his body was dug up and sold to a Doctor Hall it caused outrage among his fans, who threatened to kill the surgeon.[217] Hall agreed to return he body but kept the arm which, until very recently, was on display in Kilcullen.

Soldiers stationed at the nearby Royal Hospital Kilmainham did their best to keep watch over the graves as their comrades were also buried there, and they would sometimes shoot at resurrectionists. It is recorded that in 1825 a sentry captured Thomas Tuite, who had five bodies and pockets full of teeth in his possession.[218]

Digging up corpses was hard work and two Irishmen, William Burke and William Hare, found an easier way by murdering people.[219] The pair murdered an old beggar in Edinburgh and sold his body to Robert Knox, who ran an anatomy school, and continued to provide him with freshly murdered corpses. His students became suspicious when well known healthy individuals suddenly turned up as cadavers in the lecture hall. By the time their murder spree had come to an end in 1828 they had murdered sixteen people. Hare turned informer, Burke was hanged, and though never prosecuted, Knox became a social pariah. The public outrage which the case caused led to the Anatomy Act.

The Anatomy Act of 1832 had a massive impact on body snatching and resulted in a rapid decline of this macabre practice. According to the act unclaimed bodies or bodies donated by the family could now be used for medical research. Henceforth, an ample supply of bodies could be legally provided.

The act was just coming to force when Ireland's most famous cemetery, Glasnevin was opened in 1832. It was built with high walls and watchtowers. The watchmen, who were armed, used Cuban blood hounds to deter any nocturnal visitors. Its security from resurrectionists made it the most popular cemetery in the city and when the poet Zozimus died in 1846 he insisted on being buried there for this very reason.

The grim business did not die out entirely with the passing of the act. In 1838 thirty pounds was paid for an ankylosed skeleton of a man who had died in the Isle of Man.[220] Though his body had been broken up by his relatives to prevent his remains being exhibited, the resurrectionists disinterred it and brought it to Dublin.

Ɒan Ɒonnelly

Dan Donelly (1788-1820) was one of the greatest boxers this country ever produced. He was born into poverty to a family of seventeen down by the Dublin docks. At an early age he followed his father into carpentry to support his family.

In the years following the 1798 rebellion the people were left leaderless and in low spirits. Donnelly was just what they needed. He gave the Irish a sense of pride and self-respect at a time when it was badly needed. He soon came to be recognised as a champion of the poor and needy and became the fighting champion of the neighbourhood. Donnelly was nearly six foot (1.83m) tall and weighed almost 14 stone or 89kg.

He was a hard man to provoke into a fight but if he believed a fight was necessary, especially if a woman was being mistreated he would not shy away from it. In one incident, as he was walking by the docks he heard a woman scream and saw she was being raped by two sailors. He fought them and they fought back and beat him with stones. He managed to fight them off but his arm was left mangled. He was taken a doctor, Abraham Colles who at first wanted to amputate the arm, which would have destroyed Donnelly's boxing career. The surgeon, however, managed to put the arm back together again.[221]

His reputation as a fighter continued to grow. He took on the boxing champion of Dublin city by the Grand Canal and beat him in the 16th round. Thus Dan Donnelly became the new champion of Dublin.

It should be mentioned that boxing at that time was very different to the boxing we know today and there were a lot less rules. The obvious difference was that it was bare knuckle, which is still carried out among the travelling community. Hair pulling and headlocks were permitted. The end was signalled when the boxer could not continue or gave up. Seconds assisted the boxers between rounds. A round could last as long as six or seven minutes, or as little as 30 seconds. The round would end when one person was on the ground. He would then have 30 seconds to get up and continue the fight.

Donnelly attracted the attention of Captain William Kelly, a piper from Kildare. Kelly was a "Fancy". Fancies were aristocrats, who supported boxers. In modern parlance they would be called fight promoters. He had been in England, where he overheard a pair of English prize-fighters mocking Ireland's reputation as a nation of courageous men. Kelly was of course much put out by this and resolved to find a champion to challenge them. His search ended with Donnelly and Kelly organised a prize fight on the Curragh of Kildare. The spot chosen for the fight was a natural amphitheatre called "Belcher's Hollow". It was regularly used for fights. Donnelly's English opponent was Tom Hall, who was touring Ireland at the time showing the Irish how to box. Over twenty thousand people gathered to watch the fight. Hall gave up and Donnelly was declared champion. For the assembled crowd it was much more than a boxing match. It was a jab at their colonial masters. Thereafter "Belcher's Hollow" became known as "Donnelly's Hollow", a name it carries to this day.

Donnelly celebrated his victory a little too well and was soon broke. A fresh challenge came from George Cooper in 1815 and a new fight was arranged at Donnelly's hollow. Cooper, a bargeman of gypsy descent, was the favourite with 10/1 odds.

Bets were made back then as is still customary to this day, but people did not just bet on who would win or lose. Other factors such as who would draw the first blood or on who would score the first knockdown were also bet on. In one round, Cooper used the cross-buttock tactic which winded Donnelly. The cross-buttock belonged more to wrestling than boxing, but it was a legitimate move. With this move a boxer got in front of his opponent, and threw the other boxer over his hip, causing him to land with great force on the ground. According to folklore Donnelly was being badly beaten in the fifth round, but was saved by a lump of sugar cane slipped to him by Captain Kelly's sister.[222] Donnelly beat him in the eleventh round, when he broke Cooper's jaw. Yet again Dan Donnelly was champion and returned in triumph to Dublin.

Today on the Curragh of Kildare a grey weather beaten monument marks the site of where Donnelly beat Cooper. The inscription simply reads:

"Dan Donnelly beat Cooper on this spot 13th Dec. 1815"

Like many a sporting star he was good at making money but not so good at keeping it. He owned several pubs around Dublin, in Capel Street and Poolbeg, but he was also his own best customer and they soon went out of business. Of the four pubs he owned only Fallons in The Coombe remains. He died at Donnelly's Public House on Greek Street on 18th February, 1820 aged 32.[223] An oval wall plaque commemorates the site of his death. His funeral was a major affair in Dublin and an estimated crowd of 80,000 watched the procession.[224] His name lived on after his death. Buried at Bully's Acre, the only cemetery open to Catholics at the time, grave robbers dug up his corpse and sold it to a surgeon called Hall. His fans found out where the cadaver was and threatened to kill the surgeon. After negotiation he returned the corpse but kept the right arm. It was said to be the longest in the history of boxing and he wanted to use it for medical study. It was preserved in red lead paint and sent to a medical college in Edinburgh. From there it went on tour as part of a travelling circus. In 1904 it returned to Ireland, where it was purchased by Belfast bookmaker Hugh "Texas" McAlevey, who displayed it in his pub and then in his attic.[225] It came to Kilcullen in the 1950s as part of a Dan Donnelly pageant, where it was displayed once more in Byrne's pub "The Hideout".

The arm went on tour once more in 2006, when it flew in the cockpit of an Aer Lingus plane and formed the centrepiece of a Fighting Irishmen exhibition at the Irish Arts Center in New York City. From there it was returned to the GAA museum at Croke Park.

Faction Fighting

"The boys of Liverpool, When we safely landed,
Called myself a fool; I could no longer stand it;
Blood began to boil, Temper I was losin',
Poor ould Erin's isle They began abusin',
"Hurrah my soul," sez I, My shillelagh I let fly;
Some Galway boys were by, Saw I was a hobble in,
Then with a loud hurray, They joined in the affray.
We quickly cleared the way, for the rocky road to Dublin."
(The Rocky Road to Dublin)

The unpleasant stereotype of the fighting Irishman has its roots in faction fighting, which was widespread in the first half of the 19th century. It is difficult to fathom why two groups of people, for no particular reason, would meet to fight, though it is not uncommon for rival gangs to fight each other in big cities all over the world. It was perhaps comparable to football hooliganism. It seems to have its roots in the first half of the 19th century, where class divisions were pronounced. The two main groups that engaged in this form of fighting were the Caravats, who were landless labourers, and the Shanavests or tenant farmers.[226] It appears to have taken place all over the country and fairs and Pattern days usually had a fight associated with them. Pattern or Name Days were associated with a local saint and the local community gathered at his holy well or church.[227]

In County Dublin the Donnybrook fair was notorious for its faction fighting. Like any other fair of the time it was a gathering place for tinkers, merchants, entertainers, cattlemen and farmers. The faction fighting associated with Donnybrook was one of the primary reasons the fair, which had been in existence for several centuries, was abolished. The term "Donnybrook" is still used to describe a violent disturbance.[228]

Nobody knows for sure why faction fights broke out. Sometimes it was over a small grudge or insult, but it did not take much to get one started and, to foreign observers it seemed that the Irish fought for the pleasure of it. The British authorities did little to stop the faction fighting. After all, the Irish fighting among themselves meant they would not be fighting them.

Given that Catholics were forbidden by the penal laws to carry guns, most travellers carried a stick and were proficient in stick fighting, know as *bataireacht*.[229] The most infamous weapon used was the shillelagh. The shillelagh today is something that is sold as a kitsch souvenir to tourists, but in the 19th century was a powerful weapon. Named after the village of Shillelagh in County Wicklow, it was usually made from Blackthorn, rubbed in butter and cured up the chimney, giving it its black appearance. The name shillelagh comes from the Gaelic *sail éille,* meaning cudgel with a strap.[230] It was believed that a wound from a blackthorn stick would heal quickly, the whitethorn however was considered a much more dangerous weapon as a blow from this could result in blood poisoning. A head wound in the absence of any medical attention was highly dangerous. A particularly vicious weapon was the "loaden butt" in which the stump at the end was hollowed out and filled with lead. In close combat a short stick, "the alpeen" or "kippen" was used. It is not known whether the groups intended to kill each other, but the names the fighters gave to their weapons such as "bás gan sagart" (death without the priest) or "leagadh gan Éiri" (down without getting up) suggest they had little regard for human life.

Daniel O'Connell apppealed to the Irish to unite and this helped a little to curb the spread of faction fighting, which declined considerably after 1830. The foundation of the GAA in 1884 helped rival parishes resolve their disputes on the playing field.

the san patricios

The San Patricios was a battalion in the Mexican army which fought against the United States in the Mexican–American War (1846-1848). The battalion comprised of about 700 volunteers, nearly all of whom had deserted the US army. The battalion was led by John Riley from Clifden, County Galway, who had previously served in both the British and American armies.

What inspired these men to desert the United States army in the first place? America in the 19th century, though a melting pot of nations, had a ruling elite called "nativists" who were the descendents of the original English Protestants who came in 1620. It seemed as if those in power had brought old world intolerance with them. They had little time for Irish Catholics whom they referred to as "potato heads", or indeed for Catholics in general, and treated them terribly.

The San Patricios were by no means exclusively Irish but a mishmash of Italians, Germans, escaped slaves, Spaniards and Poles, all of whom had the unifying feature of being the underdog.

The Mexicans were aware of how Catholics were being treated in the US army and knew how they could exploit the situation. They offered them citizenship, better pay and land. Most of the Irish had been recruited directly off the boats and were not US citizens. They had suffered discrimination and hostility in the ranks of the US army and were not allowed to attend Sunday mass. The burning of Catholic churches and unprovoked attacks on Mexican civilians by the infamous Texas Rangers, known locally as *Los Diablos Tejanos*,[231] must have made them wonder why they were fighting for the United States. Why would they risk their lives for a country that treated them so shoddily? For the US army they were little more than cannon fodder and the Catholic Mexicans had much more in common with them.

Unusually for such a small unit the San Patricios were allowed their own colours. Unfortunately the colours did not survive, but they have been described as a green banner with a golden harp surmounted by the Mexican Coat of Arms, with a scroll on which was painted "Libertad por la Republica Mexicana". Under the harp was the motto of "Erin go Bragh!" On the other side was a figure of St. Patrick with the words "San Patricio"[232] underneath.

The battalion initially served as artillery, Riley being experienced in this field, but as the war progressed they were also used as infantry. While the Americans regarded them as renegades, the Mexicans looked upon them as heroes who had come to the aid of fellow Catholics. The battalion fought at the Battle of Monterrey. There were heavy losses on both sides. American soldiers had never engaged in urban warfare before and they marched straight down the open streets, and the Mexicans massacred them. The Americans had the advantage of numbers and after fierce fighting won the day.

At the battle of Cerro Gordo the US army advanced on Mexico City and the San Patricios fought a last desperate battle at Churubusco in August 1847. Much of their fire was aimed at the US officers, the ones who had most discriminated against them. The Mexicans tried to surrender but the Irish ripped down the white flag and desperately fought on until their ammunition was spent.

The battalion had been responsible for inflicting some of the heaviest casualties on the US army. Of the eighty five members of the battalion captured, seventy two were immediately charged with desertion. Two separate court-martials were held. The accused were not given representation, limited in what they were allowed to say in their defence and no transcripts of the trial were made. Riley testified at the trial that the main reason for his desertion was the shoddy treatment of Catholics in the US army, which was ignored. They were charged with desertion in time of war, which usually carried the death penalty. This usually meant death by firing squad, but to humiliate them they were sentenced to death by hanging usually reserved for spies and common criminals.

The hangings began on 10th September 1847, at San Ángel, where sixteen of them were hanged. At the execution, Patrick Dalton from Mayo was slowly strangled to death. This may have been a botched hanging but many believed it to have been deliberate as he had complained about the treatment they received as prisoners. A further four were hanged at Mixcoac.

The largest number to be hanged was at Chapultepec, on the orders of General Winfield Scott, who became a national hero in America after the war. Thirty San Patricios were executed here. The master of ceremonies was Colonel William Harney, who earned a reputation for cruelty that day. Twenty nine were brought to the scaffold. Francis O'Connor was missing as both his legs had been amputated the previous day. When the army surgeon informed the colonel that the absent soldier had lost both his legs in battle, Harney's response was:

"Bring the damned son of a bitch out! My order was to hang 30 and by God I'll do it!"[233]

The execution was choreographed to coincide with the raising of the American flag. They had been made wait on the scaffold since dawn. Surprisingly, Riley was not executed. He had deserted before hostilities had broken out. Instead he was subjected to barbaric medieval torture. He was made stand before his men who were on the gallows and branded with a two inch letter "D" for desertion with a hot-iron on the right cheek. He was given 50 lashes, which was hoped would kill him, but he did not scream. Only when branded a second time did he react, and lost consciousness. He was revived so that he could watch his men die on the scaffold. The Mexican government described the hangings as:

"A cruel death or horrible torments, improper in a civilized age, and [ironic] for a people who aspire to the title of illustrious and humane"[234]

Harney was promoted for his work to Brigadier General and would go on to receive more infamy when in 1854 he partook in the Grattan massacre of the Sioux and was referred to as a "woman killer".[235] The mass hangings made a deep impression on the Mexican civilian population. Rioting broke out in Toluca after the news reported that the executions had taken place. The Mexicans demanded that the San Patricios be treated as prisoners of war and not criminals. The Americans intended taking the remaining San Patricios back with them. The Mexicans intervened and as part of the final surrender negotiations it was agreed that the remaining San Patricios would remain in Mexico.

While most of the survivors disappeared from history, some took up the Mexican offer of land. Their existence was denied by the US authorities for decades after. It was the first and only time in the history of the United States that so many soldiers, up to 9,000, had deserted, bonded together and fought for the enemy.

The Mexicans officially disbanded the battalion in 1848. It is not known for certain what became of Riley, though it is believed that he wanted to return to his native Clifden but died of cholera. There are records of a 45 year old Juan Reley, native of Ireland, who died in 1850 in Veracruz. In 1959, a plaque was erected in Mexico City commemorating the Irish Heroes of Mexico. The inscription on the plaque would translate as:

"To the memory of Captain John Riley of the Clifden area, founder and leader of the Saint Patrick's Battalion and those men under his command who gave their lives for Mexico during the U.S.-Mexican War of 1846-1848"[236]

The battalion is still revered in Mexico and the Mexican government erected a bronze statue of Riley in his hometown of Clifden in 1999. He was played by Tom Berenger in a 1999 movie *One Man's Hero*.

Lola Montez

In a time when women were expected to obey and avoid the limelight, an adventuress such as Lola Montez attracted attention.Wherever she went, scandal followed.

Traditionally it was claimed that she was born in Limerick in 1821 as Marie Dolores Eliza Gilbert. Her father Edward Gilbert married Eliza Gilbert of Limerick in 1820 and the couple lived in Boyle, County Roscommon before moving to India via Liverpool. It was the beginning of a life spent travelling all over the world. A baptismal certificate discovered in the 1990s shows that she was born in Grange, County Sligo.[237] Given all the moving around that took place and that her mother's family was from Limerick it is easy to see how she would identify with Limerick.

Her father died of cholera shortly after arriving in India and her 19 year old mother remarried. It was decided to send their daughter Eliza back to her stepfather's family in Scotland where she was regarded as a mischievous and troublesome "Indian girl". Due to her Scottish sojourn some biographies claim that she was Scottish.

At sixteen she eloped to Ireland with Lieutenant Thomas James, but the couple separated five years later. It was then that she moved to Spain where she became an exotic dancer. In 1843 she went to Madrid and Seville to learn how to become a dancer and adopted the stage name Lola Montez, a name that gave off an aura of intrigue and the exotic. With her long black hair and wild eyes she easily passed as Spanish. It was there that she developed her spider dance, which involved her shaking fake tarantulas out of her clothes and stamping on them. The performance both shocked and excited the audience.

She began her dancing career in England but was recognised as "Mrs James" which created tongue wagging that placed her beyond the pale in polite English society, and she went to Paris where she created an aura of seductive mystery and exquisite scandal around her personality. Her performance would today be described as burlesque. Theatres at the time had never seen such an erotic performance. She had a brief fling with both the composer Franz Liszt and the novelist Alexandre Dumas. She did not stay very long in Paris either. After the 1845 death of her lover, newspaperman Alexandre Dujarier, in a duel, she left Paris. She seemed to change lovers with great frequency and Alexandre Dumas remarked somewhat prophetically in 1845 that:

> *"She will certainly bring misfortune, to whoever gets too close to her. Should anything be heard of her again it would be in connection with something terrible that has happened to one of her lovers."*[238]

She appeared on stage at the Hoftheater in Munich in October 1846. They had never seen the likes of the erotic "Spanish" dancer. Dressed in several different coloured skirts, she removed them as the spider dance progressed. The end of the dance left her in a flesh coloured top. Her burlesque style of dancing captivated the mostly male audience.

The sixty year old Bavarian monarch Ludwig I was so captivated that she soon became his mistress. According to one story he admired her ample bosom, whereupon she exposed them, but this has been discredited by most historians.[239] Not long afterwards, he bought her a palace, which was to become their love nest. Though the king was infatuated with her, Munich society looked at her differently. Not only did she appear to lack any morals but her swearing, short temper, smoking, and readiness to lash out at anyone who displeased her, as well as the huge dog that went with her everywhere, made her deeply unpopular.

She was not content to merely be Ludwig's mistress and began to involve herself in politics. By today's standards she would occupy much space in the tabloids. She advocated more liberal policies in a part of Germany still known for its conservatism. Her influence began to show and when Bavaria's President Karl von Abel refused to grant her citizenship she used her power over Ludwig to have him dismissed. Ludwig paid no heed to her critics and was completely bewitched by her. He awarded her the title of Marie, Countess of Landesfeld with an income of £2,000 a year. Due to her anti-clerical, especially anti-Jesuit policies, she soon found herself at war with the church, a most powerful institution. It is hard to know what she really wanted. Though she seemed to be a gold digger, when she was offered a large sum of money by the nobility if she disappeared she threw it in the emissary's face.[240]

The students, an influential group in the city had mixed feelings about her. In February 1848 she was attacked when she visited Munich University. She used her power over Ludwig to have the university closed down and Ludwig ordered all students to leave the city within three days. When a mob came to her palace she fired a pistol at them. The expulsion of the students had a knock on affect on those who made a living from students: publicans, prostitutes, and landlords. Despite the furore she had created Ludwig still stood by her and declared he would exchange his crown for her. Thus Lola Montez of Ireland was the catalyst for a revolution and in less than three years had cost the king his throne.

In order for peace to be restored she was expelled from Bavaria and Ludwig was forced to abdicate, handing over power to his son Maximillian. Ludwig remarked later to the French Empress Engine that:

> "I always loved the beautiful Spaniard. I know what I am talking about. It cost me the throne."[241]

She went to Switzerland but Ludwig did not join her there. His family feared he would have taken the crown jewels with him.[242] The relationship was over and Lola would have to find herself another benefactor.

She returned to England where she soon married a young cavalry officer called George Trafford Herald, who had recently inherited a sizeable sum. Problems arose when it was made known that under the terms of her divorce from Thomas James, neither party was permitted to remarry while the other was living. Once more there was a scandal and the couple fled, but their liaison was condemned to failure and ended in 1851, though some sources claim he died of drowning in Lisbon.

Her colourful life continued and she went to America in 1851, where she performed her spider dance to much success. She continued to draw attention, smoking cigars at a time when no respectable woman smoked, and drinking in saloons where women were not welcome. She branched out into other fields and composed a semi-autobiographical play "Lola Montez in Bavaria". She moved to San Francisco where she married a local newspaperman called Patrick Hull. Again the marriage did not last and ended shortly afterwards. She embarked on a tour of Australia in 1855, entertaining miners who appreciated her show while others condemned her lack of morality. She returned to America, where she moved to New York and for a time lectured on gallantry and produced a biography *"The Arts of Beauty"* (1858). She also devoted a considerable amount of her time to female outcasts.

She died of pneumonia in 1861 in New York, impoverished and forgotten about. For a woman who led such an extraordinary life, her gravestone is Spartan and lacking an epitaph, with just "Mrs Eliza Gilbert, died January 17, 1861, aged 42."[243] Though hated at the time, Germans today admire her as a woman of courage who stood up to the Church and conservatism.

the count and the kaiser

In 1853 a great crowd gathered on the Simmering Heath[244] in Vienna to watch a man being strangled to death. As was usual at such spectacles, a song, was composed mocking the soon to be deceased. The condemned man, János Libényi, had eight days previously attempted to assassinate the emperor Franz Josef, but was prevented by a man called Maximillian O'Donell[245]. Though the tale was already known to me, I arranged to meet Douglas O'Donell, a descendant of Maximillian, in Vienna for further details. Though Austrian, it was uncanny how Irish he was. The O'Donells had come over to Austria from Mayo in the mid 18th century and members of the family such as Carl Claudius O'Donell had distinguished themselves in the Seven Years War. As was usual at the time for nobility, O'Donell set up his own regiment, which existed until the 19th century. The O'Donells spoke French, the language of the nobility, with outsiders and Irish among themselves and the other Wild Geese. The Emperor Joseph II (1741-1790) was used to hearing the language and was shocked that a visiting musician, Michael Kelly of Dublin, did not understand it. Kelly explained to the emperor, in the presence of generals O'Donell and Kavanagh, (the latter having asked him a question in Irish) that it was the language of the peasantry, before realising his *faux pas*.[246] Though the status of the language had changed in Ireland it had not among the Irish nobility in exile. Maximillian was born in Vienna and brought up in Dresden. He became an aide-de-camp to the emperor after serving in the campaigns of 1848 in Italy and Hungary. Franz Josef I (1830-1916) had become emperor of the Austro-Hungarian Empire in 1848.[247]

As they walked through the city O'Donell saw a small man lunge at the Kaiser. He jumped at the would-be assassin and wrestled him to the ground. A butcher, Joseph Metternich, helped restrain him and O'Donell lashed at the assailant with his sword. Afraid that the wound might have been poisoned O'Donell sucked out any potential poison.

Though wounded, the emperor's stiff high uniform collar had prevented a much worse injury. Nobody knows for sure what motives Libényi, who was a former hussar and tailor, had for trying to assassinate the emperor, but more than likely it was hatred, for Austrian dominance in his country and the emperor's failure to quash a death sentence of Hungarian martyrs.

The assassination attempt ranks as the most famous failed assassination in the history of Austria. Though the attempt on his life was unsuccessful, the emperor's beloved wife Sissi, who used to go horse riding in Ireland,[248] was less fortunate and was murdered by an anarchist in Geneva in 1898.

A grateful emperor awarded O'Donell the Order of Leopold and granted him the unusual privilege of bearing the double headed eagle on his coat of arms. The nobility of Europe donated money towards the building of a church to gives thanks to God for saving the emperor's life. It was built on the site of the failed assassination, which today forms part of the inner city ring and is not far from a church established by Irish monks, the *Schottenkirche*.[249]It was called the Votiv (offering to God) Kirche and work on it was completed in 1879.

Traces of this assassination attempt are still around Vienna and the event is commemorated in a painting in The Vienna Museum. The same painting is on view as a mural in The Criminal Museum in the Second District.

Maximillian retired a major general in 1859 and died in Salzburg in 1895. With the collapse of the monarchy, most of the wild geese departed Austria. The O'Donells remained on in Austria and still live there today. A tale is told of one of them, who was captured by the British at Monte Casino in 1944. Because he could speak English he was given the task of interpreting and worked alongside a sergeant originally from Ireland. At roll call the prisoners were required to step forward and acknowledge their names. When the name O'Donell was called out no one stepped forward, as he standing beside the sergeant calling the roll. When it was repeatedly called out it drew the attention of an officer who roared, *"What the bloody hell is an Irishman doing in the German army?"* to which the sergeant roared back, *"What the bloody hell is an Irishman doing in the British army?"*[250]

Che Charge of the Light Brigade

"Cannon to right of them,
Cannon to left of them,
Cannon in front of them
Volley'd and thunder'd;
Storm'd at with shot and shell,
Boldly they rode and well,
Into the jaws of Death,
Into the mouth of hell
Rode the six hundred."
The Charge of the Light Brigade

Alfred, Lord Tennyson

The Charge of the Light Brigade at the Battle of Balaclava during The Crimean War (1853-56) was a military blunder and disaster, though the courage of the cavalry who were massacred by the Russian guns lives on in the famous Tennyson poem. He got the numbers wrong, but that does not get in the way of poetic licence. A considerable amount of Irishmen took part in the charge and served in the campaign. The war started when the Tsar of Russia wanted more control over the region controlled by the crumbling Ottoman Empire, known as the "Sick Man of Europe". France and Britain intervened to check Russian expansion and a fruitless war began.

The brigade was comprised of several cavalry regiments, most notably the 4th and 13th Light Dragoons, 17th Lancers, and the 8th and 11th Hussars, under the command of Lord Cardigan. Also present was the heavy brigade consisting of the 4th Royal Irish Dragoon Guards, the 5th Dragoon Guards, the 6th (Inniskilling) Dragoons and the Scots Greys. The 4th Royal Irish Dragoon Guards was raised in 1685 and disbanded in 1922. It was this regiment that fired the first shots of the Great War. The 6th (Inniskilling) Dragoons was raised in 1689 and had fought at the battle of the Boyne, and was also disbanded in 1922.

The British army of the 19th century was different to today. Commissions could be bought, which meant those in command, while of the nobility, often had little experience of leading men into battle and had little regard for human life. Several of the British commanders that day had Irish connections. Lord Raglan, the supreme commander, has a road in Dublin named after him.

Lord Cardigan, who led the charge, was unpopular among his junior officers, many of whom were veterans of Waterloo and older than him. He symbolised the arrogance and extravageance of the officer class of the time. He had entered military service in 1824 at the age of 27 and joined the 8th King's Royal Irish Hussars, buying himself the commission of Lieutenant.[251] By 1830 he was a Lieutenant-Colonel and stationed in Newbridge, County Kildare, which was the largest cavalry barracks in Ireland[252] and chosen for its proximity to the natural watering station of the River Liffey. Cardigan was dismissed from the service in 1834 as he was regarded as something of a bully, but used his influence to get back in two years later and was sent to India with the 11th Light Dragoons. Of the two years the regiment spent there he only spent four weeks with the regiment. The rest of the time was spent at leisure activities such as big game hunting. Another commander that day was Lord Lucan. He had served as MP for Mayo between 1826-30 and Lord Lieutenant for Mayo in 1845. He is remembered in the area with little fondness and recieved the title the "Exterminator" in 1845[253] when he evicted his tenants, whom he regarded as "vermin" and they starved to death. It did not endear him to the people of Mayo.

On the 25 October 1854, the infamous charge took place. More than twenty per cent of those who made the charge were Irish. Cardigan and Lucan were barely on speaking terms. Lucan had married one of Cardigan's sisters and the latter believed she was being treated badly. Lucan gave the order to attack through Captain Louis Nolan.[254] Though never having visited Ireland, Captain Nolan was born in Canada to an Irish father and was a competent cavalry officer.

Lord Cardigan gave his bugler, William Brittain of the 17th Lancers the order to sound the charge. Brittain was from Dublin[255] and his bugle had been made in Capel Street. He was injured in the charge and died of his wounds in Florence Nightingale's hospital in Scutari, Istanbul. His bugle found its way to the regimental musuem at Belvoir Castle Leicestershire.[256]

Cardigan led the charge and, reaching the Russian guns unscathed, turned back, suffering no injuries as a result. His men did all the suffering. His only concern was to report Nolan, who had fallen in the charge, for riding ahead of him in the charge. Of the 118 killed, 21 were Irish. In the aftermath of the fiasco, scapegoats were sought. Raglan blamed Lucan and Cardigan blamed Nolan for giving the "wrong" order. Lucan was recalled to England but avoided any court martial by deflecting any blame onto others. Cardigan returned to England and gave a heroic account of his exploits, a pretence which lasted only for a few months.[257]

One of the horses involved in the charge was known as Dickie Bird and was stationed at the Royal (Collins) Barracks in Dublin. His skeletal remains were discovered at the begining of this century and are now on display in the National Museum in Dublin.[258]

The Crimean war was one of the first wars where correspondents played a key role in influencing public opinion. William Howard Russell, a correpondent for *The Times*, originally from Tallaght in Dublin, was the most famous correspondent.[259] Indeed, Tennyson wrote his famous poem after reading Russell's account of the battle. Russell documented the suffering of the

British soldiers, many of whom were dying of cholera and malaria. His reports, which could be telegraphed to London, caused an outcry and he was heavily criticised by the establishment. It did however encourage people like Florence Nightingale to set up proper care for the sick and wounded. Though disliked by the establishment, Russell returned to a hero's welcome in 1856.

The Crimean war would continue for another two years after the infamous Charge of the Light Brigade, and cost 650,000 lives. It would achieve very little. It was during The Crimean War that Queen Victoria instituted a new medal for gallantry, the Victoria Cross, which is still today the highest medal for gallantry. Twenty eight Irishmen won the award in the Crimean war. Indeed, the first ever Victoria Cross was awarded to Sergeant Luke O'Connor from Elphin, County Roscommon in 1857.[260] He had joined the 17th Lancers and at the battle of Alma, though himself wounded in the chest, when the officer carrying the regimental colours was killed, he grabbed the colours, rushed towards the enemy and planted them in the ground before their lines. It inspired his comrades to attack and the position was taken. He received a commission and retired a General and was knighted. He is unique by virtue of being the only soldier in the British army to have risen from Private to General and win the Victoria Cross.

the battle of fredericksburg

The Battle of Fredericksburg, fought in December 1862, was one of the bloodiest battles in The American Civil War, and cost thousands of lives, many of them Irish. It was one of the few battles where the Irish faced each other, on opposing sides, and this will be the main focus of this article.

The Irish fighting for the North have always received more attention, chiefly because unlike the South they were organised into large brigades, such as the Irish Brigade, while the South had 45 different Irish regiments, all fighting independently of each other, making up 10 per cent of the Confederate Army. The two main Irish regiments fighting for the North were the 69th and the 116th. The 69th from New York was already famous before Fredericksburg. Shortly before the conflict had erupted they had refused to parade for the Prince of Wales, resulting in court martial for their commander Colonel Michael Corcoran, from Carrowkeel, County Sligo. The outbreak of the war meant that this court martial never took place. He had been taken prisoner the previous year, leaving Waterford born Brigadier–General Thomas Meagher[261] to assume command of the brigade. The 69th regiment was easily distinguishable by the Green Flag they carried and the sprig of shamrock they wore in their hats. A hundred years later JFK would present this Green standard to the Dáil when he visited Ireland. The 116th Pennsylvanian Infantry also partook in the assault as part of the Irish Brigade. It was led by Colonel St. Clair Mulholland, from Lisburn, Country Antrim. He was wounded in the assault and was later to receive the Congressional Medal of Honour. Meagher was also injured when a cannonball struck him in the leg. The disaster at Fredericksburg signalled the end of his career and he resigned his commission in1863.

The Union Army moved south towards Richmond and intended to cross the Potomac at Fredericksburg. The Union Army under General Burnside, numbering 114,000, was much larger than the Confederate Army of 72,000 under General Robert E. Lee. The confederates were, however, fighting on home ground and more determined. The Union Army was also under pressure from the Northern public to quell the rebellion. Burnside made several mistakes. Although his army arrived on the banks of the Potomac while the confederates were ill prepared, he had to wait until pontoon bridges arrived. This procrastination gave the confederates ample time to fortify their position and prepare for the Union assault. The assault began on 13th December and having crossed the Potomac the Union Army entered the town and ransacked it. This outraged southerners and only served to strengthen their opposition to the North. The Irish Brigade was given the order to attack the confederate positions at Marye's Heights just outside the town. Not only would it mean attacking uphill but also across open fields, giving them absolutely no cover. The Irish Brigade's chaplain, Father William Corby remarked in disbelief, *"The Generals could not be so foolish as to order us up that hill"*.[262] He was wrong. Father Corby was the most famous chaplin of the war and had told the troops that anyone who wavered or showed cowardice would be denied a Christian burial.[263] Overlooking the Irish Brigade in the confederate lines was General Thomas R. R. Cobb's brigade which included the 24th Georgia Infantry regiment which was largely comprised of Irishmen. It was 660 strong and suffered 36 casualties at Fredericksburg.[264] In later battles they were less fortunate and only 65 survived the war. Cobb was mortally wounded in the battle and replaced by Antrim-born Colonel Robert McMillan.[265] The regiment had taken up position behind a stone wall, located at the crest of the ridge, which still stands today. The wall gave them excellent cover. The confederates were confident that they would be able to repeal any assault on their positions. Indeed, the confederate artillery commander Edward Porter Alexander commented, *"A chicken could not live on that field when we open on it."*[266] Unfortunately for the Irish this would prove to be the case. The attacking 69th had to file in columns when crossing over two small bridges that spanned a drainage ditch, making them a massed target, before entering the open ground. It was a suicidal assault, doomed to fail. Nevertheless they stormed the hill shouting their war cry "Faugh an Ballagh".[267]

Watching the Union assault, Robert E. Lee wondered if Irish troops would fire on their own countrymen and sent non-Irish troops to reinforce them. It turned out to be unnecessary. When the confederates saw the green flag come up the hill they knew it was the Irish Brigade. They knew that approaching them were men who had come over from Ireland with them and men who only a year previously had been in the same army. MacMillan also saw the green colours and shouted out:

"Give it to them now, boys! Now's the time! Give it to them!"

He never wrote any regret about his decision.[268] They may have been fellow countrymen, but now they were the enemy who were trying to kill them. It was kill or be killed. The assault was repelled and the Irish Brigade massacred, although they did get closer to the confederate position than any other brigade that day. Wave after wave was repulsed by the confederate Irish. McMillan urged his men on, walking along the line exposing himself to enemy fire, apparently immune to the fear his men felt. A bullet did strike him on the neck, but he calmly picked it up and put it in his pocket. The citizens of Fredericksburg must have thought it somewhat ironic that in 1847 when the fields below Marye's Heights[269] had yielded a good corn crop it was donated to help relieve the famine in Ireland. The people this crop had helped now lay dead and dying on those same fields.[270] The Irish Brigade saw its strength reduced from 1600 to 256 men.

The total loss the Union Army suffered was 12,653 casualties, while the confederates suffered 5,377 casulties. While the South was jubilant with the result of the battle in the North, both President Lincoln and the army came in for criticism. The *Cincinnati Commercial* commented:

> *"It can hardly be in human nature for men to show more valour or generals to manifest less judgment, than were perceptible on our side that day."*[271]

Fredericksburg sent shockwaves through the Irish population in the North. In January 1863 a grand requiem was held at St. Patricks Cathedral in New York. Grief soon turned to outrage and many believed that the Irish were being needlessly sacrificed. As a result the Irish stopped enlisting. The next major battle at Gettysburg would, however, turn the tables for the Union.

the rebel sons of erin

While the Irish who fought for the Northern states are often written about, less is known about the estimated 50,000 Irish who fought for the South. The Southerners looked upon the North as something of an aggressive bully, trying to dictate how they should live their lives, and it was a sentiment with which the Irish could readily identify.

Unlike other regiments that were Irish in name only, the Tenth Tennessee Infantry Regiment was made up entirely of Irishmen and was one of only two confederate regiments made up of Irish Catholics, the others being comprised mostly of Ulster Protestants.[272] Its officers were for the most Scotch Irish, the most famous being Randall McGavock.[273] The regiment was set up at Fort Henry, on the Tennessee River, in May of 1861, a few weeks after war breaking out and Colonel Heiman assumed command.[274] It soon numbered 720 men armed with flintlock muskets. The regimental flag, which is currently on display in Nashville Museum, was made up of a golden harp with a maroon trim on a green background. Over the harp in white lettering was written "Sons of Erin" and underneath, "Where glory await you". The regiment became locally known as "The Rebel Sons of Erin" but when, later, the war took a horrific toll on its numbers, they were re-christened "The Bloody Tenth". One of the regiment's youngest soldiers was seventeen year old Patrick Griffin, who was born on St. Patrick's Day 1844, in County Galway. His parents Michael and Honora Griffin left Ireland in 1847 when The Famine was at its worst, and in their desperation, they had to leave three of their children behind. When they landed in Baltimore, Patrick's father worked laying train tracks, a job that would take the family to Nashville.

The regiment stayed at Fort Henry to drill and to train. It first saw action in February 1862 when the Union Army bombarded the fort. They were ordered to fall back to Fort Donelson on the Cumberland River where they thought they would be safe. After wading a number of streams swollen by rain and snow, and being constantly harassed by Union cavalry they eventually reached the fort late that night. They soon found themselves under attack again when Union soldiers attacked the fort. Weary and outnumbered the 10th Tennessee held them at bay for four days before being compelled to surrender. Their time in captivity was to prove harsh and they suffered under the atrocious conditions in the Union prison at Fort Warren in Boston Harbour. Five months later they were exchanged for Union prisoners and the regiment was reformed again at Clinton, Mississippi in October of 1862. When Colonel Heiman died in November 1862, he was succeeded by Colonel Randall W. McGavock. He was a highly regarded figure in Tennessee, where he had been a former mayor of Nashville. Near the end of December 1862, the regiment was ordered to Vicksburg and helped defeat General Sherman's forces at the Battle of Chickasaw Bayou. In January 1863, the 10th Tennessee was 349 strong and was serving General Gregg at Port Hudson, Louisiana, where the Union Navy bombarded them. They later engaged with Union troops at Jackson, Mississippi, and repulsed them. The 10th Tennessee then marched to Raymond, Mississippi, where, on May 12th, they fought in the Battle of Raymond, suffering 52 casualties.

At Raymond the confederate General John Gregg faced General Ulysses. The confederates were trying to prevent the Union troops from reaching the Southern Railroad and isolating Vicksburg, Mississippi, from reinforcement and resupply. It was a small but important battle in the Vicksburg campaign that thwarted Union plans.

In the midst of the battle, as the regiment awaited orders to move forward, McGavock sent a courier to find General Gregg. The courier returned, not with orders from General Gregg, but with news that the Confederate centre had been routed. McGavock then ordered his regiment into an impetuous and ill conceived assault on the centre to repel the Union soldiers. He threw back his cape and rallied his men. The red lining of his cape made him a perfect target and he was riddled with more than twelve bullets. His men carried on, only to realise that they were now being fired upon from all sides and were forced into a retreat.

Ever loyal to his commander, young Patrick Griffin took McGavock's body from the field, which led to his capture. The officer who captured him, a man by the name of McGuire, was also from Galway.[275] Impressed by the young soldier's courage and at finding a fellow Galwegian he ordered his men to place McGavock's body in one of the Union army wagons for transport into town, where a coffin was hastily put together and he was buried with full honours.

After the battle of Raymond the regiment, now numbering 328 took part with remnants of other Tennessee regiments in the Battle of Chickamauga fighting mainly as sharpshooters. The combined regiment suffered the loss and injury 224 men. Their last major battle was at Bentonville, North Carolina, in March of 1865. By the time they surrendered at Greensboro, North Carolina, in April of that year, they numbered less than 100, all of whom had been wounded several times.

The war had taken its toll on the 21 year old Griffin, who had been wounded and taken prisoner three times, and had taken part part in twenty-four engagements with the enemy. It was these engagements with which he would later regale future generations. By the time he died in 1921 he had ensured that the contribution of the confederate Irish would not be forgotten.

the molly maguires

"Make way for the Molly McGuires
They're drinkers, they're liars, but they're men
Make way for the Molly McGuires
You'll never see the likes of them again."
"The Molly Maguires"

The above lines are taken from a well known folk song. Less well known however, is who the Molly McGuires actually were. While the Irish are extremely popular in America these days it was quite the opposite in the nineteenth century. Thousands of Irish had fled post famine Ireland, but they were less than welcome in their new homeland and were placed at the lowest level of society.

The Irish worked in what jobs they could find and in Pennsylvania this was mainly in the anthracite coal mines, which included counties such as Luzerne, Carbon, Lackawanna and Northhumberland.[276] Conditions in the mines were atrocious to say the least and the mine owners showed little interest in improving them. Not only that but the foremen, usually Welsh, English or German, were inclined to cheat the Irish of their wages and this was largely tolerated.

The miners were paid only once a month and most if not all went to the 'pluck-me' or company run general store, which they were obliged to use and where they ran up a tab. The debt owed never seemed to be paid in full and customers were not permitted to see the ledger, not that it would have made much of a difference as most of the Irish would have been illiterate.

Out of this discrimination emerged the Molly Maguires, or Mollies as they were more commonly known, who were strongest between the Civil war and 1876. The origin of the term Molly Maguire is somewhat murky, but it more than likely originated in Ireland, a country with several secret organisations in the 18th century. It has been suggested that Molly was a widow evicted from her home and her supporters took on the name when they sought revenge. She may also have been the owner of a sheebeen where the group met. As with the secret societies of the old country, the activities of the Mollies included intimidation, beatings and even murder. Most, if not all, of the Mollies were also members of the legal Ancient Order of Hibernians.

The legal system as well as the police force was mostly Welsh, German, and English, and they had little sympathy for the Irish or their grievances, leaving the Mollies as the only form of support. As the grievances increased, so too did Molly activity. There were fifty unsolved murders between 1863 and 1867 in Schuylkill County, Pennsylvania and neither the public nor authorities seemed interested in solving them, such was the strength of the Mollies.

The Mollies were a thorn in the side of the industrialist Franklin Benjamin Gowen, President of the Philadelphia & Reading Railroad, who saw the Mollies as union agitators and was determined to crush any union movement. In order to crush them he would have to infiltrate them. An Irishman was required and James McParlan from County Armagh volunteered. He had only recently become a private detective working for Major Allan Pinkerton, originally from Scotland. Pinkterton ordered him to remain in the field until 'every cut-throat has paid with his life for the lives so cruelly taken'. It was a dangerous assignment that began in 1873 and would last five years. McParlan first frequented the Mollie hangouts dressed as a vagrant with very limited success. He then posed as a dandy called James McKenna and claimed to have killed a man in Buffalo. He was something of a natural entertainer and was soon a member of the Ancient Order of Hibernians, which in Pennsylvania also meant being a Molly. He soon met the 'King of the Mollies', John Kehoe from Wicklow, and James 'Powder Keg'

Kerrigan, his lieutenant. Kerrigan participated in several Molly murders but once arrested wrote a two hundred page confession which would save himself from the hangman but condemn others. His nickname was changed to 'The Squealer'.

Unlike many Mollies, McParlan could read and write and his Molly brothers appointed him secretary. His new position was ideal as he could now take his notes without arousing suspicion.

In 1874 wages for the miners were cut by 20 per cent and a strike was declared. It lasted six months and, as the company run shops would not serve striking families, women and children had to forage for food in the woods. As families starved the men were compelled to return to the mines with no concessions offered. Molly violence did not however desist. In July of 1875, Benjamin Yost, a policeman was murdered as he extinguished a street light. He had previously arrested a Molly, which made him a marked man. Not long after this, two eighteen year old Mollies, Michael J. Doyle and Edward Kelly, were commissioned to assassinate Welsh mine Superintendent John P. Jones of Tamaqua. They were caught and, unlike on previous occasions, the witnesses were not to be intimidated and over a hundred people testified against them. They were sent to the gallows in 1877.

Thomas Sanger, foreman of Heaton's Colliery in Raven Run near Girardville, and his childhood friend miner William Uren were shot dead on their way to work. Sanger died because of an alleged workplace incident and Uren was murdered so no witness would remain. The frequency of murders stirred an anti-Irish sentiment among the English and Welsh miners. It was suspected that the culprit in the Sanger-Uren murder was a Charles O'Donnell, though nothing could be proven. Patrick O'Donnell was of this family and history remembers him as the man who killed James Carey, who had informed on The Invincibles following the Phoenix Park murders. A vigilante mob went to his house and murdered him, and two children. The pregnant wife of Charles McAllister, another suspect the vigilantes seemed to know about, was murdered and her mother severely beaten.[277]

All this time McParlan had been passing on information to his superiors and Captain Robert Linden of the Coal & Iron Police. The vigilantes, though never publically identified, had all been trained by Linden, and McParlan was horrified to learn that his information was being passed on to vigilantes who murdered innocent people.[278] The operation was drawing to a close, as the Mollies suspected that an informer was in their ranks. Instead of fleeing, McParlan confronted Kehoe about the allegations and asked that a meeting of the Mollies be convened where his fellow brothers could judge him. It would also be a suitable opportunity to get them arrested. When this did not work, Gowen had his Coal & Iron Police arrest Kehoe and the other members they could catch.

The trials were not glorious events in the history of the American judicial system. No Catholics were permitted to sit on the jury and some of its members did not fully understand English, having only recently arrived from Germany. The prosecution lawyers worked for Gowen and judges were sympathetic towards him, permitting him to conduct several of the prosecutions himself, allowing him to rant on about the Mollies. Even when his statements lacked any factual basis he was not interrupted.

It was at the trial that McParlan revealed who he really was, much to the devastation of his friends, who had trusted him. Support for the Mollies began to dwindle. Labour leaders did not wish to be associated with them and they were denounced from the pulpit.

The outcome of the trial resulted in twenty men facing the hangman, though in some cases the evidence was weak and some may have been completely innocent. Alexander Campell, for example, was hanged for the murder of John P. Jones in 1875, but the evidence was based solely on the statement of Kerrigan, who was out to save his own skin. There were other irregularities about the whole affair. Although America was a sovereign nation the Mollies had been arrested by private policemen and prosecuted by mining and railroad company lawyers. Indeed, the only thing the state of Pennsylvania had provided was the courtroom and the hangman.

Ten of the Mollies were hanged – four at Mauch Chunk and six at Pottsville on 21 June 1877, a date remembered as "Black Thursday". More were to follow and at each execution the Irish community waited in respectful silence outside the prison walls. Jack Kehoe was hanged in 1878 at Pottsville for the 1862 murder of foreman Frank W. Langdon. He was pardoned in 1979 by the Pennsylvania Governor, Milton J. Shapp, who said of him:

"We can be proud of the men known as the Molly Maguires, because they defiantly faced allegations which attempted to make trade unionism a criminal conspiracy."[279]

Following the trials, James McParlan continued to work for the Pinkerton Detective Agency. Gowen committed suicide in 1889 after his railroad company fell into bankruptcy.

James 'The Squealer' Kerrigan went to live in Virginia, living under his wife's name, where he died in 1898.

Conditions for miners were slow to improve and it was not until United Mine Workers of America was founded in 1890 that an eight hour shift was introduced, children under 14 could no longer work in the mines and workers no longer had to buy at the company run shops. Since the executions, opinion has been divided on how to judge the Mollies. Ancient Order of Hibernia members who were also Mollies were airbrushed out of the organisation's history. The Mollies terrorised entire communities and murdered anyone who crossed them, though it was through great injustice that they came into being in the first place. A movie called The *Molly Maguires* was made in 1970 starring Sean Connery and Richard Harris.

mylεs κεoghn

Myles Keogh (1840-76) was a soldier who fought in three different wars and was killed in the Indian war at the Battle of the Little Bighorn. He was born to prominent and prosperous family in Orchard House, Leighlinbridge, County Carlow. Given that the family did not depend exclusively on the potato crop, they were spared the ravages of the famine, though two of his siblings did succumb to typhoid.[280] Little seems to be known about his life in Ireland or where he went to school. Some accounts claim he attended St Patricks College, but no records have been found.

Following a call to arms by the Catholic clergy, Keogh volunteered in 1860, along with over a thousand other Irish, to fight for Pope Pius IX. Given his wealthy background he was appointed Lieutenant and stationed in the Adriatic port city of Ancona. The Irish Papal battalion was a mixed bag, poorly trained and equipped with muskets from the Napoleonic period.[281]

The Papal forces were defeated in September at the Battle of Castelfidardo, and Ancona was surrounded. They had little option but to surrender and after his release from captivity Keogh went to Rome in the green uniform of the Company of St. Patrick as a member of the Vatican Guard. The pope awarded him a medal for gallantry – the *Pro Petri Sede* Medal – and also the Cross of the Order of St. Gregory – *Ordine di San Gregorio*. Keogh was a fighter and peacetime duties of the Vatican did not suit him. The clergy once more called on volunteers to fight in a foreign war and Archbishop Hughes, travelled to Italy to recruit veterans of the Papal War. Keogh resigned his commission and, in March 1862, found himself in New York holding the rank of Captain in the Union Army. He was assigned to the staff of Brigadier General James Shields from

County Tyrone and served at the battle of Antietam. He also took part in raids deep into enemy territory. At one stage he was captured but exchanged.

He continued a military career after the cessation of hostilities in 1865. Not all of America had been colonised and parts were still controlled by the Native American tribes. Keogh was now about to serve in a war that would bring about the annihilation of the Native American way of life. The Native Americans were fighting for survival, much like Keogh's countrymen during the Elizabethan conquest of the 16th century. Treaties were made and broken with the Native Americans and the white settlers had to be protected. Keogh joined the 7th Cavalry in 1866 and was assigned to Fort Riley in Northeast Kansas under the command of George Armstrong Custer. His duties included patrolling the area, keeping the peace between Native Americans and settlers. In his free time he went hunting. He was well liked by fellow officers but the isolation of the western frontier left him with little to do but drink. Alcoholism was a major problem among frontier soldiers. He returned to Carlow in 1874 and gave the estate he had inherited to his sister Margaret. Though he never married, he did become engaged to Nelly Martin of Auburn, New York. By then the Indian war was heating up. His colleague and fellow Irishman General Philip Sheridan remarked:

"The only good Indians I ever saw were dead."[282]

When he returned to duty, Custer was leading a controversial expedition through the Black Hills of what is now Montana and Dakota. By 1876 the Native Americans had organised themselves into a federation under Sitting Bull and Crazy Horse. Keogh was aware that his luck would not last forever and after sixteen years of almost constant fighting he was bound to be killed at some stage. In a letter to Nelly Martin he wrote:

"We leave Monday on an Indian expedition & if I ever return I will go on and see you all. I have requested to be packed up and shipped to Auburn in case I am killed, and I desire to be buried there. God bless you all, remember if I should die you may believe that I loved you and every member of your family – it was a second home to me."[283]

Custer made several blunders. He could have taken Gatling guns, an early form of machine gun, and he could have waited for reinforcements. His impulsiveness would cost the lives of his men as well as his own. He pursued the Native Americans right into a trap. The Little Bighorn was one of biggest concentrations of Native Americans ever assembled. It is believed that they had up to 2,000 warriors. Two-hundred and thirteen Union soldiers fell at the battle. Seven bodies were never found and the battle could only be reconstructed from the evidence later found at the scene. Strangely enough, the Native Americans were better equipped than Custer and his men, who had only single shot rifles, while their foe had repeat rifles, which could fire faster and had a greater range.

Keogh's body was found at the centre of the massacred soldiers. The only survivors' accounts of the battle are from Native American sources and, according to Two Moon of the Northern Cheyenne, a man, believed to be Keogh, rode up and down the line as they attacked shouting at his men and the Native Americans regarded him as a brave man.[284] All the bodies had been scalped save Custer and Keogh. Keogh carried his papal medal in a pouch, which the Native Americans believed to be a precious relic or some form of protection. The medal found its way back to his family.[285] He was also wearing an *Agnus Dei* (Lamb of God) on a chain about his neck, which was not removed by the Native Americans. Keogh's horse, Comanche, was the sole survivor. He was never ridden again and became the regimental mascot and was buried with full military honours when he died in 1891. The remains were later preserved and are now on display at the Natural History Museum at the University of Kansas.[286]

Myles Keogh's body was disinterred and reinterred in the family plot of Nelly Martin in Auburn, New York. She never married and laid flowers on the grave every 25th June, the date of the battle, until her death in 1927.[287]

Keogh's elegant memorial stone bears the record of his military service and a fitting epitaph from the pen of poet Bayard Taylor:

"Sleep soldier!
Still in honored rest
Your truth and valor wearing
The bravest are the tenderest
The loving are the daring".[288]

nevill coghill vc

As outlined in a previous chapter, there were many Irish recipients of the Victorian Cross and the 19th century presented many opportunities to win it. The conquest of Africa was one such place and Nevill Coghill (1852-79), from Drumcondra[289] in Dublin became one of the first posthumous recipients of the prestigious order. Coghill fell in the battle of Isandlwana and was one of two officers who tried to save his regimental colours from capture.

The Zulu king Cetshwayo was suspicious of the foreigners and remarked, *"First comes the trader, then the missionary, then the red soldier."*[290] Isandlwana was the first major battle of the Zulu war. Prior to that, traders had operated in Zululand. An important trading post was Rorke's Drift, known in Zulu as *KwaJim* or "Jim's land" after the trader James Rorke from County Cork, who was responsible for setting it up. Rorke's Drift would later be remembered for its heroic defence against vastly superior numbers of Zulu warriors, and several Irish took part in the battle. The surgeon James Henry Reynolds from Kingstown,[291] County Dublin was among them.

At Isandlwana, a force of 20,000 Zulus attacked a far inferior force of British and colonial troops.[292] Though vastly outnumbered, the British were equipped with modern Martini Henry rifles and two seven pounder artillery pieces, which, had they been deployed effectively, might have changed the outcome of the battle. The Zulus mostly carried an *assegai* or iron spear and regarded rifles as the weapons of a coward. Unlike the British soldier the Zulu warrior could not stay indefintely in the field and the invasion was therefore timed to coincide with the harvest.

The British force under Lord Chelmsford reached Isandlwana in January, but did not dig in and fortify their position and deeply underestimated the speed at which the Zulus could move. It was a mistake that would cost him dearly and when the attack came his men were completely unprepared and overwhelmed.

As the camp was being overrun, every effort was made to protect the regimental colours from capture. They symbolised the honour of the regiment and had to be protected at all costs. An unknown Irishman from the 24th Regiment defended the colours in Chelmsford's tent until he was speared to death.

Lieutenant Colonel Pulleine, Commander of the first battalion of the 24th Regiment of Foot gave the colours to Lieutenant Teignmouth Melvill and instructed him to bring them to safety. He rode away, followed by Coghill. The only way out of the massacre was through a narrow gap to the south and the two men hoped to reach the safety of the garrisoned post at Helpmekaar. [293]Coghill had injured his knee earlier on in the day, which meant that though he could ride a horse he found it difficult to walk. This is why, when the Zulus shot his horse as he crossed the buffalo river, his chances of escape deminished. British losses on the day were around 1,300, while Zulu losses were around 1,000. At the time it was the biggest loss inflicted on a European army by a native African force. Though Isandlwana proved to be something of a military disaster, and in the short term a Zulu victory, it hardened British opinion against the Zulus and the British could put far more soldiers in the field and were able to fight a longer campaign than the Zulus.

The colours were not taken by the Zulu. They were found downstream ten days later, as the level of the water had dropped by at least three feet since the day of the battle. The tattered remains were taken back to Helpmekaar and handed to Colonel Glyn, at the time in the 24th Regiment, who had received that identical Colour, as Colour Ensign, when stationed at the Curragh, County Kildare some thirteen years previously.[294]

On 2nd May 1879, a notice appeared in the *London Gazette* which stated that on account of the gallant efforts made by Lieut. Teignmouth Melvill to save the Queen's Colour of his Regiment after the disaster of Isandhlwana, and also on account of Lieut. Nevill Coghill's heroic conduct in endeavouring to save his brother officer's life, they would have been recommended to Her Majesty for the Victoria Cross had they survived.[295]Isandlwana had enraged the British public and Coghill's actions captured their imagination. The action was depicted in the movie *Zulu Dawn*. A monument was raised at the spot where the two young lieutenants fell.

When the Battalion returned to England in 1880 the famous colour was shown to Queen Victoria, who expressed a desire to see it. Though twenty three Victoria Croses were awarded during the Zulu War, the two lieutenants or at least their reatives would have to wait. Sir Joscelyn Coghill, Nevill's father, was sent a postage stamp size scrap of the Colour, enclosed in a gold and crystal locket. Despite the tattered condition, the colour remained in service until 1933 when it was placed in the Regimental Chapel of Brecon Cathedral, Wales.

Though Queen Victoria recommended the pair for the Victoria Cross it was not the custom of the time to award the medal posthumously. There were also mixed opinions about Melvill and Coghill. The public regarded them as heroes, but some of the top brass were uneasy that two officers has fled the battle on horseback while their men remained behind and fought on foot. They were both awarded the Victoria Cross in 1907 and Coghill's was sent to his brother, the artist Sir Egerton Coghill.

William Melville

In a county proud of its republican struggle not everyone in Kerry is proud of William Melville (1850-1918), founder of the British Secret Service and an inspiration for the character of "M" in the James Bond books. He was born in Sneem to James and Catherine Melville (née Connor). His father was a baker and young William attended the local national school and excelled at hurling.

He left his native town under, which the circumstances are not entirely clear, and went to work in London. Following in his father's footsteps, he initially became a baker, but deciding it was not for him he joined the Metropolitan Police in 1872. He climbed the career ladder rapidly and by 1879 he made Detective Sergeant. He married Kate Reilly from County Mayo in the same year and the couple had four children. Disaster struck when Kate died in 1889, leaving Melville with four children all under the age of seven. He did, however, remarry two years later.

In March 1883 he was recruited into a new section of Scotland Yard, known as the Special Irish Branch. London at the time was being terrorised by Fenians, who received financial backing from friends in America and who used the newly invented dynamite. In 1887 Melville uncovered the "Jubilee Plot" and, as a result of constant surveillance, the bombers had to abandon their plans. The plotters intended to blow up Westminster, Queen Victoria and the cabinet. The man behind the plot was Francis Millen of Clan na Gael. Millen was, however, also a spy working, with the approval of the Prime Minister Lord Salisbury, for the British and he concocted the plot in order to attract as many Fenians as possible and discredit the Irish Parliamentary Party. The bombers were all linked, by letters, to the head of the party, Charles Stewart Parnell, in which he apparently supported violence. It has been suggested therefore that the Jubilee Plot[296] was not about targeting Queen Victoria but Charles Stuart Parnell, the leader of the Irish Parliamentary Party. Millen was to link the Irish parliamentarians with the Fenians and then expose the links, thereby discrediting the Home Rule party. Today this would be called "dirty tricks". The incriminating letters had been supplied by Dublin journalist Richard Pigott. The matter was taken to court and the letters were shown to be forgeries, written by Pigott. *The Times*, which had published the letters, was ordered to pay Parnell £5,000 damages. Pigott committed suicide.[297]

Melville was also involved in pursuing Jack the Ripper, one of the most infamous serial killers, who operated in London's East End in 1888. Nobody was ever caught for the murders. Melville suspected an American called Francis Tumblety, who had fled London that year and had gone to France en route to America. Tumbelty may have originally been Irish and was known for his hatred of women. He kept female body parts in specimen jars. Though Melville went to France in pursuit, Tumblety escaped him.

Melville also became involved in the fight against anarchists. England had become a refuge for anarchists from all over Europe and other powers were critical of Britain's leniency towards them. Melville "uncovered" an anarchist bomb plot in the midlands town of Walsall, which showed how dangerous they could be. It is highly likely that the whole thing was instigated by Melville himself, acting on orders from above. Eighty years later it was revealed that the bombings were the idea of Auguste Coulon, who was an agent for Melville. After Walsall, nobody could accuse Melville of being soft on anarchists, and he was rewarded in early 1893 by being promoted to Head of the Special Branch. When a disgruntled ex Special Branch officer, Sergeant Patrick McIntyre, alleged publicly that Walsall was a set-up, Melville's reputation was such that it had little effect.

By the mid 1890s Chief Inspector Melville was very much in the public eye and the press in both Britain and the continent reported on his activities on a regular basis. He was increasingly called upon to protect royalty and visiting heads of state such as the Shah of Persia, which greatly raised his public profile.

He is known to have visited Sneem on several occasions and he was afforded VIP status.His visits were well reported in the media.In 1900, Melville was promoted to Superintendent and retired three years later, a decision which baffled the media. The only thing he had retired from, however, was the limelight and he was now working for the War Office as a gatherer of intelligence and controlling agents. From this point on, he became known as "M" and "William Morgan".

He was an enthusiastic supporter of the GAA in London, and brought his children up to take pride in their Irish heritage. On a subsequent visit in 1913 he had to be more wary as Irish people had suddenly decided they did not want to be British and he discovered that some were critical of those working for the British.

Germany was becoming a threat to Britain's naval superiority. The British were paranoid about spies infiltrating their military and spy mania gripped the country. In 1909 the Secret Service Bureau was set up and divided into an internal section for internal British affairs, which would later become MI5 and an external section for espionage abroad, later to become MI6. Melville's time was taken up with investigating real and imaginary reports of German spies who were supposedly photographing military and civilian installations in preparation for a German invasion.There were real German agents at work in British ports in a network managed by Gustav Steinhauer or "N", Head of the British section of the German Secret Police. He had been trained at the Pinkerton Detective Agency in Chicago and recruited his spies among German businessmen in Britain. Between 1911 and 1914 MI5 intercepted 1,189 letters from German agents. Melville knew Steinhauer personally and had worked with him when the Kaiser came to England for the funeral of his grandmother Victoria. Melville set up a register of aliens and in 1912 he uncovered Steinhauer's network of twenty one agents.

With the outbreak of hostilities in 1914, the need for spies was even greater and a spy school was established. The war saw the rapid expansion of the Secret Service. Melville is not known to have worked against Irish republicans at this time as the fight against Germany was deemed more important.[298] Melville retired in late 1917 and died of kidney failure a few months later in February 1918.

Opinions on Melville are divided. Many Kerry people have never heard of him. It is interesting to note that although Sneem commemorates her famous son Stephen Casey the wrestler and has even erected a plaque commemorating brief holidays by Charles DeGaulle, no monument to Melville exists. Helen O'Carroll, the museum curator of the award winning Kerry Museum, said of him:

"As a Kerryman born and bred, Melville is part of our story and to fit him in we must acknowledge that Irish identity encompassed a broader spectrum in the past, as indeed we are beginning to recognise that it does in the present."[299]

Others, such as Sinn Féin councillor Robert Beasley, took a different view. He remarked:

"I don't think local people would want to commemorate anything to do with the British Secret Service, whether it is in the past or today. I don't see any reason to have him honoured."[300]

the eagle of trieste

The Austrian Military Academy at Wiener-Neustadt has a room, a monument to former Imperial glory. Oil paintings of the great generals of Imperial Austria adorn the walls, all of whom were recipients of Imperial Austria's highest order The Maria Theresa Order. Introduced in 1757 by Empress Maria Theresa, the prestigious award honoured exceptional courage in wartime. Many recipients, such as Browne, Macquire, O'Donell and Lacy were Irish. One painting, depicting a young man in naval uniform stands out from the rest, that of Gottfried von Banfield, the empire's greatest air ace.

He was born in 1890 in Castelnuovo, then part of The Austro-Hungarian Empire, in present day Italy, as the youngest of five children, near the homeport of the now non-existent Austrian Navy in Pola.[301] His father was Richard von Banfield of Clonmel and Castlelyons. The von Banfields were by no means the only Irish in Trieste. With the establishment of the Austrian Imperial navy in 1720, Georg Forbes of Granard (it is interesting that most of the Wild Geese, while retaining Irish surnames took on German Christian names) became the first Grand Admiral and set up the naval base at Trieste. Admiral Richard Barry who also served in the area, organised the naval defence of Venice in 1859. The city would also later become home to James Joyce.

Richard von Banfield made his name in 1886 in the Austro-Italian war during the battle of Lissa in the Adriatic, when he sank the Italian flagship the "Re d'Italia". Years later his son Gottfried would fight the same foe, and as the most highly decorated air ace of The Austro-Hungarian Empire on a par with Baron von Richthofen, become even more famous than his father.

The young Gottfried was sent to military school at the age of eleven. Before he would be accepted, however, he had to take Austrian citizenship. He would later attend the naval academy at Fiume and graduated in 1909. After a brief spell as a frigate-lieutenant, he began pilot training. He perfected his training under the Frenchman Jean Louis Conneau, a famous pilot known throughout Europe at the time. He would later meet his teacher as an adversary in the skies over the Adriatic.

He was posted to Pola, where he began his training in seaplanes, and assumed command of the seaplane station there, which was named after him and where he would soon become something of a living legend. He flew a Lohner biplane and it was in this plane that he scored his first victories against the Italians and their French allies in June of 1915.

He later led a highly successful attack on the Italian flotilla at the central Italian port of Ancona on the Adriatic. His prowess soon earned him the title "The Eagle of Trieste". In total, he would fly 400 sorties against the enemy and was the first Imperial Austrian pilot to score a victory at night.[302]

Just how many victories he scored is a matter of dispute. Some sources say twenty, though some of these were unconfirmed. Naval pilots had the disadvantage over other aviators in that the planes they shot down were generally over water, making it more difficult to confirm a kill. His sorties were not without danger and he was lightly wounded three times and quite seriously in 1918.

In 1917, von Banfield was summoned to meet with Kaiser Karl, son of Franz-Josef who had died the previous year. He was to receive The Maria Theresa Order, the highest decoration the emperor could bestow. He was one of only 1,135 recipients of the award and the only Imperial Austrian pilot to receive such a distinction. As part of the award, von Banfield was raised to the status of Freiherr (Baron). It was the 180th time the order was bestowed, and it would be the last time in Imperial Austria. Imperial Austria collapsed in 1918, as did many other empires, and when Austria became a republic titles such as "von" and "baron" were outlawed for Austrian citizens.

With the war over von Banfield, like thousands of others, now faced an uncertain future. Italy annexed Trieste and he was for a time imprisoned by the Italian authorities. After his release, he worked for Škoda in Prague before immigrating to England in 1920, where he married Countess Maria Tripcovich of Trieste. They lived in Newscastle and had one son, Raphael Douglas, who was born in 1922. He would grow up to become a composer under the name Raffaello de Banfield Tripcovich, and died in 2008, leaving no heirs.[303]

In 1926, von Banfield returned to Trieste and took over his late father-in-law's salvage business. He also took on Italian citizenship and soon became a well-known and well-liked figure in the area, with the locals referring to him as "il nostro Barone" or "Our Baron".

His salvage business turned out to be highly lucrative. Once the Second World War started, he had plenty of work in the Adriatic and Mediterranean. His maxim was, "if it's easy it doesn't interest me". He won international acclaim when he cleared the Suez Canal of mines and debris in record time following The Suez Crisis.

He visited Ireland on several occasions. The French honoured him with the Legion d'Honnnuer in 1977 and, although now based on land he retained a passion for sailing, which he carried out until he was 90. Whenever he stayed in Vienna, sentries from the elite Garde Battalion were posted at the hotel entrance, an honour usually only afforded to presidents.

He died in 1986, aged 96. His passing brought about, not only the death of Austria's most well known fighter ace, but also the last knight of the Maria Theresa Order, ending a 230 year old tradition. For the Irish it signalled the end of 300 years of Irish military service to Austria, as von Banfield was also the last of the Wild Geese. In honour of his achievements, the graduating class of 1990 at Austria's Military academy bore his name.

the aud

"Twas on Good Friday morning,
All in the month of May,
A German Ship was signalling,
Beyond out in the Bay,
We had twenty thousand rifles
All ready for to land,
But no answering signal did come
From the lonely Banna Strand."
Banna Strand

The *Aud* was an audacious attempt to land arms and, like so many other attempts before and after it, resulted in failure and speculation of what could have been. In 1916 Ireland, being part of the British Empire, was involved in the First World War. Thousands were fighting in Belgium and France "for the freedom of small nations" and the hope of Home Rule, while a minority back in Ireland were preparing an armed rebellion against the British.

Sir Roger Casement had been knighted for his humanitarian work in the Congo. The Boer War turned him against the British Empire. He visited Germany[304] and toured the POW camps as early as 1914 looking for recruits for The Casement Brigade. It never reached brigade strength as he only found 56 volunteers.

The Germans agreed to send the Irish rebels arms and ammunition. It would provide a suitable distraction for the British and more troops committed to Ireland meant less being sent to the Western Front. The man chosen to lead the mission was Captain Karl Spindler (1887-1951) from Königswinter on the Rhine. He had joined the Merchant Navy before moving on to the navy itself.

Following boring patrol duties he was suddenly chosen for a special mission, which would bring him to Ireland within a month. He was ordered to select five petty officers and 16 crew members, who were sworn to secrecy. All had to be young, single and to have volunteered for the dangerous mission. Spindler and his crew then travelled to a Hamburg shipyard to take over the ship the *Libau*. The ship had been built in 1907 in Hull and was called the SS *Castro*, but was captured by the German Navy in 1914 and renamed the *Libau*. The crew were issued with original Norwegian seamen's clothing, which was so authentic that even the buttons were imprinted with the name of a Norwegian company. Spindler went to Berlin to meet Sir Roger Casement and finally learned the purpose of his special mission. Casement was reluctant to go with the *Libau* and it was arranged to bring him and his pair of companions to the west coast of Ireland in a German U-boat. German assistance was not as much as he had hoped for and Casement wanted to get back to Ireland as fast as possible to persuade the leaders to call off the rising. Casement was to wait at Tralee for the *Libau* to arrive.

In Lübeck, the *Libau* took on coal, water and provisions and took custody of a load of weapons and munitions. These were packed in wooden cases marked with Genoa and Naples as destination ports. The cargo of weapons included an estimated 20,000 rifles, 1,000,000 rounds of ammunition, 10 machine guns, and explosives. The majority of the rifles were the Russian Mosin-Nagant 1891, which were, despite their age, still good weapons. A cargo of wooden props for coal mines, cases of enamelled steelware, wooden doors, window frames and various other transport goods camouflaged the real cargo. Everything on board was made to look Norwegian, starting with the ship's certificate, sea charts, canned food and even the bed linen. The name *Libau* was removed and the ship became the *Aud Norge*, with "Bergen" written on its stern as its home port. The ship looked very similar to a genuine *Aud* which at that time operated under the Norwegian flag. The only thing that was missing was that nobody on board spoke Norwegian, but it was unlikely that the Royal Navy would speak Norwegian.

Spindler went on a westward course and, favoured by foggy weather, from then on navigated to the north. Now and again he met with various ships which he could not avoid if he did not want to create suspicion. Although some British guard ships were encountered in the Kattegat, the area around Jutland, there was no contact. The journey to the north could continue undisturbed. In the Skagerrak, between Norway and Sweden, Spindler finally reached a Northern latitude that would make it appear convincing that Christiania (Oslo) was his last port, when he turned off to the west. That was important, because all his documents showed this city as port of origin. A 100 nautical miles east of the Shetlands he reached the line where English warships had blocked off the North Sea to prevent break-through attempts by German auxiliary cruisers. Although the crew of the *Aud* sighted the high battle mast of a large warship it remained undetected. On the morning of 20th April the *Aud* was scarcely 45 nautical miles from Tralee bay, meaning Spindler could be at the rendezvous at the arranged time. Things were running on schedule, but they were not aware that the date had been changed from the 20th to the 23rd.

Also, the submarine which should have brought Casement did not show up. Spindler's instructions were that if, after a half-hour of waiting, none of the arranged vessels or persons made contact he should use his own discretion whether to move in or return. Unknown to him the car-load of volunteers who were supposed to meet Spindler had crashed in Kenmare, which meant there was nobody to signal him.

Casement was landed by submarine, the U-19 at Banna Strand. He was arrested shortly afterwards with his companions at an old ringfort, McKenna's fort, between Ardfert and Tralee. Among those arrested was Daniel Bailey, also known as Beverley, a sergeant in the Casement Brigade. He decided to save himself and turned informer. As a result he was never charged with any crime and continued his career in the British army.[305]

Spindler headed into Tralee Bay to explore and as suspected, found it manned by the British military. A pilot steamer the *Shatter* from the Royal Navy approached the *Aud*. Naturally the commander wanted to know why the *Aud* was anchored there and where she was bound. Spindler told him of the storm he rode out near Rockall, during which the cargo had shifted, requiring restowing. As destinations, he gave Cardiff then on to Naples and Genoa and he also showed him the ship's papers. Spindler got out some whiskey, which eased the tension, and a few bottles were passed around to the other British sailors on board. As alcohol was forbidden on British ships the gesture was gratefully received. Spindler, in return, received recent English newspapers and the converstion became jovial. Alcohol loosens tongues and the British captain revealed to Spindler that his orders were to intercept a ship which was going to land there and bring weapons to the Irish rebels. Spindler realised that the operation had been betrayed and doomed to failure. He had to get out and return to Germany.

The visit of the *Shatter* had been observed by the coastguard and reported to the Limerick naval base. The *Aud* was now going in the opposite direction to which Spindler had reported to the captain of the *Shatter*. In the afternoon another large and modernly equipped outpost boat was sighted, but the *Aud* managed to eascape. Its luck ran out when it ran into a line of warships. The game was up and, led by the auxitliary cruiser *Bluebell,* the *Aud* was escorted to Queenstown harbour in Cork. Spindler had no choice but to comply, but hoped to give them the slip. The cargo could not fall into enemy hands. In preparation for the morning, the crew put on their German uniforms.

As the *Aud* approached the entrance to the harbour it suddenly came to a stop. A small cloud of smoke was coming from its hold. The German Naval flag was now being flown from the mast and two life boats were launched, one from either side. Spindler was scuttling the ship and it did not take long to sink. The captain of the *Bluebell* noticed that Spindler and his crew had changed into German naval uniforms and raised the white flag. Had they been caught out of uniform they would have been executed as spies. Instead they were picked up by the *Bluebell* and sent to England. Spindler, who had a good command of English, was interrogated and was later involved in several escape attempts.

There were a number of reasons why the operation failed. The volunteers were poorly organised and the date for the landing changed. The *Aud* had no radio on board so it would not have been aware of this. Interestingly, though the English had known of the operation, the Easter Rising had yet to take place, so it caught them off guard. Sir Roger was hanged on 3rd August 1916 at Pentonville and reintererred at Arbour Hill in Dublin in 1965.

Spindler was released from captivitiy in 1918 and wrote a book about his Irish adventure *Das Geheimnisvolle Schiff* (The Mysterious Ship). He found an eager audience among Irish Americans. The president of the Irish Committee in New York invited Spindler to do a lecture tour of the United States in 1931 to mark the fifteenth anniversary of the Easter Rising and he went on to give lectures in Philadelphia, Chicago, Pittsburgh, Detroit, and Boston. The high point of the numerous honours conferred by the Americans was the presentation of the "Golden Key of the State of California" to Spindler by Governor Rolph, which was the first time the State had conferred this honour.[306] He returned briefly to Germany but returned to America in 1935. He was still there when hostilities broke out between America and Germany and he was interned for the duration of the war. He died in Bismarck, Dakota in 1951. The *Aud* is still forty metres under the surface of Cobh harbour and is the property of the German government. In 2012 the anchor was raised and is currently being restored. In 2006, to comemerate the 90th anniversary of the Easter Rising a plaque was placed on the *Aud* which reads:

"In Remembrance of Sir Roger Casement,
Captain Spindler and the Crew of the Aud.
Men who in 1916 risked/lost their lives for
Irish Liberty. Thank you all."[307]

the monto

Every Bloomsday (16th June), the ever popular tourist trail retraces the steps Leopold Bloom took on the fateful day in *Ulysses*. It stops short, however, of the notorious Monto, formerly one of Europe's largest red light districts, partially because it no longer exists and partially because most Irish people feel uncomfortable discussing sex. The area encompassed Talbot Street, Amiens Street, Gardiner Street, Gloucester Street (now Sean McDermott Street) and Montgomery Street[308] (now Foley Street) from where it received its moniker. It was also known as "Nighttown" and it was from the decrepit Georgian houses that the brothels operated which were also home to one of Europe's worst slums. There were several ways to access the Monto. Sailors coming up the Liffey could access it via a tunnel which ran under the Customs House. Part of the tunnel was discovered in Talbot Street.[309]

The Monto was also known for its all night bars and those who went there knew the police would not intervene. At its peak in the late 1900s and early 20th century, up to 1,600 prostitutes worked the area. The girls largely came from the countryside and were lured into the profession by promises of jobs as maids, just like modern day sex slaves from poorer countries are today. In post famine Ireland, people were less fussy about how they earned a living. Its clientele largely, but not solely as was later claimed, came from the British garrison at the Royal (now Collins) Barracks and sailors from the then thriving docks. Its more famous clientele included James Joyce, who gives a vivid description in *The Portrait of an Artist as a Young Man* and *Ulysses*, and the Prince of Wales, both of whom reputedly lost their virginity there. Indeed, when the Prince came to Dublin years later he gave his security team the slip to walk incognito through the Monto.

The Brothels, known as "kip houses", operated from crumbling Georgian buildings next to the homes of the respectable working class dressmakers, laundresses, carpenters, grocers, fish mongers and quay labourers.[310] There was a certain hierarchy among the houses. Flash houses served the wealthy and had the prettiest girls. As the girls got older they moved to cheaper houses until they moved onto the shilling houses where, old and sick, they would earn their last few pennies before they were thrown out onto the streets, riddled with venereal disease. Those with sexually transmitted diseases were sent to Westmoreland Lock Hospital on Townsend Street.[311] Set up in 1792, it provided quarantine for women who had venereal disease and was more of a prison than a hospital. It has been claimed that those worse affected by venereal diease were smothered. It was a cruel way of life for people living in hard times. It operated until 1949 and the building was demolished shortly after.

The houses were ruled by madams who were tough and brutal. The most feared madam was May Roberts, better known as Madam Oblong, who was also a money lender. She features in Roddy Doyle's *A Star Called Henry* and James Joyce's *Finnegan's Wake* and was known to have slashed the faces of girls who lied to her.[312] The first attempts to close the Monto came in 1911, when the first Catholic Commissioner of Police, Sir John Ross started raiding the brothels. The raids were a success, but the women went to Sackville (O'Connell) Street to ply their trade. Their sudden appearance there shocked the middle classes and in order to get rid of them the brothels were reopened. The seedy trade would be permitted as long as it was contained to one area.

Another madam was Betty Cooper. Samuel Beckett in his novel *Mercier and Camier* makes reference to Helen's Place, which was modelled on her brothel. Her brother, an ex-British Army soldier, James "Shankers" Ryan[313] was shot on the orders of Michael Collins in 1920 for betraying IRA volunteers Dick McKee and Peadar Clancy to the Crown Forces. The pair were arrested in The Monto, which was regarded as a refuge for the IRA and "shot while trying to escape". Given that many of the clientele were British soldiers, the pillow talk of the Monto was a valuable source of information for Michael Collins. It later became a refuge for the anti-Treaty IRA. Indeed it was said that the girls passing on venereal diseases did more harm to the British army than the IRA. It was in the Monto that Peadar Kearney from nearby Dorset Street, wrote his "Soldier's Song", which later, translated into Irish as *Amhrán na bhFiann* became the Irish national anthem.

With the withdrawal of the British army in 1922 a large part of its clientele had disappeared. A powerful enemy in the shape of the Legion of Mary had emerged and was determined to drive the madams from The Monto. The newly founded Free State had given a massive amount of power to the church and the Monto's days were numbered. The Legion had been formed in 1921 by Frank Duff, who also worked for the St Vincent de Paul and was concerned about the plight of the women in the Monto. In 1923 he started a campaign against the brothels. He received the help of the head of the Dublin police, General William Murphy, whose guards raided the brothels on 12th March 1925 and made 120 arrests. The following Sunday the Legion of Mary organised a solemn blessing, come exorcism of the Monto. It involved a procession led by Duff carrying a crucifix. They blessed each house and hung pictures of the Sacred Heart.

In June of 1925 a twenty five year old single mother, Honor Bright, or Lizzie O Neill, as she was born, was found shot dead under a bush at Ticknock in The Dublin Mountains.[314] She had been a prostitute and word on the streets was that she was going to name the father of her child. Two pillars of society, Leopold Dillon, a Garda superintendent, and Patrick Purcell, a doctor from Dunlavin, County Wicklow were tried but acquitted of her murder. It ruined Dillon's career and Purcell emigrated.[315]

Prostitution in Ireland continued but without official recognition of any kind. When John Ford directed his movie *The Informer* in 1935 there is a scene where the protagonist Gypo Nolan goes into a brothel. In order to get past the censor the prostitutes were made to wear hats, thus making it look less like a brothel. With no work and no other skills, many of the girls found refuge in the notorious Magdalene Laundries which operated between 1766 and 1996. They were a kind of labour camp where fallen women ostracised by family and by society could work to atone for their "sins" and be swept under the carpet. Once admitted they could only be released if collected by family or had some place to go. Many stayed until they died, working free of charge, washing and ironing sheets, for a business that made a profit. The last Magdalene to close was in Foley Street in the heart of the former Monto. Forty elderly penitents were still working there shortly before it closed. Society did not want to know about them. An ugly reminder of forgotten history emerged when the nuns sold a former laundry and the corpses from an unmarked grave had to be reinterred in Glasnevin. It was discovered that many had no death certificates and could not be identified.

The Monto would have faded away completely were it not for the song written by George Desmond Hodnett, music critic of the *Irish Times*. Hodnett wrote *Take me up to Monto* in 1958 as a satirical ditty. Due to its historical references many believe it to be much older than it is. It was not intended for widespread consummation, but that changed when the *The Dubliners* adopted it.

ERSKINE CHILDERS

It was the ultimate paradox; an Englishman fighting for Irish freedom, only to be killed by the very people for whom he had fought and ruined his reputation. Robert Erskine Childers was born in Mayfair, London in 1870. His father was an oriental scholar while his mother Anna Mary Henrietta née Barton, was Irish, from an Anglo-Irish family in Annamoe, County Wicklow, otherwise known as the Protestant Ascendcy.[316] One wonders at this point whether or not to call him English at all, and Childers may be a prime example of how we define Irishness. Other nationalists such as James Connolly were born in Scotland, but are not referred to as Scottish. Similarly, Patrick Pearse, born to an English father, is rarely called English. When Childers senior died of TB, young Erskine was sent to live with his Irish relatives for a period while his mother convalesced.

He studied law at Cambridge and was a firm believer in the British Empire, which as nothing unusual, even in Ireland. When the Boer War (1898-1902) started he wasted no time in volunteering for service in the artillery. After a three week voyage he arrived in South Africa. He saw action but contracted trench foot, a type of disease usual among soldiers standing in wet boots and socks, and was sent back to England in 1900. While visiting Boston in 1903, his car broke down outside the home of Doctor Hamilton Osgood and his daughter Mary "Molly" Alden. The couple married the following year and had three sons, of whom; Erskine, born in 1905, was to become President of Ireland. As a wedding gift his father-in-law had a 28-ton yacht, *Asgard*, built for the couple. The yacht would later play an important role in Irish history.[317]

Childers was also a writer and his book *Riddle of the Sands* published in 1903, proved highly influential. The plot concerned two Englishmen who sail through the Frisian Islands, as Childers did himself in 1897, where they find the Germans preparing for war. The book was an inspiration for later spy novels and one of the first in which a specific foreign government is positioned as the enemy.[318] It was of course a time when German expansion caused concern among the British. It convinced the British public that more spending on the navy was required.

At what point did a man who fought for the Empire suddenly risk everything and become an Irish Nationalist? There does not appear to have been any definite turning point. By 1914 Ireland was in turmoil. Nationalists wanted Home Rule, which meant the return of the Irish parliament, which closed in 1800, but to remain within the Empire, similar to the Hungarian model. Unionists feared that Home Rule would be "Rome Rule", in other words that the Catholic Church would call the shots, and landed a consignment of arms at Larne. The Unionists paradoxically declared their loyalty to the Crown, but declared they were ready to fight the Crown if Home Rule were to be introduced. The government considered sending troops north, but the officers at the Curragh declared they would not move against the Unionists. Inspired by this, the Irish volunteers decided to smuggle in a consignment of arms, and Childers offered to bring them in on the *Asgard*. In May of 1914 Childers and Darrell Figgis travelled to Germany and bought a consignment of 1,500 Mauser Model 1871 rifles and 49,000 rounds of ammunition. Figgis was a writer and Irish volunteer. He fell from grace after the Treaty and committed suicide in 1925, and is a character that appears to have been written out of the history books. The consignment arrived at Howth in July. The delivery was an open secret and though the volunteers were not challenged at Howth, a crowd of Republicans was fired upon in the city centre by The King's Own Scottish Borderers and three people were shot dead.[319]

Home Rule was shelved when the war broke and the Irish volunteers split. Most of them went to "fight for the freedom of small nations" and believed that by showing their loyalty they would receive Home Rule after the war, which they also believed would over by Christmas. A militant minority refused to enlist in the British army and prepared for armed insurrection. Childers volunteered for service with the Royal Navy. He served in the Gallipoli campaign and was awarded the Distinguished Service Cross. Republicans could hardly hold his service in the British armed forces against him, as celebrated IRA commanders such as Tom Barry had also worn British khaki. Childers was against the 1916 rising for which he had helped supply arms and was even more against the executions of the leaders that followed.

When the first Dáil met at the Mansion House in Dublin in 1919, Childers was made Director of Publicity. Prominent Nationalists such as Arthur Griffin had little time for him and regarded him as a renegade and possible spy. Childers was with the official Irish delegation at the Paris Peace talks. He wanted to remind the conference that Britain had gone to war for the "freedom of small nations" and it was hardly apt that she deny a small country like Ireland self-governance. The delegation was ignored.

In 1920 Childers published "Military Rule in Ireland", a strong attack on British policy. At the 1921 elections, he was elected to the Second Dáil, as Sinn Féin member for the Kildare Wicklow constituency and published the pamphlet "Is Ireland a Danger to England?" which attacked the British prime minister, David Lloyd George. He served as secretary to the Irish delegation at the Anglo-Irish Treaty talks, where the Irish delegation faced highly skilled British negotiators. The Irish delegation knew how to fight a guerrilla campaign but had poor negotiating skills. The treaty they settled for divided the Irish people. Childers was something of an unwavering idealist who wanted the Ireland for which the men of 1916 had fought. This did not include compromise, and those compromising the republican ideals felt uncomfortable with him around. He opposed the treaty and men who had fought alongside each other now drifted apart and prepared to kill each other.

Childers became chief propagandist of the Republican movement and went on the run. The *Dáil* introduced an Army Emergency Powers Resolution in September of 1922 establishing martial law powers and new capital offences for the carrying of firearms without a licence. In Britain he was regarded as a traitor and former allies such as Winston Churchill, who had been a great admirer of his novel, now said of him:

> *"No man has done more harm or done more genuine malice or endeavoured to bring a greater curse upon the common people of Ireland than this strange being, actuated by a deadly and malignant hatred for the land of his birth."*[320]

Although Childers was risking his life for a cause in which he believed, he was still regarded by many in the IRA as a "bloody Englishman". Though he had military experience, he was not given a fighting role. On 10th November, Childers was arrested by Free State forces at his home in Glendalough, County Wicklow. It was probably not the best place to be, given that he was number one on the wanted list of Republicans and his home would be an obvious place to check. He was tried by a military court on the charge of possessing a Spanish-made "Destroyer" .32 calibre semi-automatic pistol, which was in violation of the Emergency Powers Resolution. The small pistol had been a gift from Michael Collins when the two were on the same side. Collins had by this stage been shot and The Free State was executing captured Republicans as reprisals. Childers was convicted and sentenced to death on 20th November. He appealed the sentence and his appeal was still pending when he was shot by firing squad on 24th November at Beggar's Bush Barracks. The barracks is now called Cathal Brugha after an anti-treaty IRA man who fought against and was killed by the Free State army. [321] He bore no malice or ill will to those who were about to kill him. In an extraordinary gesture he shook hands with each of the firing squad. He also made his 16-year-old son, also called Erskine, promise that he would seek out and shake the hand of every man who had signed his father's death warrant. His last words were to the firing party:

"Take a step or two forward, lads. It will be easier that way."[322]

His execution was politically motivated. Though a brilliant mind, he had made enemies who were determined that he would make no further contribution to the development of the nation he had helped create. The execution was brutal and undemocratic, but the act which had condemned him was designed to get the gun out of Irish politics and bring peace. He was buried at the barracks until 1923, when his body was reinterred in the republican plot of Glasnevin Cemetery. The infamous pistol found its way into the National Museum, where it is currently on display.His widow did not want anything written about her late husband to be published until fifty years after his death. It was only in 1977 that a biography based on his papers was written. Indeed, it was only in the seventies that a civilised discussion on the Civil War could take place at all. His son Erskine Childers became president in 1973, but only served a year, dying suddenly of a heart attack, the only Irish President to die in office. His monument is alongside that of Samuel Fergusson and Douglas Hyde in St Patrick's Cathedral. His daughter Nessa went on to become a politician for the Labour Party.

ERNIE O'MALLEY

Ernie O'Malley (1897-1957) fought for Irish freedom and has been sometimes referred to as the intellectual of the IRA, proving that he was more than a mere gunman. He led a somewhat colourful life and cheated death on several occasions.

He was born in Castlebar, County Mayo to a family of eleven children. The family moved to Dublin in 1911 and at the outbreak of the Great War his brother Frank enlisted in the British army.[323] Ernie would later use his brother's uniform to buy a pistol in Dublin. He was a medical student at UCD at the time of the Easter Rising and found himself in the city centre. It was a rising that would not have been supported by his family. He bumped into friends who tried to persuade him to defend Trinity College against the rebel forces. He declined and decided his sympathies lay with rebels. In the aftermath of the rising he dropped out of university and joined the IRA in 1917, unknown to his family, and became a training officer travelling the country. Thus he experienced at first hand the war from all over the country.

Like any war, it was not a pleasant affair and in his memoirs he does not hold back or paint a romantic view of the conflict. Few realise that when Frank O'Connor wrote his famous short story *Guests of the Nation*, that it was based on true events that occurred, not in Galway, but in Fethard County Tipperary. Three British officers had been captured and, as the British were executing captured IRA men, the three were executed. It was a far from glorious event and O'Malley makes no attempt to glorify the terrible deeds of war.[324]

O'Malley was captured by the British in Kilkenny in December of 1920 and found to be carrying a handgun and the names of all the members of the 7th West Kilkenny Brigade, all of whom were subsequently arrested. The British knew the man they had arrested was definitely involved with the IRA, but they never realised just how big a fish they had caught. O'Malley gave his name as Bernard Stewart and was taken to Dublin Castle, where he was badly beaten. Due to be executed, he escaped from Kilmainham Jail with the help of a sympathetic British soldier two months later and the British never realised that they had had a top IRA man.[325] A truce was declared not long after and Irish independence loomed. O'Malley opposed the infamous Treaty which gave Ireland partial independence and which created the divided Ireland that still exists. Those in favour of the treaty argued that it was a stepping stone towards independence. The young guns of the IRA believed they had brought the most powerful empire in the world to its knees and saw no reason why they should not continue the struggle for complete independence. The majority of Irish people were happy that the hostilities were over. O'Malley occupied the Four Courts which was bombarded by cannons the Free Staters had borrowed from the British. The Four Courts Garrison surrendered after a two day bombardment but O'Malley escaped yet again from captivity and made his way to Carlow via the Wicklow Mountains. The other leaders who had occupied the Four Courts were executed. He returned to Dublin and was recaptured after a shoot out with Free Staters in Ballsbridge in November of 1922. He was severely wounded in the incident, being hit over twenty times. Three bullets were to remain in his back for the rest of his life. Fortune still favoured O'Malley, as the surgeon who examined him was a former classmate who exaggerated the extent of the injuries. The Free Staters were executing anyone caught in possession of a firearm, but at the same time a repeat of the James Connolly type execution was not desired and thus his life was spared once more. It was at this time that he first started recording his experiences, which would later provide important documentation for students of Irish history.

He survived his wounds and was sent to Mountjoy where he went on hunger strike for forty one days protesting against the continued imprisonment of republican prisoners. While still on hunger strike he was elected TD for Dublin North and became one of the last prisoners to be released.[326]

His fighting days were now behind him and in an effort to regain his health he went mountain climbing in the Pyrenees. He returned to Ireland in 1926 where he continued his medical studies, but never graduated. He embarked on a tour of America to raise funds for a republican paper, *The Irish Press*. It was to become the voice of Fianna Fáil and would run from 1931until 1995.

His travels took him throughout the US and into New Mexico where, living amongst Native Americans, he began work on his memoirs. He was well versed in English literature and, perhaps because he had lived life on the edge with several near death experiences he identified with the romantics. He said of his writing:

"Writing has helped me to work certain prejudices out of my system, to clarify experience."[327]

His first book *On Another Man's Wound* was an account of his War of Independence experiences. It appeared in 1936 and was an immediate success. A subsequent book *The Singing Flame,* an account of the Civil War, a highly sensitive topic, was only published in 1978. In the 1950s *Raids and Rallies,* an account of his and other fighters experiences, based on interviews he conducted with veterans appeared and was also published. The books became invaluable sources for those studying the fight for Irish freedom and were praised for their literary quality. He met Mabel Dodge Luhan, who introduced him to literary figures such as D.H. Lawrence and Aaron Copeland. In 1930 he studied at the Mexico City University of Arts and worked as a secondary school teacher. He returned to America and met Helen Hooker, a wealthy young sculptor. When Fianna Fáil was elected to government he returned to Ireland and received a pension for his combat contribution and married Hooker in London in 1935. The couple settled in Newport, County Mayo but were later to divorce. He also wrote poetry and became a contributor the literary and cultural magazine *The Bell*.[328]

He spent the war in Ireland and volunteered for the Local Security Force, an auxiliary police force. He was friends with John Ford and became an advisor to *The Quiet Man*[329] and the IRA character in the movie was based on O'Malley. In 2001 he was further fictionalised in the drama *Rebel Heart*. Ken Loach in *The Wind That Shakes the Barley* partially based his character of Damien on O'Malley. His war wounds were a constant source of pain and he was given a state funeral when he died in 1957.

paddy mayne

Paddy Mayne was a warrior and a founding member of the SAS, an elite unit of the British army which has not always enjoyed popularity in this country. He was born Robert Blair Mayne in Newtownards, County Down, and would later acquire the nickname "Paddy" when he joined the British army.[330] He excelled at both rugby and boxing, becoming the Irish Universities Heavyweight Champion in August 1936. He won his first Ireland cap in 1937 and would go on to win five more as a lock forward, going on tour with The British Lions to South Africa.[331]

He had joined the Reserve Artillery in March of 1939 and held a commission. With the outbreak of the war he served with The Royal Ulster Rifles. After Dunkirk he joined the newly formed commandos, an elite unit which carried out raids behind enemy lines, and was assigned to No. 11 Scottish Commando. Training involved a six week intensive commando course at Achnacarry in the Scottish Highlands with a focus on fitness, speed marches, weapons training, map reading, climbing, small boat operations and demolitions both by day and by night.

His first taste of action was against the Vichy French in Lebanon as part of the Litani River Operation. His actions on the raid impressed a fellow officer, Scotsman Captain David Stirling[332] who was setting up a new unit called the Special Air Service and he asked Mayne to join it. It was called "air service" to give the enemy the false impression that it was a paratrooper regiment. Stirling believed a small motorised team of highly trained soldiers with the advantage of surprise could inflict far greater harm on the enemy than an entire regiment.

Before Mayne could join the unit Stirling first had to get Mayne out of prison[333] as he had been incarcerated for hitting his

Commanding Officer, Lieutenant-Colonel Geoffrey Charles Tasker Keyes and was awaiting court martial. Sterling made Mayne a *Dirty Dozen*-style offer, which he gladly accepted. Keyes himself would later be killed in a raid against Rommel and was awarded a posthumous Victoria Cross.

The regiment initially consisted of five officers and 60 other ranks. Its first operation was a parachute drop in November of 1941 and turned out to be something of a flop, with twenty two men either killed or captured. Parachute drops were clearly not going to work and it was Mayne who came up with the idea of using jeeps. The next mission, a raid on three airfields, was more successful and would be become characteristic of surprise hit-and-run raids for which the unit would become famous. Sixty aircraft were destroyed and no casualties suffered. It was successes such as these that would keep the regiment, known as 1 SAS, in existence and its critics at bay.

By 1944 Mayne had become a lieutenant colonel and now commanded the SAS Regiment. Sterling had become a prisoner of war in Tunisia. He would later escape, get recaptured and was eventually sent to Colditz where he spent the rest of the war.

Working with resistance groups in the Dijon and Burgundy region Mayne led the regiment in operations that interupted German communications and hampered German reinforcements being sent to the front in Normandy. It was dangerous work and Mayne, as a Special Forces soldier could expect no quarter if captured. The more successful they became the more reprisals were exacted on the local civilian populace. It was highly unusual for such a senior officer to be in the thick of the action and those who served with Mayne looked upon him as indestructible. His leadership and disregard for danger inspired those who served with him. After France the regiment moved into the Netherlands, Belgium and into Germany.

In 1945 Mayne was recommended for a VC, but the accuracy of the citation had been questioned by those present, one of whom noted that his account of the incident had been altered in the final version.[334] Mayne was supposed to have "single-handedly" rescued a squadron of his troops who were, trapped by heavy gunfire near the town of Oldenburg in North West Germany. He was, however, accompanied by John Scott who gave him covering fire. Though he had received a VC recommendation from Montgomery himself, he was in the end awarded a bar to his Distinguished Service Order. It is a matter that still irks his supporters.[335]

In May 1945, 1 SAS went to Norway with the rest of the SAS Brigade, where they had the task of disarming the German troops in the Bergen area. They had served their purpose and the regiment was disbanded in the UK in October of the same year. He remained in the army for a while after the war, getting a posting with the British Antarctic Survey in the Falklands and South Georgia, but back injuries sustained during the war kept him away from the type of operations he craved.

He had become one of the most highly decorated soldiers of the British army and, for showing courage and leadership under fire had been awarded the Distinguished Service Order with three bars, only seven of which had been awarded in the war. For his actions in liberating France the French Government awarded him the Legion d'honneur and the Croix de Guerre. However, the Victoria Cross eluded him.

While he had been in his element during the war, peace time did not suit him and he found the changeover from soldier to civilian difficult. He returned to his native Newtownards and resumed his work as a solicitor, becoming secretary to the Law Society of Northern Ireland. He had experienced much during the war and was surrounded by people who could not identify with what he had experienced, so he rarely spoke of his war time experiences. He took up gardening and became a well known face at the local pubs, where it was not uncommon for him to be involved in pub brawls. He was killed in a traffic accident in 1955 while returning from a Free Mason meeting, when his car hit a parked lorry and crashed into an electricity pole a few hundred metres from his home. He was only forty. He is buried in Movilla Cemetery in Newtownards, where there is also a bronze statue of him in Conway Square.[336]

the Diamantis

Ireland was largely spared the ravages of The Second World War. Indeed, there was no mention of the word "war" and it was officially referred to as "The Emergency", with the newly founded Free State declaring itself neutral, albeit in favour of the Allies.

Germany knew that in order to win the war they would have to cut off supplies to Britain. The U-boat campaign played a pivotal role in this and German U-boats operated off the Irish coast. The British, fearful that the U-boats would seek shelter and even supplies in neutral Ireland put pressure on the Irish government.

The war came to the south coast when survivors of the Greek ship *Diamantis* were landed in Ventry harbour in County Kerry. The bizarre thing is that their rescuers were also those who had torpedoed their ship. Along with the Laconia incident, it was one of two incidents where the Germans risked their lives to help shipwrecked survivors.

Captain Werner Lott (1907-97), commanding the U-35 had intercepted the *Diamantis* off Land's End. He signalled to the ship that he needed to check if they were carrying supplies to the British, which would legally entitle him to sink it. He fired a warning shot across their bow and the crew rapidly abandoned ship.[337] Although the crew had made it to the lifeboats, the sea was rough and some of the boats started to capsize. Lott was not obliged to pick up survivors. Indeed, during the later Laconia incident the submarine which picked up survivors was bombed by the Americans despite the presence of a Red Cross flag. Lott knew that they would drown if he did not intervene and gave the order to pick up the crew. An examination of the Greek ship's papers showed that the *Diamantis* was carrying 4,000 tonnes of Iron ore from South Africa to England.

It was the confirmation he needed and Lott gave the order to sink the *Diamantis* fifty miles from Land's End.

Lott now had a situation on his hands. Submarines were notorious for their lack of space and provisions. The U-boat had a crew of forty three. An extra twenty eight people on board would be a tight squeeze. They had to be placed on board as RAF spotter planes patrolled the area and to stay on the surface was too dangerous. The Greeks requested that they be brought to England, which was not an option as it meant that Lott and his crew would either be captured or killed. He decided to bring them to the south west coast of Ireland. At least there they would not be fired upon. The U-boat submerged before the RAF turned up and headed towards Ireland. They resurfaced when darkness fell, as a U-boat travelled faster on the surface. They arrived at Ventry harbour, stopping a few metres from the shore. The Greeks were brought ashore in a small boat, two at a time, while a crowd of locals looked on. None of the German crew actually set foot on Irish soil.

The landing was witnessed by twelve year old Jimmy Fenton, who was amazed that the Greeks were full of praise for a man who had sunk their ship. According to one of the Greek sailors, Paderas Panagos, the Germans had given them food and cigarettes.

News of the event was reported in *The Kerryman* on 7th October 1939, which stated that the crew were treated hospitably at Maurice Clery's in Ballymore. Five of them were suffering from shock and taken to Dingle hospital, but were soon well enough to accompany the remainder of the crew to Dublin.

The event made international headlines and Lott was widely praised for his chivalry. Though the Greeks were in his debt, Lott received no thanks from his own government. The Irish Free State authorities had complained to the German government about the breach of their neutrality, which got him a reprimand.

It was not the first time the war had come to the Dingle Peninsula. On 14th September 1939 a RAF plane which was on patrol looking out for U-boats was forced to land in Ventry Harbour with engine trouble.[338] The pilot, Lt. Brooke and a mechanic went ashore with a broken fuel pipe, and waved down a passing motorist, Brendán O'Connell, a civil engineer who drove them to Dingle, where a mechanic repaired the pipe.[339] The two airmen should have been interned, but were let go. Dingle would also later be the spot where a German spy, Walter Simon would be landed by the U-38 in June of 1940. He immediately raised suspicions when he asked about the next train, not realising the line had long since closed. He was followed to Dublin, where he was arrested and interned.[340]

As the war progressed such acts of humanity, on both sides, would become rarer. Lott's war was of a short duration and the U-35 was sunk in November of that year off the Norwegian coast. The crew made it to the surface and were picked up by the British. Lott and his crew were extremely fortunate. Of the 35,000 German sailors who served on the U-boats 28,744 were killed in action. Lott surrendered to Lord Louis Mountbatten and the two became lifelong friends. Imprisoned in the Tower of London in primitive conditions, Lott would later help Hans von Werra escape, the only German POW to escape from the British and make it back to Germany.

After the war Lott returned to Germany to look after his wife, who had been confined to a wheelchair after injuries sustained in a bomb blast. He devoted his life to social work and became the director of a large rehabilitation centre. He finally set foot on Irish soil in 1984 when he went to visit the Dingle Peninsula.[341]

HERMANN GÖRTZ

While Hitler's plans for Ireland are still regarded as at a matter of speculation, he did send a number of spies into the country. It was of great concern to the Allies that the Free State would be used to transmit weather reports, useful for U-Boats, to Germany, or indeed that neutral Ireland become a safe haven for spies to infiltrate Britain. The most famous of these spies was Dr. Hermann Görtz[342](1890-1947).

Görtz had fought in the First World War and had interrogated allied prisoners, a skill that would later have its use. After the war he trained to be a lawyer and went to England on his own bat in the 1930s to write a book on the expansion of the RAF, or so he would claim at his trial for spying at the Old Bailey in 1935. He was accompanied by a secretary, nineteen year old Marianne Emig, who posed as his niece. They lived in Broadstairs, Kent and the pair befriended a local RAF man, Kenneth Lewis, whom they duped into giving information.[343] He was amazed at how much they knew about the RAF and when he became concerned about telling them military secrets Görtz assured him that England and Germany would be on the same side in the next war. His "niece" maintained regular correspondence with Lewis and was happy to get photos of RAF planes which the unwitting Lewis sent her.

When the landlord of the house Görtz had been renting called by, he found a note his tenant had left, which he believed referred to Görtz's motorbike. Believing that someone had stolen the motorbike while Görtz was away, the landlord rang the police. They searched the property but did not find the motorbike. What they did find were maps and drawings of the local RAF bases. Emig was in Germany when Görtz was arrested and, under the circumstances, was reluctant to return to England. His trial attracted considerable media attention at the time and he was sentenced to four years. Following his release in 1939 he was deported back to Germany.[344]

In 1940, Britain faced a serious threat of invasion and in May of that year Görtz parachuted into Ireland as part of a fact finding mission which had been given the codename "Operation Mainau". He landed at Ballivor,[345] County Meath, although he was supposed to have landed in Tyrone. He was wearing his Luftwaffe parade uniform and First World War medals. Still dressed in his uniform, he went to the local Garda station to find out where he was and look for directions. The Guards seemingly found nothing unusual about the apparition that appeared before them and gave him the necessary directions. He then walked the eighty odd miles to Laragh, County Wicklow, the home of Iseult Stuart, wife of Francis Stuart who was in Germany at the time, and daughter to Maud Gonne. Both women had been love interests of the poet William Butler Yeats. In Berlin, Francis Stuart had told him that if he ran into difficulty he was to go to her and he now availed of the offer.

From Wicklow he went to Dublin to meet IRA activist Stephen Carroll Held at number 245 Tempelogue Road. Held, having first made contact with Oscar Pfaus from the Abwehr, the German secret service, had travelled to Germany a few weeks previously to deliver to the Abwehr, Plan Kathleen.[346]Plan Kathleen was a grandiose plan conceived by IRA man Stephen Gaynor, which outlined a proposed invasion of the north, similar to the invasion of Norway, and was approved of by Stephen Hayes, Acting Chief of Staff of the IRA. As part of the plan an amphibious assault was to be made at Lough Swilly. German paratroopers would land in the Divis Mountains and Lisburn, while the IRA would attack from the south at Leitrim. The plan called for 50,000 German troops, but contained no details of coastal defences in the North or other vital information. The Abwehr had been told that the IRA in Ireland was 5,000 strong and all that they needed was guns, which they wanted to be brought ashore along the west coast.

Görtz, who had looked at the plan a fortnight before dropping into Ireland, thought it somewhat far-fetched. He wanted the IRA to cease hostilities in the Free State, where they were more active than in the North, and concentrate their energy on fighting the British. He was shocked to find that the IRA was not the guerilla movement he had been told it was. He found it to be unreliable and completely disorganized. In terms of numbers it seemed nowhere near the size he had been told in Berlin. It proved to be more of a liability to the Germans and other German spies were told to avoid contact with the IRA.

While Görtz was staying with Held, the house was raided on 22 May. While Görtz escaped through the back garden, Held was not so fortunate and was given a given a five year prison sentence for his involvement in the affair. The guards found $20,000 in the house, as well as details on Irish harbours, bridges and the distribution of the Defence Forces. The plans for Plan Kathleen were also uncovered and handed over to the British. Görtz managed to stay at large until November 1941. When a known IRA man, Pearse Paul Kelly visited Stuart's house, the guards raided and arrested both Kelly and a German who called himself Heinrich Brandy. Brandy soon revealed his true identity to be Hermann Görtz.[347] Stuart was also taken into custody. She was imprisoned for a month, but was acquitted when brought before a court.

Görtz was not the only spy to arrive in Ireland. Others such as Günther Schütz were sent to collect weather reports and assess the effect of German bombing in the north. He was supposed to be dropped off at Newbridge in September 1940 but landed in Wexford and was arrested almost immediately.[348] It is possible that this was the intention. The news of German spies arriving in Ireland would unsettle the Allies. Although the agents were informed in depth about Ireland by the professor of Celtic Studies, Ludwig Mühlhausen, they had very poor English and were bound to stand out. None of the spies were allowed to associate with German prisoners of war in the Curragh. Schütz tunnelled his way out of

Mountjoy in 1942 and found refuge in an IRA safe house. He was later recaptured and survived the war. Following this escape attempt Görtz and the other spies were transferred to Costume Barracks in Athlone, where they spent the rest of the war. In 1946, Görtz applied for asylum, but his application was turned down. He was released the following year and went to live with Bridie and Mary Farrell. His days, however, in Ireland were numbered. On 23rd May, 1947, he was requested to report to the Aliens' Office in Dublin, where he was told a plane was ready to return him to Germany. Knowing that he would probably face a prison sentence or worse in occupied Germany, he swallowed a poison capsule and died within a few seconds.[349] He was buried at Deansgrange cemetery in Dublin with a swastika draped over the coffin. He was later re-interred in the German cemetery at Glencree in 1974. All Irish government communications with Görtz were ordered destroyed.[350] He is said to have designed his own gravestone, a sword wrapped in ivy, which is also at Glencree. In 1984 he was the subject of a RTÉ drama *Caught in a Free State*. The German war cemetery at Glencree, the resting place of 134 Members of the Luftwaffe and Kriegsmarine, is itself worth a visit. At the entrance, engraved on a rock, is a poem written by Stan O'Brien:

"It was for me to die
Under an Irish sky
There finding berth
In good Irish earth
What I dreamed and planned
bound me to my Fatherland
But War sent me
To sleep in Glencree
Passion and pain
Were my loss my gain:
Pray as you pass."

James Brady

While the activities of William Joyce and Francis Stuart have been well documented over the years, very little is known about the handful of Irishmen who fought on the German side in the Second World War. These men were not part of the Legion of St George, a group of Englishmen in the Waffen SS, as is often believed, but more specialised commandos. The most prominent of these were James Brady of Strokestown, County Roscommon and Frank Stringer from Gravelstown, County Meath. It is also believed that a Patrick O'Neill from Donegal served as a doctor with a SS penal battalion and was killed in action in 1944, though this has never been satisfactorily confirmed.[351]

Brady was born in Strokestown in 1920. His mother died when he was very young and in 1938 he went to Liverpool and enlisted in the Royal Irish Fusiliers. He was stationed on the Island of Guernsey, where he and Frank Stringer were involved in a fracas in a pub.[352] After hitting the policeman who had come to arrest them they were both sentenced to a term in the local jail. When the regiment pulled out of Guernsey it seemingly forgot about Brady and Stringer. They were still in jail when the Germans took possession of the island in July 1940 and were subsequently transferred from the prison to a prisoner of war camp in France.

In May 1941, about fifty Irish POW's, including Brady and Stringer, were segregated from the other prisoners and sent to a camp at Friesack in Northern Germany under the supervision of the *Abwehr*, or the German counter-intelligence. They were chosen by Helmut Clissmann, from the elite Brandenburger unit, who would later settle in Ireland.[353]

A number of British POWs of an Irish background were kept there. It was intended that they were to form the nucleus of an Irish Brigade. It was not a new idea and, just as Roger Casement had sought to form an Irish Brigade in the First World War, so too did Seán Russell.[354] He was not alone in this idea. Eoin O'Duffy also wanted to raise a brigade from Ireland to fight Russia as he had done in Spain, though his plan was not taken seriously by the German authorities. The recruits were treated well, given freedom of movement, good food and money. Other Irish men to receive specialised training in bomb making at Friesack included Sergeant John Codd from Mountrath, County Laois, William Murphy from Enniscorthy, Patrick O'Brien from Nenagh and Andrew Walsh from Fethard, County Tipperary. Little or nothing is known about most of them, though Codd is known to have returned to Ireland with his German wife in 1945 and was arrested by G2 or the intelligence wing of the Irish army.

The brigade was intended to appeal to Irish Nationalists, but as with the previous German Irish brigade it met with very limited success and it was decided to train them as spies instead. Helmut Clissmann, who later dropped into Ireland, was involved in their training.

That was not entirely successful either. They had been told that they were being transferred to a camp with better conditions for the Irish. This is all some of them wanted and they had no intention of serving the Germans. The men were put under immense psychological pressure to cooperate and when the idea of dropping them into Ireland was deemed unworkable those unwilling to further cooperate were sent to Sachsenhausen concentration camp.

The espionage side of things had little appeal for Brady and Stringer and in September of 1943 they both transferred to the Waffen SS, where they received further training along with other European volunteers at Sennheim in Alsace. Brady adapted the alias De Lacy and would reach the rank of SS-Unterscharführer (Sergeant) before the war was out, while Stringer, who became known as Le Page, never rose above the rank of Private.

It was in France that they received their blood groups tattooed on their left arms, which was common to all members of the SS. Their in-depth training there lasted until March of 1944. They were not satisfied being normal infantry men and sought more of a challenge. They were sent to a special camp at Friedenthal, near Berlin and became part of the elite commando SS-Jaegerbatallion 502, which had been set up by Otto Skorzeny. Skorzeny was famous all over Europe for his daring rescue of Mussolini and would move to Ireland after the war. From there they were then posted to SS-Jagdverbände Mitte. It was one of these units that infiltrated the American lines dressed as Americans during the battle of the Bulge, which spread panic through the American lines. While Brady and Stringer didn't participate in this operation, they did take part in a cunning plan to kidnap the son of Hungary's regent Admiral Horthy, who had been planning to surrender to the Russians. The regent did not initially sway when his son was kidnapped but did when the SS kidnapped him as well and the operation in October 1944 was a success.[355] In spite of this success, the Third Reich was collapsing and in January 1945 Brady was wounded during a Russian attack on the river Oder and had to be hospitalised. He fled from the hospital shortly before the Russians overran it. At the war's end he avoided captivity by going underground with other SS men. He did not seem content with a life on the run, however, and he turned himself in to the British authorities in Berlin in September of 1946. From there he was brought to London, where in Mayfair in December of that year he was court-martialled and received a 12 year sentence. Stringer had surrendered to the Americans, who handed him over to the British. He too faced court-martial; and here it was proven that he had been a serving member of the British army when he had joined the German army. He was released from prison in 1950 and returned to Ireland. What became of him after this, or indeed any of the Irish men mentioned in this article, is not known.

fethard-on-sea

A sleepy rural Wexford town in 1957 made headlines both nationally and internationally when the Protestants of the town were the subject of a boycott. Sectarianism is a malaise that has affected this island for centuries and while many Irish Catholics can readily quote anti-Catholic sectarianism, anti-Protestant sectarianism is often overlooked.

The furore started with Seán and Sheila Cloney (née Kelly), a mixed married couple. He was Catholic and she was Protestant. It was at a time when mixed marriages were not commonplace. Both came from the town and married in an Augustinian church with a blessing at an Anglican one in London in 1949. By marrying a Catholic she was consenting to a 1908 papal decree by Pope Pius X called the *Ne Temere* Decree,[356] which meant that any children born to the couple would have to be raised as Catholics. The couple had three daughters, Mary, Eileen and Hazel, who was born after the controversy.

Protestantism had been the official religion of the island under colonial rule, but this had changed with Independence, when the newly founded Free State acknowledged the special position of the Catholic Church, the religion which the majority of its citizens professed. While ethnic cleansing was not as rampant as with the Ethnic Germans in Czechoslovakia in 1945-46, non Catholics in Ireland after 1922 were expected to keep their heads down and their mouths shut. It was forbidden for Catholics to enter a Protestant church. Thus when Douglas Hyde, the first president of Ireland and eminent Gaelic scholar died in 1949, government ministers did not attend the funeral service at Saint Patrick's Cathedral, but waited outside. The exception was Dr Noël Browne, a man ahead of his time, and who met his Waterloo when he took on the Church with his Mother and Child Scheme.

When the time came that Eileen was of school going age the local priest Father Stafford visited the family and demanded that she be sent to the local Catholic school. Perhaps he should have remembered the old adage, "you get more flies with honey than you will with vinegar", and Sheila Cloney did not appreciate someone coming into her home making demands. At the same time it was not the done thing to defy the Catholic Church, but Sheila resented the priest's involvement and was not going to be pushed around by anyone. Her decision required a considerable amount of courage. The previous year two Jehovah's Witnesses were attacked by a mob led by Fr Patrick Ryan in Clonlara,[357] who burnt their pamphlets and told them never to come to the town again. When the Jehovah's Witnesses complained to the guards no charges were brought against the mob. Quite the opposite happened, and when the matter came to court the two Jehovah Witnesses were ordered to pay £100 each. The then Taoiseach John A. Costello expressed his support for the church.

The priest put pressure on Seán and it drove a wedge between the couple. Feeling isolated, Sheila packed her bags and left with the children. She found refuge in Northern Ireland, a sectarian state fearful of Catholic oppression. The case of Sheila Clooney was embraced as a prime example of what would happen to all Protestants in a United Ireland. A few days later a Belfast barrister, Desmond Toal arrived at the Cloney household to inform Seán Cloney that his wife and children had sought refuge in Belfast. She would only be prepared to return if he sold the farm, emigrated to Australia and have the children raised as Protestants. He refused.

Matters escalated when Father William Stafford announced from the altar a boycott against the local Protestants. As a result nobody went into the two Protestant shops, the Protestant school lost a Catholic teacher, and the Protestant music teacher lost twelve of her thirteen pupils. Protestant farmers could not bring in their crops as nobody was willing to help them and nobody was willing to buy their produce. The boycott was nothing new to Ireland. The word itself had been coined in Mayo, when this form of protest was successfully used against Captain Boycott. It was a tough time for Seán Cloney. The only ones in the village to support him were old IRA men who had had their own troubles with the church.[358]

Bishop Browne of Galway threw oil on the fire when he came out in public support of the boycott. He told a meeting in Wexford:

> *"There seems to be a concerted campaign to entice or kidnap Catholic children and deprive them of their faith. Non-Catholics, with one or two honourable exceptions, do not protest against the crime of conspiring to steal the children of a Catholic father. But they try to make political capital when a Catholic people make a peaceful and moderate protest."*[359]

Not everyone shared his view. A Catholic barrister, Donal Barrington, who would later become a judge, counteracted this Episcopal view by calling the boycott "the most terrible thing that has happened in this country since the Civil War".[360] The affair was covered by *Time* magazine which coined the term "fethardism" to mean a boycott along religious lines. Aware of the negative press Ireland was receiving on the international stage it was up to the Taoiseach Eamonn DeValera to put a stop to it. In July, in a speech to the Dáil he said:

> *"If, as head of the government, I must speak, I can only say from what has appeared in public that I regard this boycott as ill-conceived, ill-considered and futile for the achievement of the purpose for which it seems to have been intended, that I regard it as unjust and cruel to confound the innocent with the guilty, that I repudiate any suggestion that this boycott is typical of the attitude or conduct of our people and that I beg of all, who have regard for the fair name, good repute and well-being of our nation, to use their influence to bring this deplorable affair to a speedy end."*[361]

Sheila, who was by now living on the Orkney Islands, decided to come home. So that no side would be seen to win it was decided that Sheila Cloney would educate her children herself. Though her opinions never changed, she never again spoke publically of the affair. The events that transpired that summer were made into a film, *A love Divided* (1999) with Orla Brady playing the role of Sheila. The film itself caused controversy as it over dramatised some events and added in events that never happened. Sheila Cloney died in 2007. Both she and her husband lived long enough to get an apology from the Catholic Church in 1998.

Almost three decades later the town of Fethard-on-Sea would once more hit the headlines when it was revealed that the notorious child abuser Seán Fortune had abused children there until 1987. Child abuse until the nineties was something of a known unknown that was swept under the carpet by both church and state, and the general public acquiesced. Seán Cloney helped compile a list of Fortune's abuses.[362] Fortune himself committed suicide before his trial in 1999.

michael manning

Twenty four year old Michael Manning, executed in 1954, was the last man to hang in Ireland. In a drunken act of stupidity he raped and murdered a 64 year old nurse, Catherine Cooper. The tragedy of the case is that his actions seemed to be momentary madness, rather than those of cold, calculating murderer, but he had made a mistake and it would cost him his life. Fellow inmates recalled that Manning appeared to be completely normal. Manning's body was buried in an unmarked grave in a yard at Mountjoy Prison as was usual at the time.[363] The hanging inspired a play by Ciarán Creagh. Creagh's father, Timothy, was one of the two prison officers who stayed with Michael Manning on his last night and *Last Call*[364] is loosely based on what happened that night. It was shown in Mountjoy Prison's theatre for three nights in June 2006.

It is interesting to note that in ancient Ireland, hangings were not the norm. An *éiric*, a form of compensation had to be paid to the victim's relatives and only if they could not pay was a hanging carried out.

Women convicted of murder were burnt at the stake. Dorcas or Darkey Kelly, a madam and serial killer wrongly thought to have been a witch was burnt in Baggot Street in 1761.[365] Five bodies were found at her brothel, The Maiden Tower, in the heart of the city, known as "Hell" in the Christchurch area.

Public hangings were usual until 1868 and in Dublin they were performed at St. Stephen's Green or Newgate Prison which closed in 1863 and was located in the area around the Cornmarket. The Cornmarket was also a place where public floggings were administered. Outside of Dublin the victim was hanged before their house. Carlow doctor Samuel Haughton (1821-1897) developed the humane "Standard Drop" method of hanging that came into use in 1866.[366] Until this time, those condemned to hang were "hanged by the neck until dead" which could take a while. The victim also had to endure a jeering mob. With Haughton's method, the exact length of rope and the exact depth of fall could be calculated, determined on the victim's weight, to bring about immediate death. The system of hanging in Britain was similar if not identical, to that of Ireland.

William Marwood[367] (1820–1883) created the "long drop" which he used for the first time in 1872. With this method the prisoner's neck was broken instantly at the end of the drop, resulting in the prisoner dying of asphyxia while unconscious.[368] It was Marwood who hanged *The Invincibles*, a gang who had assassinated Lord Frederick Cavendish, the Chief Secretary for Ireland, and Thomas Henry Burke, the Permanent Under-Secretary for Ireland, at Kilmainham Jail in 1883. The leader of the gang, James Carey, had been arrested and, in order to save himself, betrayed the group. He was subsequently killed by Patrick O'Donnell in Cape Town. Reference is made to this in the song *Take me up to Monto*.

Many who were executed were believed to be innocent. The most notorious case was the Maamtrasna Murders of 1882[369] on the shores of Lough Mask, where an entire family was murdered. Both the trial and the executions were covered in considerable detail at the time and three men were sentenced to death by hanging at Galway Jail.[370] Marwood officiated. One of the men, Myles Joyce was believed to be innocent.[371] His trial had been conducted in English but he understood little or no English and was not provided with an interpreter. His name has yet to be cleared.

Executions very often created martyrs. One only has to think of The Manchester Martyrs of 1867 or the executions of the 1916 leaders, which actually popularised a most unpopular rising. Not learning from this blunder, the English hanged an eighteen year old medical student and IRA volunteer Kevin Barry. The departure of the British in 1922 did not put a stop to executions, nor did it stop the creation of martyrs. The Free State government executed several anti-

Treaty IRA men, often without trial. The more famous victims were Rory O'Connor, Joe McKelvey, Richard Barrett, and Liam Mellows, shot by firing squad without trial as a reprisal for the shooting of Seán Hales, something they had not been involved in. They were chosen to represent each of the four provinces. The Civil War came to an end in 1923 but the bitterness it left behind still lingers.

Business for the hangman in Ireland was slow in the 1930s and only five people were executed. The Emergency (1939-46) led to an increase in IRA activity and a fearful government dealt severe penalties to those involved. Former head of the anti-treaty IRA and now Taoiseach Eamon De Valera did not intervene when two IRA men were hanged in Belfast gaol. In the Free State five IRA men were shot by firing squad. Two of them, Maurice O'Neill and Richard Goss, had shot but not killed a guard, and became the only people executed by the state for a non-murder crime. One volunteer, Charlie Kerins was hanged.[372]

Manning was hanged by Albert Pierrepoint, who had made his debut hanging in Ireland. For Pierrepoint executions were something of a family business. Both his father and uncle were involved in the grisly trade. Ireland did not have its hangman, partially because no suitable candidate could be found for the job, a job not much in demand, and partially because it suited a long tradition of the Englishman executing the Irishman. Pierrepoint had trained an Irishman at Strangeways prison, who was supposed to be the state executioner, but as Pierrepoint pointed out in his autobiography that he did not have the stomach for it.[373] It was in 1932, at Mountjoy Jail that Albert Pierrepoint, accompanied by his uncle, witnessed his first hanging when Patrick McDermott, who had murdered his own brother, was executed. Uncle Tom had previously sent off the last woman to be executed in Ireland in 1925. Annie Walsh, aged 31, was convicted of murdering her husband, who was twice her age. Her lover, her husband's nephew, was also hanged. Albert Pierrepoint had more business in England and went on record as performing the fastest hanging in the world when he hanged James Inglis, whom he advised to go quickly and without fuss. Inglis was pronounced dead within seven seconds of leaving his cell.[374]

After Michael Manning's execution all sentences were commuted to life even when the accused was sentenced to death. Mamie Cadden, for example, was sentenced to be hanged in 1957 for murder after performing an illegal abortion on a woman who died; the sentence was commuted to life imprisonment. The death penalty was abolished in 1964, though it remained on the statue books for murders of The Garda Síochána. A powerful deterrent was needed to protect the unarmed police force, but again this was never carried out, even when members of the force were brutally slain. It was finally removed from law in 1990. Recent changes to the constitution provide that the penalty cannot be reintroduced even in war or a state of emergency.[375]

POSTSCRIPT

"Out of Ireland have we come,
great hatred, little room,
maimed us at the start.
I carry from my mother's womb
a fanatic heart."[376]
William Butler Yeats

Irish society is in a constant state of transition and Irish history is constantly being rewritten. The once deeply Catholic country, rocked by child abuse scandals, is currently becoming deeply secular. From the poverty of the eighties, we encountered extreme wealth during "The Celtic Tiger" and lost it all again. Joining the British army no longer has a stigma attached. Indeed, Irishmen who deserted the Free State army to fight for the British in World War Two are now looked upon as heroes. Even the statelet of Northern Ireland was officially recognised by the Irish people when they voted to amend articles two and three of the constitution in 1999. Though Irish unification was important, especially when listening to rebel ballads in pubs, it was ultimately not worth shedding any blood over. The words of Phil Coulter's much loved song *The town I loved so well* are apt:

"For what's done is done and what's won is won
and what's lost is lost and gone forever
I can only pray for a bright, brand new day
in the town I loved so well."

When Queen Elisabeth made her historic visit in May of 2011 her first stop was at the Garden of Remembrance, just a few metres from

O'Connell Street, to honour the Irish who fought for Irish freedom, against the British. She laid a wreath there before moving on to Island Bridge to pay her respects to those Irish who fought in The Great War, on the side of the British. It was a simple but powerful gesture. She also visited Croke Park, scene of the 1920 massacre. Though the visit resulted in the largest security operation in the history of the state, it was a success. Her visit was an acknowledgement of Irish sovereignty. The visit would have been unthinkable only a decade previously and heralded a new beginning in the relationship between two islands which had fought each other for centuries and a further stepping stone towards the peace brought about by The Good Friday Agreement of 1998.

BiBLiOgRapHy

Books

Broderick, Marian, *Wild Irish Women – Extraordinary lives from History*, Dublin 2005

Cannan, Fergus, *Galloglass 1250-1600*, Oxford 2010

Corkery, Daniel, *The Hidden Ireland*, Dublin 1924

Corless, Damien, *GUBU Nation*, Dublin 2005

Dames, Michael, *Mythic Ireland*, London 1992

Danaher, Kevin, *Gentle Places and Simple Things*, Dublin 1984

English, Richard, *Ernie O'Malley IRA Intellectual*, Oxford 1998

Enno, Stephan, *Spies in Ireland*, Dublin 1963

Fennell, Paul, *Haunted-A Guide to Paranormal Ireland*, Dublin 2006

Furlong, Nicholas, *Diarmait King of Leinster*, Cork 2006

Greene, Miranda, *Celtic Goddesses*, London 1997

Hayes-McCoy, G.A., *Irish Battles-A Military history of Ireland*, Belfast 2009

Hopkins, Frank, *Rare Old Dublin: Heroes, Hawkers and Hoors*, Dublin 2008

Hull, Mark M., *Irish Secrets-German Espionage in Wartime Ireland 1939-45*, Portland 2003

Joyce, P.W., *A Child's History of Ireland*, Dublin 1898

Kelly, Fergus, *A Guide to Early Irish Law*, Dublin 2003

Kelly, Maria, *A History of the Black Death in Ireland*, Stroud 2001

Kennealy, Ian, *Courage and Conflict-Forgotten Stories of the Irish at War*, Cork 2009

Lamb, Roger, *Memoir of My Own Life*, Dublin 1811

Lenihan, Michael, *Hidden Cork*, Cork 2009

Lewis, Arthur H., *Lament for the Molly Maguires*, Oxford 1964

Little, George A., *Malachi Horan Remembers*, Dublin 1945

Logan, Patrick, *The Holy Wells of Ireland*, Buckinghamshire 1980

Lyons, Mary Ann and O Connor, Thomas, *Strangers to Citizens-The Irish in Europe*, Dublin 2008

Mac Coitir, Niall, *Irish Trees, Myths, Legends and Folklore*, Cork 2003

Maletzke, Elsemarie, *Dublin ein literarische Portraet*, Frankfurt 1996

MacArdle, Joesph, *Irish Rogues and Rascals*, Dublin 2007

McCarthy, Cal, *Green, Blue and Grey, The Irish in the American Civil War*, Cork 2009

McCormack, John, *Twists of Fate*, Dublin 2005

Meehan, Carey, *The Travellers Guide to Sacred Ireland*, Glastonbury 2002

Nicholls, K.W., *Gaelic and Gaelicized Ireland in the Middle Ages*, Dublin 2003

Ó Cróinín, Dáibhí, *Early Medieval Ireland 400-1200*, Longman 1995

O'Donell, Vincent, *O'Donnells of Tyrconnell-A Concise History of the O'Donnnell Clan*, Inver 198, reprint 2000

O'Malley, Ernie, *On Another Man's Wound*, Cork 2012

O'Malley, Ernie, *The Singing Flame*, Cork 2012

O'Reilly, Terence, *Hitler's Irishmen*, Cork 2008

Ó Ríordáin CSsR, James J., *Early Irish Saints*, Dublin 2007

Ó Tuama, Seán, *An Duanaire 1600-1900: Poems of the Dispossessed*, Dublin 1981

Ó Tuama, Seán, *Caoineadh Airt Uí laoghaire*, Cork 1961

Pierrepoint, Albert, *Executioner: Pierrepoint*, Kent 1974

Pollard, H.B.C., *The Secret Societies of Ireland – Their Rise and Progress*, Kilkenny 1998

Power, Patrick C., *Sex and Marriage in Ancient Ireland*, Cork 1997

Richards, A. P., *Irish Murders*, New Lanark 2006

Roche, Richard, *The Norman Invasion of Ireland*, Dublin 1995

Ronan, Gerard, *The Irish Zorro*, Dingle 2004

Severin, Tim, *The Brendan Voyage*, London 1976

Simms, George Otto, *Brendan the Navigator – Exploring the Ancient World*, Dublin 2006

Slavin, Michael, *The Ancient Books of Ireland*, Dublin 2005

Spindler, Karl, *Das geheimnisvolle Schiff*, Berlin, 1921

Stephan, Enno, *Spies in Ireland*, London 1963

Uíbh Eachach, Vivian, *Fiach mac Aodha Ó Broin*, Indreabhán 2003

Wilde, Sir William, *Irish Popular Superstitions, London 1852*

Journals and periodicals

Crewe, Ryan Dominic, *Lamport, William (Guillén Lombardo) (1610-1659)* in *Irish Migration Studies in Latin America* 5:1 (March 2007), pp. 74-76.

Barfield, Doreen, *"'For Valour' at Fugitives' Drift, An account of the award of the Victoria Cross to Lieuts. Melvill and Coghill for heroism at Fugitives' Drift after the disaster of Isandhlwana"* in *Military History Journal Vol 1 No 6 – June 1970*

Frieder Berres: „*Kapitän Karl Spindler. Erinnerungen an einen außergewöhnlichen Königswinterer Bürger, der in die Seekriegsgeschichte einging*". in: „*Jahrbuch des Rhein-Sie Kreises*", 1998, S. 98–114.

Hogan, Patrick M., *"The Undoing of Citizen John Moore – President of the Provisional Government of the Republic of Connacht, 1798"* in *Journal of the County Galway Archaeological and Historical Society*, Vol. XXXVIII, 59-72.

Mitchell, James, *"Mayor Lynch of Galway: A Review of the Tradition"* in *The Journal of the Galway Archaeological and Historical Societe* Vol. 38, (1981/1982), pp. 31-44

Ó Cochláin, Rupert S., *"Count O'Donnell and the Austrian Emperor"* in *The Irish Sword*, No. 8, 1956

Ó Cochláin, Cathach, *"Battle book of the O'Donnells"* in *The Irish Sword: the journal of the Military History Society of Ireland*, Vol. VIII, No. 32, pp. 157-177, Summer, 1968

Ó Danachair, Caoimhín, "*Armada losses on the Irish coast, with map*" in *The Irish Sword: the journal of the Military History Society of Ireland, Vol. II, No. 9*, pp. 320-331, Winter, 1956

Petrie, Sir Charles, "*The Irish Brigade at Fontenoy*" in *The Irish Sword: Journal of the Military History Society of Ireland,* Volume I, No. 3, 1951-52, pp 166-172

notes

1   William Butler Yeates Quotes at:
http://www.quoteoasis.com/authors/y/william_butler_yeats_quotes.html

2   http://quotationsbook.com/quote/13650/#sthash.BMvcUULS.dpbs

3   *Lindeman, Micha F, Crom Cruach* at
http://www.pantheon.org/articles/c/crom_cruach.html

4   Thurneysen, Rudolf, *Die Irische Helden und Königssagen bis zum 17.Jahrhundert.*
Halle 1921. Reprint: Hildesheim 1980.

5   Dames, Michael, *Mythic Ireland*. London: Thames & Hudson, 1996.

6   See *The Rolling Sun from Boheh* in The Mayo News at:
http://www.mayonews.ie/index.php?option=com_content&view=article&id
=17572:see-the-rolling-sun-from-boheh&catid=23:news&Itemid=46

7   The Sacred Island, Available at:
http://www.carrowkeel.com/sites/croaghpatrick/reek2.html

8   *The Metrical Dindshenchas*, available at:
http://www.ucc.ie/celt/published/T106500D/text007.html. My thanks to
Beatrix Färber for allowing me to use this translation.

9   Crom Cruach at: http://en.wikipedia.org/wiki/Crom_Cruach.

10   http://www.flickr.com/photos/mickbourke/5451239533/

11   Marsh, Richard, *The Killycluggin Stone –County Cavan* at:
http://mazgeenlegendary.wordpress.com/2011/01/19/the-killycluggin-stone-county-cavan/

12   Greene, Miranda, *Celtic Goddesses*, London 1997.

13   For more information see http://corofin.galway-ireland.ie/knockma.htm

14   *Mongfind* at: http://en.wikipedia.org/wiki/mongfind

15   Other theories suggest the same comes from 'stoney river' or 'settlement of
the foreigners'.

16   River Shannon: Facts About the Longest River in Ireland at
http://primaryfacts.com/555/river-shannon-facts-about-the-longest-river-in-ireland/ (accessed 13/03/13)

17   Kelly, Fergus, *A Guide to Early Irish law*, Dublin 2003

18   Power, Patrick C., *Sex and Marriage in Ancient Ireland*, Cork 1997

19   *The Chieftain Clan O'Flaithbheartaigh-Kings and Queens of Connemara* at:
http://laffertyhistory.webs.com/connemaraspiratequeen.htm

20   Slavin, Michael, *The Ancient Books of Ireland*, Mcgill Queens Univ Press 2005.

21   *Becoming a King in Medieval Ireland* at:
http://earlymedievalirishtuath.wikispaces.com/Becoming+a+king

22   *The Battle of Cooldrumman* at:
http://www.oracleireland.com/Ireland/history/battle-culdema.htm. Battles at
the time tended to be small so this would have been a significant amount.

[23] http://en.wikipedia.org/wiki/cumdach

[24] Cathach of St. Columba at:
http://en.wikipedia.org/wiki/cathach_of_st._columba

[25] Ó Cochláin, Rupert, *Cathach, The Battle book of the O'Donnells* in *The Irish Sword: the Journal of the Military History Society of Ireland*, Vol. VIII, No. 32, pp. 157-177, Summer, 1968.

[26] http://en.wikipedia.org/wiki/Clonfert_Cathedral

[27] Simms, Otto, *Brendan the Navigator – Exploring the Ancient World*, O'Brien 2006.

[28] Saint Brendan's Island at:
http://en.wikipedia.org/wiki/Saint_Brendan%27s_Island. Accessed on 4/05/13.

[29] The Voyage of Bran at: http://en.wikipedia.org/wiki/The_Voyage_of_Bran

[30] Severin, Tim, *The Brendan Voyage*, Hutchinson 1978.

[31] Papar at: http://en.wikipedia.org/wiki/Papar

[32] http://www.heritageisland.com/attractions/craggaunowen-the-living-past

[33] This cathedral contains one of the finest medieval doorways in Ireland. http://www.megalithicireland.com/Clonfert%20Cathedral.html

[34] Some accounts say he was from Scotland. For centuries no distinction was made between the Scots and the Irish. Indeed the Romans referred to Ireland as both *Hibernia* and *Scotia*.

[35] http://virginia.ie/index.php?page=st-killian-s-heritage-centre—-mullagh-co-cavan

[36] The text of which is available at http://www.irishcultureandcustoms.com/Poetry/PangurBan.html

[37] Johannes Scotus Eriugena at:
https://en.wikipedia.org/wiki/Johannes_Scotus_Eriugena.

[38] Saint Killian at: http://en.wikipedia.org/wiki/Saint_Killian

[39] http://www.virgilofsalzburg.com/

[40] Virgil von Salzburg at: http://de.wikipedia.org/wiki/Virgilius_von_Salzburg

[41] Gordan, P. Paulus, *St. Virgil-The History Of St. Virgil Of Salzburg: His Life and Work* at http://www.stvirgil.org/virgil.html?id=1095779848

[42] *The Inhabitants of the Earth* at:
http://vserver1.cscs.lsa.umich.edu/~crshalizi/White/geography/inhabitants.html

[43] http://vserver1.cscs.lsa.umich.edu/~crshalizi/White/geography/inhabitants.html

[44] Hugh Redington Norman and Rae Keck, Karen, *St. Virgil the Geometer, Abbot-Bishop of Salzburg, Enlightener of Carinthia* at http://www.voskrese.info/spl/XvirgilSalz.html (accessed 24/04/12)

[45] St. Virgilius of Salzburg at:
http://www.catholic.org/saints/saint.php?saint_id=2018

[46] A thousand years after its establishment the original Viking settlement was uncovered. Unfortunately its location was prime real estate and the authorities felt the need to destroy it forever by pouring concrete over it and building the

massive structure which became the Dublin City Council Civic Office.

[47] Isolde's Tower, Dublin at http://www.hidden-dublin.com/foot/foot04.html

[48] Maletzke, Elsemarie, *Dublin ein literarisches Portraet*, Insel Taschenbuch, Frankfurt 1996.

[49] Pronounced /gur-um-la/. She features in the historical novel *Lion of Ireland* by Morgan Llywelyn (2002 Tor Books).

[50] *The Story of Burnt Njal(Njal's Saga) Part 11: Sections 147 – 158*
Online Medieval and Classical Library Release #11 at: http://omacl.org/Njal/

[51] *The Battle of Clontarf-Brian Boru's Last Costly Victory* at
http://www.doyle.com.au/battleclontarf.htm

[52] *The Story of Burnt Njal(Njal's Saga)Part 11*: Sections 147 – 158 at:
http://omacl.org/Njal/11part.html

[53] Joyce, P.W., *A Children's history of Ireland*, Dublin 1898.

[54] *The Story of Burnt Njal(Njal's Saga) Part 11: Sections 147 – 158* at:
http://omacl.org/Njal/11part.html

[55] Unfortunately this is only a copy; the original was removed by the city of Dublin in the 17th century and destroyed.

[56] *The Story of Burnt Njal(Njal's Saga) Part 11: Sections 147 – 158* at:
http://omacl.org/Njal/11part.html (accessed 20/04/12)

[57] Cearbhall MacDunlainge at http://www.stevenroyedwards.com/cerball.html

[58] *The Annals of Innisfallen* at:
http://www.ucc.ie/celt/published/T100005B/index.html.M928.10. My thanks to Beatrix Färber for allowing me to use this translation.

[59] Wynne Foot, Arthur *Account of a Visit to the Cave, Co Kilkenny, with some remarks of human remains found therein* at:
http://www.archive.org/stream/journalofroyalso11royauoft#page/64/mode/2p

[60] Buckley Laureen, *Dunmore Cave – A Viking Massacre Site*
.http://tbreen.home.xs4all.nl/PAISN/3-DUNMORE.html

[61] http://www.excavations.ie/Pages/Details.php?Year=&County=Kilkenny&id=1839

[62] http://irishhistorypodcast.ie/2011/07/05/dunmore-cave-following-in-the-footsteps-of-1100-year-old-murderers/

[63] *Saint Colman of Stockerau* at http://saints.sqpn.com/saint-colman-of-stockerau/

[64] *Die Legende vom Heiligen Koloman* at:
http://www.sagen.at/texte/sagen/oesterreich/niederoesterreich/weinviertel/kolmann.html

[65] Koloman (Heiliger) at : http://de.wikipedia.org/wiki/Koloman_(Heiliger). The stone is located just inside the gift shop on the right hand side.

[66] Roche, Richard, *The Norman Invasion of Ireland*, Anvil Books Dublin 1970, reprint 1995.

[67] Furlong, Nicholas, *Diarmait King of Leinster*, Cork 2006.

[68] Some still survive, such as the crowning stone of the O'Connors now at

Clonalis House, County Roscommon.

[69] The High King or *Ard Rí* was akin to emperor. The last one was Rory O'Connor (died 1198) who was buried at the Cathedral at Clonmacnoise.

[70] Lough Derg also known as "Saint Patrick's Purgatory" is in County Donegal. According to legend Christ showed Patrick a cave there which was a gateway to hell. It was made famous all over Europe by a 12th century text *Tractatus de Purgatorio Sancti Patricii* describing the journey of a knight into purgatory. It proved to be a medieval best seller making Lough Derg one of the most popular European places of pilgrimage.

[71] The name simply means 'son of Gerald'. The Irish version became "Mac Gearailt".

[72] More information is available here: http://en.wikipedia.org/wiki/Laudabiliter

[73] *The Annals of Innisfallen* at http://www.ucc.ie/celt/published/T100004/AI1170.4. My thanks to Beatrix Färber for allowing me to use this translation.

[74] His tomb was destroyed several centuries ago and replaced by an unrelated effigy from a church in Drogheda. It is nevertheless still referred to as "Strongbow's tomb".

[75] Furlong, Nicholas, *Diarmait King of Leinster*, Cork 2006.

[76] *Gods & Goddesses Dian Cécht* at http://www.sheeeire.com/Magic&Mythology/Gods&Goddess/Celtic/Gods/Diancecht/Page1.htm

[77] Logan, Patrick, *The Holy Wells of Ireland*, ColinSmythe Limited Buckinghamshire1980.

[78] Meehan, Carey, *The Travellers Guide to Sacred Ireland*, Gothic Image Publications Glastonbury 2002.

[79] I can highly recommend *Ancient & Holy Wells of Dublin* by Gary Branigan(The History Press Ireland 2012).

[80] Logan, Patrick, *The Holy Wells of Ireland*.

[81] Burr Davis, Boccaccio on the Plague at: http://www.history.vt.edu/Burr/Boccaccio.html (accessed 13/04/13)

[82] Kelly, Maria *A History of the Black Death in Ireland*, Tempus 2001.

[83] Kelly, Maria, *A History of the Black Death in Ireland,* Tempus 2001.

[84] Others argue that the name comes from a tannery that existed there.

[85] Kelly, Maria *A History of the Black Death in Ireland*, Tempus 2001.

[86] Cannan, Fergus, *Galloglass 1250-1600 Gaelic Mercenary Warrior*, Osprey 2010.

[87] Heath, Ian, *The Irish Wars 1485-1603*, Osprey 1993.

[88] Nicholls, K. W., *Gaelic and Gaelized Ireland in the Middle Ages*, Lilliput Press 2003.

[89] Massing, Jean Michel, *Albrecht Dürer's Irish Warriors and Peasants* in *Irish Arts Review* at http://irishartsreview.com/irisartsreviyear/pdf/1994/20492793.pdf.bannered.pdf (accessed 20/02/12)

[90] Alasdair Mac Colla at http://en.wikipedia.org/wiki/Alasdair_Mac_Colla

91 Hayes-McCoy, G.A., *Irish Battles – A Military history of Ireland,* 1969, reprinted Belfast 2009.

92 *The Battle of Knockdoe 1504* at: http://www.aoh61.com/history/knockdoe.htm

93 Hardiman, James, *Hardiman's History of Galway Chapter 4: From 1484 to the commencement of the Irish Rebellion in 1641* at: http://www.galway.net/galwayguide/history/hardiman/chapter4/knoc_tuadh.html (accessed 15/04/12).

94 *Ireland's greatest Gaelic lords gathered at Knockdoe* in *The Galway Advertiser,* 8 July 2010, at: http://www.advertiser.ie/galway/article/28336.

95 More information available at http://en.wikipedia.org/wiki/Francisco_de_Cuellar (acccessed on 03/05/12). There is also an excellent account of his Irish adventure in *Endurance – Heroic Journeys in Ireland* by Dermot Somers (O'Brien 2005).

96 http://www.irishwrecksonline.net/Lists/GalwayListA.htm

97 Ó Danachair, Caoimhín, *Armada Losses on the Irish Coast* in *The Irish Sword*: the Journal of the Military History Society of Ireland, Vol. II, No. 9, pp. 320-331, Winter, 1956

98 Pronounced /tie-ga na bwilla/.

99 Hardiman, James, *Hardiman's History of Galway Chapter 4: From 1484 to the commencement of the Irish Rebellion in 1641* at: http://www.galway.net/galwayguide/history/hardiman/chapter4/spanish_armada.html

100 *Galway and the Armada* at: http://places.galwaylibrary.ie/history/chapter58.html

101 Rynne, Etienne, *Tourist Trail of Old Galway,* Ireland West Tourism, Galway1977, reprint 1985.

102 Mitchell, James, *Mayor Lynch of Galway: A Review of the Tradition* in *The Journal of the Galway Archaeological and Historical Society* Vol. 38, (1981/1982), pp. 31-44

103 *Lecture on James Joyce's Galway* 31May 2012 in The Galway Advertiser at: http://www.advertiser.ie/galway/article/52507/lecture-on-james-joyces-galway

104 From which the phrase 'beyond the Pale' originates.

105 Even today it is a remote spot. Photos of the valley are available here: http://wicklowdailyphoto.blogspot.ie/2010/09/battle-of-glenmalure.html (accessed on 30/12/12).

106 Uíbh Eachach, Vivian, *Fiach mac Aodha Ó Broin,* Indreabhán 2003.

107 Torpey, Michael, *The massacre at Dun an Oir* in *The Clare Champion* at: http://www.clarechampion.ie/index.php?option=com_content&view=article&id=8148:the-massacre-at-dun-an-oir&catid=76:history&Itemid=55

108 Uíbh Eachach, Vivian.

109 Mac Eiteagáin, Darren, *Feagh McHugh O'Byrne and the Ulster Princes:his Role in their Dublin Castle escapes* at: http://www.byrneclan.org/feagh_mchugh_dublin_escapes.htm

110 Disney made a film based on Red Hugh called *"The fighting Prince of Donegal---"* (1966). A contemporary account of the escape *Beatha Aodha Ruaidh*

Uí Dhomhnaill was written by Lughaidh Ó Cléirigh in the early 17th century.

[111] Mac Eiteagáin, Darren, *Feagh McHugh O'Byrne and the Ulster Princes:his Role in their Dublin Castle escapes* at:
http://www.byrneclan.org/feagh_mchugh_dublin_escapes.htm
(accessed 3/05/13).

[112] Some accounts say that she was kept in a cage for several days.

[113] O'Byrne, Emett, *A striking and wicked beauty-Rose O'Toole of Glenmalure Part 1* at: http://www.independent.ie/regionals/braypeople/lifestyle/a-striking-and-wicked-beauty-28830675.html

[114] McArdle, Joseph, *Irish Rogues and Rascals*, Gill and MacMillan 2007.

[115] Semple, Patrick, *Miler McGrath* at:
http://www.patricksemple.ie/other/mcm.php

[116] *Miler Magrath* at: https://en.wikipedia.org/wiki/Miler_Magrath

[117] McArdle, Joesph, *Irish Rogues and Rascals*, Gill and MacMillan 2007.

[118] McArdle, Joesph,

[119] Kirby, Brian, *Meiler Magrath's Clerical Career* at:
http://www.scoilnet.ie/hist/docs/meiler%20magrath.pdf

[120] Quoted from
http://archiver.rootsweb.ancestry.com/th/read/IRL-TOMBSTONE-INSCRIPTIONS/2005-05/1115694313

[121] *The real Zorro was Irish* at http://www.examiner.com/article/the-real-zorro-was-irish

[122] Ronan, Gerard, *The Irish Zorro*, Brandon 2005.

[123] Ronan,Gerard, *The Irish Zorro*.

[124] Legends of Máire Rua at :
http://www.clarelibrary.ie/eolas/coclare/places/the_burren/maire_rua_legends.htm (accessed on 03/03/13)

[125] Leamaneh Castle at http://en.wikipedia.org/wiki/Leamaneh_Castle

[126] Leamaneh Castle at
http://www.all-ireland.com/attractions/munster/clare/leamanehcastle.htm

[127] This practice is described in more detail in the book *To Hell or Barbados: The Ethnic Cleansing of Ireland* by Sean O'Callaghan (Brandon 2001)

[128] *Saint Oliver Plunkett* in http://livingspace.sacredspace.ie/F0701s/. (accessed on 15/04/13)

[129] http://en.wikipedia.org/wiki/Oliver_Plunkett

[130] *Titus Oates* at:http://www.historylearningsite.co.uk/titus_oates.htm

[131] Spartical Educational *Titus Oates* at
http://www.spartacus.schoolnet.co.uk/STUoates.htm

[132] St Oliver Plunkett-St. Peter's Church, Drogheda at
http://www.saintoliverplunkett.com/stpeters.html (accessed on 1/05/13)

[133] A nice version of this song is sung by the Donegal group *The Cassidys*.

[134] Upshaw.Tom, *A Short History of the Irish Palatines, at:*
http://www.teskey.org/palhist.html

135 Ronan, Sean G., *The Palatines in Ireland-An Account of their Settlement in the 18th Century* http://www.gladleh.com/gen/ambassador.htm (accessed 14/04/13)

136 http://www.irishpalatines.org/

137 Sometimes written as Bonny without the 'e'.

138 Arditti, Michael, *Women pirates of the West Indies* at http://www.michaelarditti.com/non-fiction/women-pirates-of-the-west-indies/ (accessed 3/05/13)

139 Broderick, Marian, *Wild Irish Women-Extraordinary lives from History.*

140 Vallar, Cindie, *Friends and Enemies* at http://www.cindyvallar.com/friendsenemies.html. (accessed 03/05/13)

141 *18th Century Women Pirates: Anne Bonny And Mary Read* at http://www.essortment.com/18th-century-women-pirates-anne-bonny-mary-read-20352.html. (accessed 03/05/13)

142 http://en.wikipedia.org/wiki/A_General_History_of_the_Pyrates

143 Anne Bonny, created by SJ Corcoran October 27 2007 at http://www.findagrave.com/cgi-bin/fg.cgi?page=gr&GRid=22488988

144 Penal Laws at http://saints.sqpn.com/ncd06402.htm. (accessed 03/05/13)

145 Henley, Jon, *Stranger than fiction: the true story behind Kidnapped*, in *The Guardian*, Thursday 18 February 2010 at: http://www.guardian.co.uk/books/2010/feb/18/kidnapped-stevenson-true-story-annesley (accessed 03/05/13)

146 'Birthright': *The Astonishing Story Behind 'Kidnapped'* at: http://www.npr.org/templates/story/story.php?storyId=12346373

147 There is an interesting article on the subject at: http://www.sligoheritage.com/archBarbados.htm. See also O'Callaghan, Sean, *To Hell or Barbados.*

148 Ekirch, Roger A., *Kidnapped!* at: http://www.common-place.org/vol-11/no-01/ekirch/ (accessed 20/05/12)

149 The Battle of Fontenoy 1745 at: http://www.britishbattles.com/battle_fontenoy.htm

150 Petrie, Sir Charles, *The Irish Brigade at Fontenoy* in *The Irish Sword: Journal of the Military History Society of Ireland*, Volume I, No. 3, 1951-52,

151 Henry, William, *The Battle of Fontenoy* in *The Galway Independent* 6/02/13. http://galwayindependent.com/stories/item/5812/2013-6/The-Battle-of-Fontenoy

152 The text of her poem is available here-http://www.bartleby.com/250/87.html

153 Bereford Ellis, Peter, *Remember Fontenoy!* in *Irish Democrat* at: http://www.irishdemocrat.co.uk/features/remember-fontenoy/

154 Galloping Hogan at: http://en.wikipedia.org/wiki/Galloping_Hogan

155 A biography 'Freney the Robber' was written in 2009 by Michael Holden.

156 Danaher, Kevin, *Irish Customs and Beliefs*, Mercier 1964.

157 Lyrics at: http://www.justanothertune.com/html/brennanonthemoor.html

158 Danaher, Kevin, *Gentle Places and Simple Things*, Dublin 1984.

[159] Danaher, Kevin, *Gentle Places and Simple Things*, Dublin 1984.

[160] "Captain Gallagher-The Irish Highwayman" in "Tales from the West of Ireland" by Sean Henry at http://www.stand-and-deliver.org.uk/highwaymen/gallagher.htm. (accessed 20/04/13)

[161] Danaher, Kevin

[162] Danaher, Kevin

[163] The poem is pronounced /kweena Art-ee-Leera/. There are several translations available. I recommend the version found in *An Duanaire 1600-1900: Poems of the Dispossessed* by Seán Ó Tuama.

[164] Pronounced as /ev-leen/.

[165] Corkery, Daniel, *The Hidden Ireland*, Dublin 1924.

[166] Corkery, Daniel.

[167] Readers may find it unusal that I write O'Connor with an apostrophe and Ó Laoghaire without. The apostrophe here is unusual in Gaelic. The 'O' and 'Mac' identifies the Gaelic surname. It used to be said that:
"By Mac and O
You'll always know
True Irishmen they say'.
But if they lack
The O and Mac,
No Irishmen are they".
At Ellis Island the American authorities changed Gaelic names and the 'o' and 'mac' were often removed. It is not unsual for Irish people today when encountering a *gaeilgeoir* to 'translate' their name.

[168] Pronounced as /o-leer-a/

[169] Edmund Burke vs. the Catholic Penal Laws posted on December 4, 2008 at http://proecclesia.blogspot.ie/2008/12/edmund-burke-vs-catholic-penal-laws.html. (accessed on 03/05/13)

[170] Now called Carriganimmy. It is found in the area of Muskerry 19 km north of Macroom on the R582.

[171] Ó Tuama, Seán, *Caoineadh Airt Uí Laoghaire*, Baile Átha Cliath 1961, reprint 1979.

[172] Lenihan, Michael, *Hidden Cork*, Cork 2009.

[173] Corkery, Daniel, *The Hidden Ireland*. Dublin 1924.

[174] Lamb, Roger, *Memoir of my Own Life*, Dublin 1811.

[175] The older spelling of "Welsh" was with a "c" instead of a "s".

[176] Lamb, Roger, *A Journal of Occurrences*, Dublin 1809.

[177] Cheaney, Janie B., Charles,Earl Cornwallis at http://www.his.jrshelby.com/kimocowp/cornwal.htm. (accessed 3/05/13)

[178] Robert Graves at:http://en.wikipedia.org/wiki/Robert_Graves. (accessed 13/05/12)

[179] Code Duello at: http://en.wikipedia.org/wiki/Code_duello

[180] Martin, Richard (1754-1834), of Dangan and Ballynahinch, co. Galway and

16 Manchester Buildings, Mdx.Published in The History of Parliament: the House of Commons 1820-1832, ed. D.R. Fisher, 2009 at http://www.historyofparliamentonline.org/volume/1820-1832/member/martin-richard-1754-1834

[181] http://brendano7.com/2010/07/20/duelling-in-eighteenth-century-ireland/

[182] Danaher, Kevin.

[183] McNamara, Robert, Famous Duels of the 19th century at: http://history1800s.about.com/od/majorfigures/ss/duels19thcentury_3.htm (accessed on 20/02/13)

[184] Pollard, H.B.C., *The Secret Societies of Ireland-their Rise and Progress*, The Irish Historical Press, Kilkenny 1998.

[185] Full text of the poem is available at http://carriganimawhiteboys.com/cathcheimanfhia.html

[186] Bunbury, Turtle, *The Whiteboy Insurrection in Macroom, 1822* at: http://www.turtlebunbury.com/history/history_irish/roadshow/whiteboy.htm (accessed 14/05/13)

[187] *Castlepollard Massacre* at http://www.castlepollard.ie/History_page.html (accessed 03/05/13)

[188] O'Connell, Morgan John, Mrs, *The Last Colonel of the Irish Brigade, Count O'Connell, and old Irish life at home and abroad, 1745-1833,* London, K. Paul, Trench, Trübner & co., ltd. 1892. The subject also featured in a TG4 documentary by Manchán Magan called *Cé a chónaigh i mo Theachsa.*

[189] Tom Crean, Thomas Ashe, Marie Antoinette & Dingle Peninsula at http://www.dodingle.com/Heritage/famous_peninsula_people.html

[190] Irish surname search – Rice, (O'Mulcreevy) at: http://www.goireland.com/genealogy/family.htm?FamilyId=280

[191] General Arthur Dillon at http://www.virtualarc.com/officers/dillon/. (accessed 03/05/13)

[192] James O'Moran / Thomas Ward at http://www.irishmeninparis.org/soldiers-and-politicians/james-o-moran-thomas-ward (accessed 03/05/13)

[193] http://www.advertiser.ie/galway/article/47963/dick-martins-reputation-as-a-duellist-struck-terror-into-his-creditor

[194] The episode inspired Thomas Flanagan to write a thinly fictionalised account *The Year of the French* (Macmillan 1979) which in turn was made into a mini series by RTÉ in 1984.

[195] Coyne, Kevin *The Moores of Moorehall* at http://www.mayo-ireland.ie/Doon/moores.html(accessed on 05/05/13)

[196] Fennell, Paul, *Haunted-A Guide to Paranormal Ireland.*

[197] Hogan, Patrick M., "The Undoing of Citizen John Moore – President of the Provisional Government of the Republic of Connacht, 1798", *Journal of the County Galway Archaeological and Historical Society*, Vol. XXXVIII.

[198] Hogan, Patrick M., 'The Undoing of Citizen John Moore – President of the Provisional Government of the Republic of Connacht, 1798', in *Journal of the County*

    Galway Archaeological and Historical Society, Vol. XXXVIII, 59-72.

[199]   Coyne, Kevin.

[200]   *John Moore* at: http://en.wikipedia.org/wiki/John_Moore_(Irish_politician)

[201]   *Reader's Digest Illustrated Guide to Ireland, March 1934* at:
http://www.rootsweb.ancestry.com/~irlros/executioner.htm
(accessed13/05/12)

[202]   Broderick, Marian, *Wild Irish Women – Extraordinary lives from History*, O'Brien
2004.

[203]   'Lady Betty' and the ' enemy of romance' in *The Galway Advertiser*, 22
September 2011 at: http://www.advertiser.ie/galway/article/44186/lady-betty-
and-the-enemy-of-romance

[204]   Wilde, Sir William, *Irish Popular Superstitions, London 1852.*

[205]   http://www.bbc.co.uk/radio4/womanshour/05/2006_18_fri.html   (accessed
20/04/12)

[206]   This site has a nice picture of the jail:
*http://elsidodotcom.wordpress.com/2012/01/18/roscommon-jail-micro-mall-and-
innovative-hangwoman-betty-2/* (accessed 20/04/13)

[207]   *The Colleen Bawn(1803-1819)* at:
http://www.clarelibrary.ie/eolas/coclare/people/bawn.htm

[208]   Broderick, Marian, *Wild Irish Women – Extraordinary lives from History*, Dublin
2005.

[209]   *John Scanlan and Stephen Sullivan – The murderers of the Colleen Bawn* at:
http://www.exclassics.com/newgate/ng584.htm(accessed on 20/01/13)

[210]   Richards, A.P. *Irish Murders*, Geddes and Grosset 2002.

[211]   Ó Tuama and Kinsella, *An Dunaire1600-1900, Poems of the Dispossessed.*

[212]   His monument is on display at St Patrick's Cathedral in Dublin. His most
famous piece *Carolan's Concerto* is a gem of harp music.

[213]   For an English translation I recommend *An Duanaire 1600-1900: Poems of the
Dispossessed* compiled by Seán Ó Tuama.

[214]   This piece known as *A Child's Hymn of Praise* was written by the poet Jane
Taylor (1783-1824) in her *Hymns for Infant Minds* (1810).

[215]   Little, George A., *Malachi Horan Remembers*, Dublin 1945.

[216]   The Legend of Margorie McCall ~ 1705 at
http://www.lurganancestry.com/mmccall.htm.(accessed on 3/05/13)

[217]   Hidden Ireland:The capital's oldest graveyard at:
http://www.thejournal.ie/hidden-ireland-the-capitals-oldest-graveyard-
609289-Sep2012/ (accessed 3/05/13)

[218]   http://en.wikipedia.org/wiki/Body_snatching

[219]   MacGowan, Douglas, *William Burke & William Hare-The Grave Robbing Business*
at http://www.trutv.com/library/crime/serial_killers/weird/burke/index_1.html.
(accessed 15/03/13)

[220]   Hickey, Eileen M., *The Background of Medicine in Ireland* at:
http://europepmc.org/articles/PMC2479627/pdf/ulstermedj00186-0004.pdf

221   Dan Donnelly at: http://en.wikipedia.org/wiki/Dan_Donnelly_(boxer)

222   http://en.wikipedia.org/wiki/Dan_Donnelly_(boxer)

223   Abel, Allen, *Donnelly's Arm* at:
http://sportsillustrated.cnn.com/vault/article/magazine/MAG1006267/2/

224   Jackson, Ron *Legend of Dan Donnelly's arm* at
http://www.fightnews.com/Boxing/legend-of-dan-donnellys-arm-
56429(accessed on 03/05/13)

225   Myler, Patrick, *"Irish Dan Donnelly: still on Tour 178 years after his Death"* in *The Ring*.

226   Rural unrest in northern Tipperary 1750 to 1850 at:
http://www.grantonline.com/grantfamilygenealogy/Tipperary/
Shinrone/rural_unrest_in_northern_tippera.htm

227   Nolan, Willie, *Historical People of Ballingarry*, at:
http://ballingarry.net/people/jim_kennedy.html (accessed 22/04/13)

228   http://www.wordnik.com/words/donnybrook

229   *Bataireacht-Irish Stick Fighting* at:
http://www.irish-stick fighting.com/000001986c14e8d05/0000009eff1103412/
index.html (accessed 20/04/13)

230   http://en.wikipedia.org/wiki/Shillelagh_(club)

231   "Los Diablos Tejanos" at:
http://www.imageswest.digitalimagepro.com/tejanos.html

232   Kennealy, Ian, *Courage and Conflict-Forgotten stories of the Irish at War*, Cork 2009.

233   Minster, Christopher, *The Saint Patrick's Battalion* at:
http://latinamericanhistory.about.com/od/Mexican-AmericanWar/a/The-Saint-
Patricks-Battalion_2.htm (accessed 22/04/12)

234   *The San Patricios and the Mexican War of 1847*
http://www.turtlebunbury.com/history/history_irish/history_
irish_sanpatricios1847.htm (accessed 22/04/12)

235   *Praise, Condemnation for Massacre of Sioux Indians* at:
http://www.newsinhistory.com/blog/praise-condemnation-massacre-sioux-
indians (accessed 23/04/13)

236   Clifden and Connemara Heritage Society at:
http://www.clifden2012.org/history/the-san-patricios/itemlist/category/16-the-
san-patricios.html (accessed 22/04/12).

237   Lola Montez at:http://en.wikipedia.org/wiki/Lola_Montez

238   D'Auvergne, E. B. , *Lola Montez – the Adveneuress of the Forties* at
http://www.gutenberg.org/ebooks/38512 (accessed 23/05/12)

239   *Die Welt, Die Stripperin und die Revolution*, (in German) 29/06/07.

240   *Journey to the East – Lola Montez* at:
http://www.roguery.com/golden/road/LOLA.HTM

241   http://www.gutenberg.org/files/21421/21421-h/21421-h.htm

242   http://history.knoji.com/lola-montez-the-dancer-who-brought-down-a-king-
part-two/

243   Lola Montez at:

http://www.findagrave.com/cgi-bin/fg.cgi?page=gr&GRid=726

244   Some accounts say he was actually executed at Spinnerin am Kreuz.

245   Written with one 'n' and pronounced in the French style.

246   *Die Wildgaense-The Wild Geese, Special exhibition Book*, Heersgeschichtliches Museum, Vienna 2003.

247   O'Cochlain, Rupert, *Count O'Donnell and the Austrian Emperor* in *The Irish Sword*, No. 8, 1956.

248   *Sissis Reitpeitsche in Irland aufgetaucht* (in German) at http://www.gaelnet.de/2010/09/28/sissis-reitpeitsche-irland-aufgetaucht/ (accessed 10/04/13)

249   As explained previously the Irish abroad in the medieval period were referred to as "Scots".

250   This tale was recounted to me by Count Douglas O'Donell.

251   Bloy, Marjie, *James Thomas Brudenell, seventh Earl of Cardigan 1797-1868*, at: http://www.victorianweb.org/history/crimea/cardigan.html

252   The barracks was used until the Civil War, but today only a single wall remains.

253   Woodham Smith, Cecil, *Lord Lucan and the Irish potato famine*, at: http://www.victorianweb.org/history/famine2.html

254   The Battle of Balaclava at: http://www.britishbattles.com/crimean-war/balaclava.htm

255   http://comeheretome.com/2010/03/09/from-capel-street-to-the-crimea/

256   *The Balaklava Bugle* at: http://www.bbc.co.uk/ahistoryoftheworld/objects/rJ49c3NITF aqZOHa09NjXg

257   *The charge of the light brigade and the Crimean War* at: http://www.oxforddnb.com/public/themes/92/92728.html

258   http://www.museum.ie/en/news/press-releases.aspx?article=dc986faf-b552-4366-9ca8-9eb614c720fb

259   *William Howard Russell* at: http://en.wikipedia.org/wiki/William_Howard_Russell

260   Tiernan, Danny, *Luke O'Connor was the first soldier to receive the Victoria Cross* at: http://www.irishidentity.com/extras/hidden/stories/lukeoconnor.htm

261   Hickman, Kennedy, *The Battle of Fredericksburg* at: http://militaryhistory.about.com/od/civilwar/p/fredericksburg.htm (accessed13/04/12)

262   http://en.wikipedia.org/wiki/Battle_of_Fredericksburg

263   http://www.angelfire.com/ny5/pinstripepress/FatherCorby.htm

264   Robert McMillan, 24th Georgia Infantry: 'A Gallant Irishman at Fredericksburg' at http://irishamericancivilwar.com/2012/12/13/robert-mcmillan-24th-georgia-infantry-a-gallant-irishman-at-fredericksburg/

265   McCarthy, Cal, *Green, Blue and Grey-the Irish in the American Civil War*, Collins Press 2009.

266   http://www.imdb.com/character/ch0175490/quotes

[267] A corrupt form of the Irish "fág an bealach"(clear the way). It became the motto for numerous Regiments of Irish descent. It is still used as a motto by the Royal Irish Regiment.

[268] McCarthy, Cal.

[269] http://www.civilwar.org/battlefields/fredericksburg/maps/maryesheightsmap.html

[270] McCarthy, Cal.

[271] Battle of Fredericksburg at:
http://en.wikipedia.org/wiki/Battle_of_Fredericksburg

[272] McCarthy, Cal, *Green, Blue and Grey – the Irish in the American Civil War*. Collins Press 2010.

[273] Rodgers, Thomas G., *Irish-American Units in the Civil War*, Osprey 2008

[274] *Who is the Tenth Tennessee?* at: http://www.tenthtennessee.org/ (accessed 10/06/11)

[275] Blackwell Drake, Rebecca, *The Exploits of Patrick Griffin: "He Must Have Been Irish"* at
http://www.battleofraymond.org/history/griffin1.htm (accessed 15/07/12)

[276] Lewis, Arthur H., *Lament for the Molly Maguires*, Longmans 1965.

[277] *Molly Maguires – The Irish in the Coal Fields* at:
http://www.aoh61.com/history/molly_coal.htm

[278] Lewis, Arthur H., *Lament for the Molly Maguires*.

[279] *Molly Maguires* at:http://en.wikipedia.org/wiki/Molly_Maguires

[280] Myles Keogh at: http://en.wikipedia.org/wiki/Myles_Keogh.

[281] Byrne, Liam and Maureen *Myles Walter Keogh* at:
http://www.tinryland.ie/index.php?history/article2. (accessed on 13/04/13)

[282] Often misquoted as "the only good Indian is a dead Indian."

[283] Pohanka, Brian C. *Myles W. Keogh's Life and Times* The Irish Knight at:
http://custer.over-blog.com/article-14349757.html

[284] http://en.wikipedia.org/wiki/Battle_of_the_Little_Bighorn (accessed on 3/05/13)

[285] Apparently the medals were sold at auction.
http://www.cowansauctions.com/item.aspx?ItemId=41175 (accessed 20/03/13)

[286] Comanche (horse)at: http://en.wikipedia.org/wiki/Comanche_(horse).

[287] http://www.tinryland.ie/index.php?history/article2

[288] http://custer.over-blog.com/article-14349757.html

[289] http://www.evi.com/q/obituary_of_nevill_josiah_aylmer_coghill

[290] Young, John, *The Defence of Rorke's Drift* at:
http://www.rorkesdriftvc.com/battle/full_defence_account.htm

[291] Now called Dún Laoghaire or Dunleary.

[292] The Battle of Isandlwana at:
http://www.britishbattles.com/zulu-war/isandlwana.htm

[293] Lieutenant Nevill Josiah Aylmer Coghill, 24th Regiment at:
http://www.northeastmedals.co.uk/britishguide/zulu/vc_nevill_

josiah_aylmer_coghill.htm (accessed10/05/12)

294 Barfield, Doreen, *"For Valour" at Fugitives Drift, An account of the award of the Victoria Cross to Lieuts. Melvill and Coghill for heroism at Fugitives' Drift after the disaster of Isandlwana* in *Military History Journal Vol 1 No 6 – June 1970.*

295 List of Zulu War Victoria Cross recipients at: http://en.wikipedia.org/wiki/List_of_Zulu_War_Victoria_Cross_recipients

296 See also http://london-bombs.blogspot.ie/2005/07/jubilee-plot-of-1887.html

297 Richard Pigott at: http://en.wikipedia.org/wiki/Richard_Pigott

298 Fleming,Diarmaid, *Irish spymaster 'M' sparks debate* at http://news.bbc.co.uk/2/hi/uk_news/northern_ireland/7163329.stm (accessed on 05/05/13)

299 O'Carroll, Helen, *William Melville-Spymaster* at: http://www.kerrymuseum.ie/forum_1.html (accessed 23/05/12)

300 Peterkin, Tom, *Irish inspiration for Bond character M* in *The Telegraph.* 2 Jul 2007 at: http://www.telegraph.co.uk/news/uknews/1556242/Irish-inspiration-for-Bond-character-M.html

301 Die Wildgaense-The Wild Geese, Special exhibition Book, Heersgeschichtleise Museum, Vienna 2003.

302 Knights of the Air: Gottfried von Banfield at: http://www.dieselpunks.org/profiles/blogs/knights-of-the-air-gottfried (accessed 13/06/11)

303 Further biographical details are available here: http://en.wikipedia.org/wiki/Raffaello_de_Banfield

304 There is a small guest house in Riderau on the shores of lake Ammersee with the inscription, *Hier wohnte im Sommer 1915 Sir Roger Casement. Ein Märtyrer für Irlands Freiheit.Ein hochherziger Freund Deutschlands in schwerer Zeit.Er besiegelete die Liebe zur Heimat mit seinem Blute."*
"Sir Roger Casement, a martyr for Ireland's freedom, resided here in summer 1915. A magnanimous friend of Germany in difficult times. He sealed the love for his country with his blood."

305 *Daniel Bailey, Irish Brigade Sergeant* at: http://www.irishbrigade.eu/recruits/bailey.html

306 Heimatverein Siebengebirge e.V. Königswinter at: http://www.heimatverein-siebengebirge.de/aktivitaet/artikel/spindlere.html

307 Libau at:http://de.wikipedia.org/wiki/Libau_(1911)

308 Monto at: http://en.wikipedia.org/wiki/Monto

309 Finn, Clodagh, *Dublin: A new city afoot* at: http://www.independent.ie/lifestyle/travel/inside-ireland/dublin-a-new-city-afoot-26560868.html (accessed 20/04/13)

310 *The Bloomsday world tourists never get to hear about* in *The irish independent* by Maggie Armstrong Tuesday June 14 2011 (accessed 14/04/12)

311 Hopkins, Frank, *Rare Old Dublin: Heroes, Hawkers and Hoors*, Dublin 2008.

312 Scanlan, Billy, 02 Jun 2003, *TAKE ME BACK TO MONTO* at

http://www.hotpress.ie/archive/2658236.html

313 Pierse, Michael, *The miracle of Monto?A chequered history, from prostitution to pilgrimages* at:
http://republican-news.org/archive/2002/September05/05mont.html

314 Blain, Emma, *An Honour Killing* at: http://www.herald.ie/entertainment/hq/an-honour-killing-1398843.html

315 The Irish Independent, *Death in a Lonely Spot*, 2 February 1926.

316 Even today many Irish do not consider Protestants to be "Irish" even though they have roots going back several centuries in this country.

317 The yacht is still in existence and though unseaworthy was recently restored and is currently on display at The National Museum at Collins Barracks in Dublin.

318 Talbot, Paul *The Riddle of the Sands* at
http://www.scandalpark.com/blog/books/the-riddle-of-the-sands/ (accessed on 20/03/13)

319 The Massacre of Bachelor's Walk at:
http://www.turtlebunbury.com/history/history_irish/history_irish_bachelors_walk.htm

320 http://www.scandalpark.com/blog/books/the-riddle-of-the-sands/

321 Another paradox is that the army barracks in Galway is named after Liam Mellows who also fought against the Free State army and who was executed without trial by the Free State forces.

322 Conroy, James *Childers, Erskine: Patriot or Traitor?* at http://www.irish-society.org/home/hedgemaster-archives-2/people/childers-erskine-patriot-or-traitor (accessed on 20/03/13)

323 Ernie O'Malley at http://www.cairogang.com/ira-men/o'malley.html (accessed 20/03/13)

324 O'Malley, Ernie, *On Another Man's Wound*, London and Dublin 1936, reprint Dublin 2002.

325 O'Malley, Ernie, *On Another Man's Wound*, London 1936 (reprint Anvil 2002).

326 O'Malley, Ernie, *The Singing Flame*, Dublin 1978.

327 English, Richard, *Ernie O'Malley IRA Intellectual*, Oxford 1998.

328 Ernie O'Malley & Achill Island at:
http://www.achill247.com/writers/eomalley4.html

329 A romantic comedy drama film from 1952 and though "stage Irish", it proved to be a success.

330 http://en.wikipedia.org/wiki/Paddy_Mayne

331 Paddy Mayne at: http://en.wikipedia.org/wiki/Paddy_Mayne

332 http://www.specialoperations.com/Foreign/United_Kingdom/SAS/Founding_Fathers.htm

333 Hunter, Simon, *Blair Mayne SAS diary released* at:
http://www.bbc.co.uk/news/uk-northern-ireland-15036691

334 http://www.ww2awards.com/person/42139

[335] Peterkin, Tom, *50 years after his death, maverick colonel may yet receive the VC* (14/12/05) at: http://www.telegraph.co.uk/news/uknews/1505430/50-years-after-his-death-maverick-colonel-may-yet-receive-the-VC.html

[336] http://www.our-wee-country.com/blair-mayne-statue-mrvisk.html

[337] http://www.independent.ie/national-news/town-to-honour-wwii-uboat-crew-for-saving-28-sailors-lives-1890213.html (accessed 20/02/12)

[338] Foreign Aircraft landings Ireland 1939-1945 at http://www.csn.ul.ie/~dan/war/crashes.htm (accessed 30.05.12)

[339] 'Submarines in the bog holes': West Kerry's experience of World War II The Kerryman, 01 October 1999 at: http://www.u-35.com/sources/Kerryman1999.htm (accessed 30/05/12)

[340] *Tralee and Dingle Light Railway* at: http://en.wikipedia.org/wiki/Tralee_and_Dingle_Light_Railway

[341] http://www.u-35.com/sources/Kerryman1984.htm

[342] I have chosen the German spelling of his name. In English without the *umlaut* it is written as 'Goertz'.

[343] Hermann Goertz at http://www.nationalarchives.gov.uk/releases/2003/november14/Goertz.htm Document reference: KV 2/1319-1323 (accessed 13/03/12)

[344] http://www.nationalarchives.gov.uk/releases/2003/november14/Goertz.htm Document reference: KV 2/1319-1323

[345] Enno, Stefan, *Spies in Ireland*, Stackpole 1965.

[346] Plan Kathleen at: http://en.wikipedia.org/wiki/Plan_Kathleen (accessed 15/06/12).

[347] http://www.nationalarchives.gov.uk/releases/2003/november14/goertz.htm

[348] Hull, Mark M. *Irish Secrets: German Espionage in Wartime Ireland 1939-1945*, Dublin 2004.

[349] Hull, Mark M. *Irish Secrets: German Espionage in Wartime Ireland 1939-1945*, Dublin 2004.

[350] http://www.independent.ie/unsorted/features/the-spy-who-was-left-out-in-the-cold-26095995.html

[351] O'Reilly, Terence *Hitler's Irishmen*, Cork 2008.

[352] O'Reilly, Terence.

[353] Hull, Mark M. *Irish Secrets. German Espionage in Wartime Ireland 1939-1945*

[354] There is a statue of Seán Russell in Fairview Park, Dublin which has been much vandalised over the years.

[355] Vest, Rob, *Otto Skorzeny: The Scar-Faced Commando* at: http://homepages.ius.edu/RVEST/SkorzenyDr2.htm

[356] Ne Temere at: http://en.wikipedia.org/wiki/Ne_Temere

[357] For more information on this incident see *GUBU Nation* by Damian Corless (2005 Merlin Publishing).

[358] Torpey, Michael, *Boycott at Fethard on Sea* in *The Clare Champion* at: http://www.clarechampion.ie/index.php?option=com_content&id=2371:boycott.

The Catholic Church would not give the sacraments to many IRA members during the War of Independence. During the Civil War they were excommunicated.

359   Fethard Boycott Recalled *in The Mayo News, 23/05/07.*

360   Torpey Michael.

361   *Fethard Boycott Recalled in The Mayo News, 23/05/07.*

362   *Fethard-on-Sea boycott* at: http://en.wikipedia.org/wiki/Fethard-on-Sea_boycott

363   Corless, Damien, *You shall hang by the neck* in *The Irish Independent*, 21/11/09.

364   http://en.wikipedia.org/wiki/Ciaran_Creagh_(Irish_writer)

365   http://www.herald.ie/news/truth-about-darkey-kelly-burned-as-a-witch-250-years-ago-but-who-was-really-a-serial-killer-27970534.html

366   Carlow County – Ireland Genealogical Projects – Samuel Haughton at: http://www.rootsweb.ancestry.com/~irlcar2/Sam_haughton.htm

367   http://en.wikipedia.org/wiki/William_Marwood

368   Collins, R.D.,*William Marwood – Hangman, Executioner,Cobbler*, at: http://www.horncastlediscovered.com/william-marwood.htm

369   O'Gorman, Ronnie *The Maamtrasna Murders, August 17 1882* at: http://www.advertiser.ie/galway/article/21496

370   The jail was closed in 1939 and a Catholic Cathedral built on the site in 1965. A cross in the adjacent carpark marks the spot where Joyce and the other unfortunates were buried.

371   http://www.coimisineir.ie/downloads/Information_Note. The_Maamtrasna_case.pdf (accessed on 20/04/13)

372   1169 And Counting… at: http://1169andcounting.blogspot.ie/2004_02_22_archive.html (accesseded on 20/03/13)

373   Pierrepoint, Albert, *Executioner Pierrepoint*, Kent 1974.

374   Pierrepoint, Albert, *Executioner Pierrpoint*, Kent 1974.

375   http://en.wikipedia.org/wiki/Capital_punishment_in_Ireland

376   Taken from the poem *Remorse For Intemperate Speech* available at: http://www.poemhunter.com/poem/remorse-for-intemperate-speech/

Lightning Source UK Ltd.
Milton Keynes UK
UKOW05f0834041013

218454UK00003B/8/P